Onward Christian Athletes

Onward Christian Athletes

Turning Ballparks into Pulpits and Players into Preachers

Tom Krattenmaker

ROWMAN & LITTLEFIELD PUBLISHERS, INC.
Lanham • Boulder • New York • Toronto • Plymouth, UK

ROWMAN & LITTLEFIELD PUBLISHERS, INC.

Published in the United States of America
by Rowman & Littlefield Publishers, Inc.
A wholly owned subsidiary of The Rowman & Littlefield Publishing Group, Inc.
4501 Forbes Boulevard, Suite 200, Lanham, Maryland 20706
www.rowmanlittlefield.com

Estover Road
Plymouth PL6 7PY
United Kingdom

British Library Cataloguing in Publication Information Available

Library of Congress Cataloging-in-Publication Data
Krattenmaker, Tom.
  Onward Christian athletes : turning ballparks into pulpits and players into preachers /
Tom Krattenmaker.
    p. cm.
  ISBN 978-0-7425-6247-9 (cloth : alk. paper) — ISBN 978-1-4422-0129-3 (electronic)
  1. Sports—Religious aspects—Christianity. 2. Christian athletes—United States/ 3.
Christianity and culture—United States. I. Title.
  GV706.42.K73 2010
  201'.6796—dc22   2009027159

Printed in the United States of America

♾™ The paper used in this publication meets the minimum requirements of American
National Standard for Information Sciences—Permanence of Paper for Printed Library
Materials, ANSI/NISO Z39.48-1992.

~

Contents

~

Introduction

"You knew I was gonna do it," the jubilant quarterback said with a shrug and a quick look at his network television interviewer, "but I gotta do it!"

And, yes, he was right. Whatever we thought of the good or the bad of the deed that Kurt Warner had to perform, none of us who knew anything about the freshly crowned football champion could claim surprise. Like Fox television analyst and host Terry Bradshaw, like many of the seventy thousand fans inside that stadium, like many of the tens of millions of us watching on television, lots of us *did* know that the Super Bowl-bound quarterback was going to use his moment on the victory platform, in the live TV spotlight, to champion the cause dearest to his heart. From the moment he threw the game-winning touchdown pass to complete his reascension to the top of the pro football world, we in fandom knew—knew with eye-rolling dread, some of us, or with proud anticipation—that Warner, leader of the newly minted National Football Conference champion Arizona Cardinals, was going to proclaim his devotion to Jesus.

We knew because Warner, like so many of his professional athlete brothers today, can't seem to let his moments of high-profile good fortune go by without bringing his Christian religion into it, and without making sure that God becomes part of it for us spectators, too.

Bradshaw—a God-fearing retired quarterback himself, and one who had experienced championship glory in his own playing career—asked Warner how it felt to know that he was about to become the third oldest quarterback ever to play in the Super Bowl. The question hardly mattered, it seemed. Warner had something to say, and he was bound to say it.

"You know, everybody is gonna be tired of hearing this, but I never get tired of saying it," Warner began amidst a swirl of confetti. "There's one reason I'm standing up on this stage today. That's because of my Lord up above." Pointing upward now and raising his gaze to the sky, Warner brought home the point. "I gotta say thanks to Jesus! You knew I was gonna do it. But I gotta do it!"

His religious duties and impulse thusly fulfilled, Warner thanked and praised the stadium full of fans and concluded with a joyful shout: "We're going to the Super Bowl!"

The Cardinals and their 37-year-old leader indeed were on their way to the Super Bowl. Two weeks later, in front of the massive television audience that only the pro football championship can command, Arizona fought valiantly against the heavily favored Pittsburgh Steelers, only to see a last-minute Pittsburgh score reverse the Cardinals' lead and give the game to Pittsburgh. Thus was lost to Warner—and the evangelical culture that understood and shared his compulsion to talk about Jesus—the chance to display his Christianity once more on the grandest victory stage. (In his generally gracious post-game TV concession remarks, Warner had not a word to say about his Lord, suggesting that the religious obligation to proclaim Jesus belongs only to the victors.)

Owing to its status as America's most-watched television property, the Super Bowl surpasses all other games, shows, awards programs, and the like to rank as the country's top advertising event. Thirty-second spots cost as much as $2.7 million in 2008 (although slightly less in 2009, the year of what some called the "Recession Bowl"), and the commercials, with all their creativity, tech wizardry, and crass hilarity, generate nearly as much buzz as the game itself.

The concept of using sports to advertise services and products also goes a long way toward explaining Kurt Warner's seemingly forced "thanks to Jesus!" pitch in the post-game interview, and a multitude of similar Christian displays furnished game after game, year after year, by the contestants in America's big-time sports. For advertising—advertising Jesus and the religion that revolves around him—well describes the nature of Warner's gambit in his moment of championship glory.

Unpack Warner's Jesus proclamation, and one begins to understand the dynamics of a Christianity-in-sports movement that, for all its highly visible manifestations, has a little-seen and a less-well-understood history, logic, infrastructure, subplot, and set of implications. Unpack Warner's championship moment, and you begin to see the contours of this book, of my attempt to uncover the large part of the religion-in-sports iceberg hidden beneath the water.

More than most evangelizing athletes, Kurt Warner tipped his hand in his January 2009, post-game proclamations, revealing the not-exactly-spontaneous nature of players' shout-outs to the Lord. "I gotta do it," Warner admitted. Such is the religious duty that pro athlete Christians are taught to accept and fulfill by a network of evangelical chaplains and sports ministry organizations that have long appreciated the "advertising" value of big-time sports, and have long worked to harness the sports industry's influence to push out their salvation message and draw new people into the flock.

Warner telegraphed something else that's important to know about evangelical Christianity in big-time sports: the ever-present push-back. "Everybody is gonna be tired of hearing this," Warner admitted before thanking Jesus, as if to give all the nonevangelical spectators the chance to brace themselves or hit the "mute" button. Warner is certainly right: Many, many people *do* grow weary of hearing multimillionaire athletes proclaiming their Christian faith in ways, and in moments, that sometime seem to trivialize religion's rich complexity as powerfully as they offend and divide portions of the viewing audience.

Yes, we did know that Kurt Warner was going to turn his victorious moment into a plug for his evangelical faith—because we're accustomed to hearing victorious players wax religious this way in a day and age when sports are not only hugely popular, but often drenched with Christian religion.

But what we as an American society don't know or understand so well is the how, and the why, and the "what does it all mean?" Lots of us in fandom's nonevangelical majority might roll our eyes or cringe when players wear their faith on their sleeve, but we have failed to articulate a compelling case against sports-world religion in its present form, or even establish the fact that we, the public, have a right to make that case. Nor have we done enough to concede the aspects of Christianity in sports that are inevitable, understandable, legitimate, and even constructive in exerting a moral influence on a sector that, with all its gaudy excesses, unbridled greed, and staggering amounts of money changing hands, could really use some positive moral force.

And short of banning religion in sports—a nonstarter in a culture that values religious freedom—we have failed to shape a vision for a more appropriate, fair, and thoughtful form of faith in sports.

Consider the pages that follow my earnest attempt at starting the completion of all that unfinished business.

*

When I think about religion in sports, my train of thought inevitably takes me back to Metropolitan Stadium. I was eight years old the first time I saw the hometown Minnesota Twins in that old ballpark in suburban Minneapolis, on the plot of land now occupied by the Mall of America. Coming through the upper-deck tunnel, getting my first glimpse of the green diamond below, I was enthralled. I remember Minnesota right fielder Tony Oliva making a diving, backhanded catch at that first game of mine, injuring his shoulder in the process and getting helped off the field. My second game came the following year, 1969. Harmon Killebrew hit a game-winning home run to beat Oakland and sent us home happy, and the Twins were on their way to the West Division championship.

One of my earliest trips to "The Met" was not for a game at all. The Twins and that stadium in Bloomington had a powerful hold on my imagination, so when a friendly neighborhood family invited me to join them for an event at the ballpark featuring Twins pitcher Al Worthington, I eagerly accepted. Instead of a game, I had my first encounter with evangelical Christianity.

The headline act at this religious revival, Worthington spoke not so much about his baseball career, but about his relationship with Jesus Christ. The concept was new to me, growing up as I was in a (marginally) Catholic family. The Twins' closer invited the unconverted in the seats to stand up and accept Jesus as their savior. Feeling confused and conspicuous, not wanting to displease the people who had invited me, I rose. Thus unfolded the first of several occasions in my young life when I accepted Jesus with the encouragement (and under the pressure) of the agents of evangelical Christianity.

As implied by the serial nature of my conversions, none took. Yet my fascination with evangelical religion, equal parts attraction and revulsion, never left for long.

In high school, my wanting to be one of the popular kids drew me to Young Life meetings, where the pull was social, and the message—a surprise to me the first time I attended—was religious. Sure, I thought, I'll live this Christian life, as long as it means I'll fit in with the group!

It was the same story, writ larger, when I went through my Campus Crusade for Christ period during college. The desire to be with fraternity friends—and meet women—lured me to my first meeting of "Greek Life," a Campus Crusade outreach program aimed specifically at the fraternity and sorority set. Before long, I was attending lectures and retreats, joining others from the button-down-shirt-and-khaki crowd for barbecues at the leader's home, and meeting one-on-one with my assigned Campus Crusade staffer. He, like the Twins pitcher years before, encouraged me to have that personal relationship with the Lord. I tried. But nothing really changed. I began to wonder about the ministry's teachings. Maybe it was my intellectual side getting in the way, or maybe the occasional whiffs of the ministry's conservative cultural and political direction, which seemed suspect to my developing political awareness. My interest waned—for a time.

Like my fascination with evangelical religion, my devotion to sports never left me for long. As a boy, I played sports, watched sports, and simulated sports with dice games. Despite the decade and a half of mediocrity that followed their 1970 division championship, the Twins held my imagination through my high school and college years and my young adulthood. As a young reporter working in Southern California, I trekked to Anaheim whenever Minnesota was in town to play the Angels, witnessing, among other moments, the major league debut of a fireplug named Kirby Puckett, who treated me to a 4-for-5 performance that night at the "Big A." Puckett was on his way to big things, as were the Twins. As an Associated Press reporter in Minneapolis, I covered the World Series victory celebrations in 1987 and witnessed firsthand the way a team could unite and excite a community. During that championship run and its aftermath, we Minnesota people seemed to have far more in common than we had differences. What we had in common was Kirby Puckett and our world champion Twins.

Four years later, as a transplant on the East Coast, I sweated it out in front of the television as the Twins won their second World Series championship. My future wife and I endured all ten innings of the seventh and final game, finally rising in relief and happiness when the Twins pushed across the game- and World Series–winning run.

After lying dormant for many years, my interest in evangelical Christianity returned in my adulthood—this time in an intellectual form. Graduate study at the University of Pennsylvania, directionless at first, found me gravitating toward courses on religion and, eventually, a decision to concentrate my master's study in a program called Religion in Public Life. Given my youthful dalliances with evangelical Christianity, and my growing fascination with the powerful impact of theologically conservative Christians on America's politics and culture, it seems inevitable, in retrospect, that evangelicalism would become the focus of my research and my eventual thesis.

Because of my enduring sports fandom, and because of something most intriguing happening in the sports world that drew so much of my attention, it was also inevitable that my research would link strongly to the professional sports sector. What was happening, of course, was the ever more conspicuous presence of evangelical Christianity in the game. I knew religion and big-time sports had long been partners of sorts—I had, after all, attended that Al Worthington event at the Met when I was a boy—and, like most sports fans, I had become accustomed to players like Reggie White unabashedly declaring their Christian faith in the 1980s and 1990s. But something different—something bigger by degrees and bolder in shape and form—seemed to be afoot in sports as the 1990s wound down and the new century began. My mind and eyes sharpened by my coursework, my perspective broadened by my many readings, I was watching sports not just for the entertainment value anymore, but as a window to a changing national culture.

Anyone watching cannot help but notice it: Baseball players pointing skyward as they cross home plate, eyes gazing at the heavens; pro football gladiators joining hands in prayer with teammates and opponents alike at midfield after three hours of organized violence, for all the stadium to see; an NBA Finals MVP praising God on national television as he kisses his trophy and declares, "God is good!" We sports fans have all seen and heard it: Pro athletes turning the post-game interview into opportunities to proclaim Jesus; players claiming that they perform their heroics on the field or court to "glorify God"; ministries turning ballparks into revival halls on "faith nights." These are the visible manifestations. As I was learning through my research, they were anything but random, and not entirely spontaneous. They signified something bigger, something deeper.

For one, this heightened presence of Christianity in the sports world mirrors the trend in society—the forceful public presence of conservative Christians in so many public venues in America. As I was also beginning to see, this trend in sports is more than just an organic development or a reflection of the times. The athletes' gestures and shout-outs to God are fruits of a campaign by well-organized, well-financed evangelical sports ministries committed to leveraging sports to reach and change the broader American culture. Pro athletes, it turns out, may well be one of the most heavily proselytized segments of our society, eyed by the evangelical ministries as a uniquely advantageous gateway to the hearts and minds of America.

It is my personal story and perspective, combined with the important but scarcely examined penetration of evangelical religion into big-time sports, that form the basis for this book.

As you will read in the chapters before you, I am not against religion; nor am I against religion in sports. And while I am not an evangelical Christian, I am not the least bit opposed to the Christian faith. Quite the opposite, actually. I don't propose to do away with religion in sports. I propose that we make it better.

The story about evangelical religion in our professional sports is anything but fixed. True, there appears on the surface to be very little that has changed about certain aspects of evangelical engagement with sports since Frank Deford published his seminal critique of Christian sports ministry—"Sportianity," as he called it—more than thirty years ago. Deford's chief indictment in that three-part *Sports Illustrated* series was that sports ministry barely concerned itself with the exploitation and abuses wrought by the big-business enterprise of pro sports, that the sports world representatives of Jesus were chiefly concerned with exploiting sports' clout and visibility to market their religious message. It's not a flattering portrayal: Evangelicals out to exploit the exploiters, rarely if ever raising a voice of Christian conscience against the sports industry's "sins."

But as I complete the journey of writing this book, I am struck by how much is changing, by how much has already changed since the mid-part of this decade, when religious and political conservatives seemed to have taken control of the country—taken control of politics, culture, and sports—with no sign of letting go.

Those who pay attention to politics know that the outsize influence of conservative Christians on American politics has waned. Barack Obama, whose stands on abortion and many other issues are anathema to the Christian Right, has won the White House. The moment captured in this book's opening chapter, one that fused Christianity, sports, and hard-right politics in a particularly stark and dubious way, should be seen as a snapshot of an evolving organism. It is not the case that the Christian Right has faded away. Far from it. Or that its ethos, politics, and theology no longer infuse religion in professional sports. They absolutely do. But, as has become ever clearer to me in my interactions with today's sports world Christian missionaries, change is in the air. It turns out that a movement thought incapable of change by so many of us progressive skeptics *is* beginning to change. Its leading-edge innovators and pioneers are in the midst of reinventing the Christian presence in sports, in ways that are promising for those of us inside and outside the evangelical orbit. I don't know how far they will get. I wish them well.

Readers should be aware of a few key methodological decisions I made in structuring this book and the research that informs it. The athletes and ministry undertakings described in the following chapters come almost entirely from the "big three" professional sports leagues in America: Major League Baseball, the National Basketball Association, and the National Football League. I believe the ideas evoked through these stories and analyses apply well beyond these three predominant leagues—well beyond sports, even. (So stay with me, those of you who are not interested in what might appear to be a "sports book.") I do not mean to slight the other professional sports leagues, most of which have interesting religious dynamics; nor do I wish to overlook women's sports, whose rising stature is testament to the progress of which our society is capable. But in the interest of a manageable body of material, and because the issues that concern me are especially poignant with respect to the massively popular NFL, NBA, and Major League Baseball, these three leagues provide most of the grist for my storytelling and analyses.

You will find lots from the political arena, too. For as you'll see, politics are never far away when one begins to peel back the surface layers to examine what's really going on when it comes to evangelical Christianity in professional sports. Not that the athletes and chaplains and other agents of faith in the game are primarily political actors. But politics have a huge and largely unexamined influence on the shape and direction of religion in sports, a politics very much of the Christian Right variety. Indeed, an understanding of religion in sports is impossible without an examination of the politics, just as an understanding of popular religion in twenty-first-century America is incomplete without a grasp of what is happening in big-time sports.

Only by examining religion in sports through the lens of politics can we begin to thoughtfully critique the movement. As I have continually asked myself, why should the public care if evangelical Christianity dominates religious practice in the sports world? How does the public have a stake in the issue? Whose interests are harmed by the evangelicals' engagement with sports—or by their "infiltration," if you'd like to put it in darker terms? As I've been told by certain readers of my newspaper and magazine articles on faith in sports, fans who have a problem with athletes spouting off about God need not pay attention. Live and let live.

They're right. There is nothing particularly wrong with athletes who express their faith in the stadium and the media; in a country that cherishes religious freedom, they have every right. That is not what this book is primarily about. But a deeper point prevails. The public *does* have a stake in what happens around religion in major league sports. For as you'll see in the stories and explorations awaiting you, pro sports have a very real public mission, and the rights and responsibilities that accrue thereto. If pro leagues and teams are going to expect public financing of stadiums, the continuation of their crucially important antitrust exemption, and all the other forms of support provided by their communities, they are accountable to the public. If they're going to get us to watch games by telling us it's "our" team, then they need to respect the larger swath of *us*.

The public, I'm afraid, is not always well served by the shape and form of religion in pro sports. Given the evangelical Christian dominance of religion in the game, and given that the movement promotes an exclusive theology (and politics) counter to the interests of the majority of us in a religiously, politically diverse America, it seems clear that those who run pro sports are not fulfilling their obligation to ensure that the religious playing field is level and fair.

But these are not the times for more harsh polemics about all that is wrong with evangelical America. So let me be adamant in saying that I do not wish solely to expose and critique all that is objectionable about religion in pro sports, but to show, too, what is good (or at least more complicated than we thought), and begin to imagine something better at the intersection of religion and pro sports.

Let me be clear, too, in stating that if there's fault to assign for the situation at hand, a fair amount of it belongs to secularists and nonevangelical believers who have stood by, watching idly, while their born-again fellow citizens have seized control of religion in the game. Anyone who has immersed himself in evangelical America as I have in researching this book begins to see that evangelicals often gain the upper hand in given settings because, to use a sports cliché, they simply out-hustle the rest of us. Don't count on the evangelicals to do the legwork to ensure that Jews and Muslims and agnostics and pluralists and Catholics and liberal Protestants have a voice in the pro sports world. The responsibility for inclusion falls only partly on those who run our teams and leagues. Those of us who resent the absence of our voices and perspectives in sports-world religion need to assert ourselves, as the evangelicals have done.

So, too, must the nonevangelical "rest of us" demonstrate the capacity for open-mindedness and nuanced thinking that supposedly sets us apart from the conservative Christians whose alleged rigidity we so often lament. As I wrote in one of my USA Today columns, those of us with a secular, blue-state habit of mind tend to cling too tightly to the old story lines—the story lines frozen in 2004. Evangelical America has never been as lockstep monolithic as we've been tempted to think, and its citizens have been busting out in all sorts of surprising and encouraging ways in the closing years of the decade. Evangelicals in sports are hardly the leading agents of the cultural change, but nor are they immune to it. And when you start to talk with the chaplains and ministry staffers, it becomes more and more difficult to cling to stereotypes; you find that they are, by and large, very decent human beings who treat people well and aim to serve, and who care deeply about their faith's reputation. We of the blue-state mentality may need to adjust our story about those "crazy" evangelicals.

This book is largely about what is, and has been, with regard to Christianity in pro sports. But it's also about what might be.

Yes, the title of this book is at least a little cynical. The crusader overtones of Christian Right rhetoric—evoked by my riffing on that revered martial hymn "Onward Christian Soldiers"—are worrisome to me, and a discredit to the very fine religion known as Christianity. Too often, that crusader form of faith—rigid, militaristic, nationalistic—is what prevails in the professional sports leagues. Too often, it's a form of faith that tends to separate us all into opposing sides and make unwelcome judgments about those on the "wrong" side of the line. As the newspaper columnist Ray Waddle aptly observes, "the fateful merger of piety and aggression haunts the world."[1]

At the same time, though, I do not advocate a complete separation of church and sport, and I can guarantee that Christian athletes will be coming to a stadium near you for the foreseeable future. So let's make the best of it. Sports ministry is not fixed in stone. Change is possible, and, frankly, pro sports could really use some "good" religion—religion that summons our better selves, serves our least advantaged fellow citizens, and exerts moral resistance against aspects of sports culture that are harmful and exploitive.

So I mean it when I say it, too:

Onward, Christian athletes.

Note

1. Ray Waddle, "Mixing the Gospel and Modern Sport is a Bit Strange," *The Tennessean*, January 3, 2009.

CHAPTER 1

~

On Any Justice Sunday

Evangelicals, Pro Sports, and the (Conservative) Campaign for Jesus

Herbert Lusk's journey had taken him from the Meadowlands end zone to Greater Exodus Baptist Church. The eyes of millions of television viewers were on him now as the charismatic African American preacher began to rise thunderously to the occasion.

Eighteen years earlier, in October 1977, Lusk had followed his religious impulse and, upon completing a long touchdown run for the Philadelphia Eagles, had kneeled in prayer in the New York Giants' end zone. Up until the moment that Lusk's bended knee hit the artificial turf of that stadium just outside of New York City, religion had run strongly through the veins of the professional football world—but mainly out of view, confined to locker rooms, private conversations, and pious minds and hearts. Lusk, in his act of reverence, humbleness, and gratitude, had turned the opponent's end zone into his place of *public* prayer. "During that run, I couldn't wait to get on my knees and thank God for it," Lusk recalled years later, his voice bubbling with joy as he thought back on the moment. "I got right down on my knees and I praised God for it. I don't recall anyone doing that before me. I think it became contagious."[1]

A large measure of the old gridiron competitor seemed to be coming through now on the brightly lit pulpit of Greater Exodus as the minister began working up a theatrical and rhetorical head of steam. Lusk was on his home turf this time, appearing to revel in his role as the head of this flourishing Christian congregation on Philadelphia's rundown north side and as host of an event that, for the moment, had made his church the center of the Christian Right universe. In a performance that was equal parts halftime pep talk, taunting of the opponent, and fire-and-brimstone sermon, Lusk recalled the volleys of criticism he'd absorbed for agreeing to host the night's big event, Justice Sunday III. "I've been called a sellout," Lusk declared. "I've been called an Uncle Tom. And the *New York Times* called me a maverick to the black church." The crowd murmured.

Seated around Lusk at the altar of his packed church, having already spoken or waiting to take their turn at the microphone, were some of the biggest names in Christian conservative politics—Rick Santorum, the junior U.S. senator from Pennsylvania; Jerry Falwell, the founder of the Moral Majority; James Dobson, the founder and leader of Focus on the Family; and Tony Perkins, head of the Family Research Council. The latter was the chief organizer of this, the third rendition of Justice Sunday, an event billed as a stand of resistance by people of faith against the supposed tyranny of a liberal judiciary bent on leading America away from its Christian heritage. The leaders were gathered in north Philadelphia on the eve of Senate confirmations hearings for Samuel Alito, nominated by President Bush for the U.S. Supreme Court—a choice that had greatly pleased a Christian Right movement that considered itself responsible for the president's reelection and was counting on Bush to reciprocate. Although only six hundred people could squeeze into Lusk's sanctuary, many more were experiencing the moment live over several Christian television networks and the Internet.

"Well, my friends, I just want the *Times* to know that if a maverick can be defined as one who is pro-life, then I'm a maverick," Lusk continued, his raspy voice growing louder, applause beginning to rise from the congregation. "And if being a maverick means I'm one who supports the original intent of God Almighty to have a husband and a wife, then I want you to mark, right next to my name, Herbert Hoover Lusk, the Second, *maverick!*"

Seated with Lusk and the other speakers, waving her hands rapturously, was a woman whose surname was the most prominent of all—Alveda King, niece of none other than Martin Luther King Jr. A darling of the Christian right for her outspoken anti-abortion stance and blood connection to the late civil rights prophet, King had invoked the themes and emotions of her uncle's movement in her address moments before, leading the throng in a rendition of that old social justice standard "We Shall Overcome."

Oppression—not of African Americans, but of Christians—had been King's theme, and now Lusk was invoking the same rallying cry as he rose toward his combative crescendo.

"My friends, I want you to know the foundation has been tampered with. . . . We are facing, like we never have before, this hostility against the people of God. My brothers and sisters, I want you to know I will not go down lightly.

Don't fool with the church, because the church has buried many a critic, and all the critics that we have not buried, we're making funeral arrangements for them!" The congregation roared.

Lusk's rallying of the troops at Greater Exodus that winter night in Philadelphia captured a moment in time and showcased a long-developing relationship that had come into full bloom in the early years of the new century. The players in this powerful triumvirate: evangelicals, political and cultural conservatives, and, perhaps surprisingly at first glance, the world of professional sports.

How fitting that a pro footballer-turned-minister, the very father of the end zone prayer, played this crucial role in an event stunning for its melding of white conservatives and black Christians—groups often out of sync in American politics—and for its linking of religion, race, politics, culture, and sports. Because if one were to choose a human symbol of the complex dynamics that have turned pro sports into a vehicle for the promotion of Christianity, and the conservative cultural and political worldview right alongside it, no person would serve quite like Herbert Lusk.

Why Lusk?

There is his religious piety: In an age when religious gestures on the field are both conspicuous and commonplace, Lusk is the one who started it all with that fateful display in the Giants end zone back in the 1970s. Lusk is right—his act of kneeling in the end zone *was* contagious, and barely a pro football or baseball game passes today without Christian combatants praying at the mound or home plate, pointing triumphantly to the heavens after a touchdown or home run, or praising their God in post-game interviews. These gestures are emblematic of something deeper in sports: an engagement by evangelical Christians that has progressed to the point where born-again believers make up something approaching 40 percent of the rosters of many major league teams in baseball, basketball, and football.

There is the nature of Lusk's Christian faith: Lusk is an evangelical, an adherent to and promoter of the conservative branch of Christian belief that dominates religious practice and expression in our major professional sports leagues. It has, among its principal tenets, the conviction that believers are called upon to spread the good news of the Bible so that others, too, may accept the lordship of the savior, Jesus Christ, and thus earn their salvations.

There is his political stance: As a friend of George W. Bush and a major recipient of funds from the then-president's faith-based initiatives program, as an ally of staunch Christian political conservatives such as Tony Perkins and James Dobson, and as a man who hits hard on anti-gay and anti-abortion notes when he applies his religion to the public issues of the day, Lusk has been known as a "card-carrying" member of the Christian Right.

And there is his race: Lusk is African American. Given the social justice tradition of the black Christian church in America, the combination of his race and religion, in a different time, might have compelled him to stand for progressive-leaning racial and social justice, in the mold of a Jackie Robinson or Gale Sayers. But where faith, sports, and politics intersect today, you will find few black Christian sports stars standing up for so-called liberal issues. Like Lusk, they are more likely followers and promoters of a Christian Right movement that has not found much room on its agenda for the issues—racial equality, economic justice, peace—that found their voice in Martin Luther King Jr.

On that given Sunday in north Philadelphia in 2006, pro sports, evangelical religion, and conservative politics came together in a particularly stark framing of a powerful current in American public life. Yet on *any* given Sunday in the National Football League, or in the National Basketball Association or Major League Baseball for that matter, the same dynamics are there together, too—perhaps subtly, but together just the same.

Depending on one's religious and political leanings, all this might be worthy of cheers, not concerns. After all, in a sports culture awash in immorality and self-seeking, what could be wrong with some good old religion and traditional values, with a perspective larger than oneself? Let it be said that the Herb Lusks of the sports/culture/politics realm—all the current and ex-athletes who carry the banner for Christ—do considerable good in their congregations and communities, that they often demonstrate outstanding personal morality, and that they have every right to hold and promote their beliefs in a country that cherishes religious freedom.

But whatever one's opinion about the rights and wrongs of Christianity in sports, it is well worth understanding that the pious proclamations and parades on our athletic fields of battle are more than isolated, spontaneous occurrences. In potent and well-organized combination, pro sports and evangelical Christianity have been coming together in the nation's stadiums as part of a concerted campaign for Jesus and, often with it, a sustained drive to shape American culture in the mold of the leaders who joined together at the pulpit of Greater Exodus Baptist Church on a Sunday night in Philadelphia—Tony Perkins, James Dobson, Jerry Falwell, and the Reverend Herbert Hoover Lusk, the Second.

*

When tens of millions of fans plop down in front of their televisions for their Sunday football bounty, ease through the turnstiles at major league ballparks, or settle into their courtside seats at posh NBA arenas, it is doubtful that many of them are thinking of Jesus Christ as somehow central to the spectator experience they are about to enjoy. So it would probably come as news to the vast majority if someone were to inform them that the game is not principally about the entertainment, competition, or athletic artistry, or about the emotional lift we experience when our teams wins, or about the beer and snacks, or about the social bonding that takes place between citizens of a given city as they root for the home team, or even about the sexual titillation served up by the alluring women in the dance teams and beer commercials. No, the game is principally about advancing evangelical Christianity.

Advancing Christianity? Yes, according to a network of evangelical ministries that help place Christian chaplains with all the teams in major league baseball, basketball, and football. Yes, according to these well-funded, politically well-connected organizations like Athletes in Action, Baseball Chapel, and the Fellowship of Christian Athletes that proudly describe their mission as one of using sports to promote Christianity. Yes, according to numerous players like onetime major league baseball player Morgan Ensberg, who during his playing days declared, "The entire reason I play baseball is so that I get a chance to speak about Christ."[2] *Absolutely*, according to a sizeable subset of pro athletes typified by NFL safety Michael Boulware, who said his participation in the 2006 Super Bowl was "about Jesus Christ . . . and what he did on the cross. That's what I'm really here for—to advance his kingdom, not just win a game."[3]

Obviously, statements by pious players about pro sports existing primarily to advance religion do not mean sports have become that which the Christian athletes cite. But nor is it wise for those of us with a different view of sports to dismiss such claims as obviously nonsense. For in treating sports as a vehicle for advancing the evangelical message and worldview, Christian athletes *make* sports that vehicle, at least in part.

That is not particularly astounding in view of the fact that professional sports are just one of numerous public venues being influenced and used—commandeered, if you prefer—by evangelical Christians intent on making their mark on American culture. The evangelical engagement with sports is best understood in the context of what is happening more broadly in American culture: a quarter century of hard work by evangelical Christians to assert themselves in the public square, to grab hold of the tools of culture—television, movies, technology, media, politics, sports—and use them to spread their message and their values. The infusion of evangelical Christianity in major league sports has been one of the most visible manifestations—one of the most potent thrusts—of this counteroffensive by evangelical America to influence our culture and turn our country in a more Christian, and more conservative, direction.

Fans cannot help but be aware of the index fingers raised to the sky, of devout players thanking their maker in victory interviews and performing good deeds in their communities in the name of their savior. Some might recall the several occasions when anti-Semitic and anti-gay bigotry have seeped out of locker rooms and into the media. Yet they see only the nose of the camel. A Christian network of considerable breadth, depth, and influence has been operating behind the scenes, with the quiescence of league and team managements, to convert players and enlist them in an effort to sway others who play and follow sports.

To its credit, the movement brings pro athletes something they very much need: encouragement to become better individuals. Even critics of the ministries must acknowledge that a sports-industrial complex awash in sexual aggression, greed, and a win-at-all-costs obsession is in dire need of perspective and morality. Numerous players are encouraged to become better husbands, fathers, and teammates thanks in part to the teachings of the Christian ministries. The unique pressures of their line of work often leave them in need of spiritual guidance and counseling—resources energetically provided by the ministries operating in sports.

So, too, must skeptics acknowledge the marketing logic behind Christian outreach through sports. Major league players and their industry exert a powerful hold on the attention of the American public. Sports are used to sell innumerable products, from deodorant and athletic gear to satellite television systems and beer. As those in ministry ask, why not "sell" something truly important through sports—like Jesus and a shot at eternal salvation?

There is truth as well to the ministries' defense of their mission as a solution to a logistical problem. Pro ballplayers typically cannot make it to church on Sunday, so the ministries are bringing church to the players. But here's the rub: The Christian vanguard in sports isn't bringing *religion* to clubhouses so much as a potentially divisive brand of evangelical Christianity. And often attached to it, as will be explored in later chapters, is something beyond just religion—a conservative worldview that is frequently indifferent if not outright hostile to the plights of racial, religious, and sexual minorities and committed to a highly debatable vision for America.

To a committed Christian athlete, it makes eminent sense to conceive of major league sports as an instrument for the advancement of evangelical Christianity. To the evangelical mind and heart, faith infuses all parts of one's life, and believers have an obligation to share the good news of Jesus however and wherever they can. Yet the conception of sports as an entity that exists chiefly for the promotion of one form of religion (implicitly at the expense of other religions and of *non*religion) is strange and jarring to large numbers of us, religious or not, who have grown up knowing and loving the game in a much different way—loving it, despite its excesses, for its always-gripping combination of drama, excitement, and fun, for its ability to crush us and thrill us, for the way it can inspire us to high-five the stranger next to us in the sports bar or the box seats. The steady infusing of evangelical Christianity into the fiber of sports culture has happened so gradually that many of us barely noticed; indeed, its deeper sources and purposes have escaped attention almost entirely. It is time we understand it for what it is.

Crucial to this entrenchment of conservative religion in sports are the managements of our professional leagues and teams, without whose cooperation and blessing the ministries like Athletes in Action and Baseball Chapel would not enjoy the access to pro locker rooms and the athletes who populate them. While avoiding any frank public discussion of the matter, the executives of pro sports have found common cause with the evangelicals (despite the curious fact that two of the commissioners of the "big three" major league sports are Jewish).

But management skipped a crucial step as it decided, consciously or otherwise, to swing open the clubhouse doors and grant privileged access to evangelical Christianity: They never consulted us—the nonevangelical fans who have helped make sports the colossus they are by caring enough to buy the tickets, watch the games, read the sports pages, listen to the sports-talk radio chatter, finance the stadiums, and (through our elected representatives) provide the crucially important antitrust exemptions that make major league sports possible in their current, lucrative configuration—all while never once being asked if we wanted our pastime turned over to purposes that are, for many of us, contrary to our interests.

How did all this happen?

*

The story goes back some two thousand years to the apostle Paul, the father of all Christian evangelists, the Christian convert who traveled around the civilized world in the first century telling the story of the crucified and risen Jesus and building what would become the Christian church. Preaching to fledgling congregations, sending letters of instruction to newly formed Christian fellowships, Paul vouched for Jesus' divinity, testified to Christ's exclusive ability to redeem sinners, and charged new and would-be converts with the imperative to live a reborn Christian life. Evangelical Christians, in a very real sense, follow in Paul's footsteps today. The charge to evangelize comes from an even more revered source—Jesus himself. If you want to know what animates the evangelism of fervent Christians today, look up Matthew 28:19-20 in the New Testament. It is there that you will find Jesus' "Great Commission," his charge to followers to "go and make disciples of all nations, baptizing them in the name of the Father and of the Son and of the Holy Spirit, and teaching them to obey everything I have commanded you."

Jump to 1954, and meet a young, little-known college football coach who is seeking an audience with a famed pro sports executive who has already sealed his legacy as the man who brought Jackie Robinson to the Brooklyn Dodgers and thus integrated major league baseball.

Don McClanen, the coach of Eastern Oklahoma A&M, has dreams of founding an organization dedicated to nurturing a stronger relationship between his two most passionate interests: faith and sports. In his words, he wants to form "a ministry of coaches and athletes" dedicated to promoting the Christian faith to the nation's athletes, and to the "harnessing of heroes to reach those who idolized them for a life for the Lord."[4] His idea, in sum, is to use sports and their cultural influence to spread the gospel. His name for the new organization: the Fellowship of Christian Athletes (FCA).

McClanen believes he identified just the man he needs to win visibility and credibility for his cause. Given Branch Rickey's strong and well-known Christian faith, the young coach is confident he can win him over. Without an appointment, McClanen travels to see Rickey, who has moved on from his Brooklyn Dodgers post and is working as general manager of the Pittsburgh Pirates. After hearing out his ardent visitor, Rickey comes to share McClanen's excitement for this venture. Rickey helps organize funding, recruits prominent Christian athletes and other key allies, and places his name and stature behind the new ministry. As McClanen will later put it, Rickey "put the FCA on the road."[5]

That road has been paved with figurative gold. Many cousin ministries have followed FCA onto the playing field—including Baseball Chapel, which provides chaplains to all major league and minor league baseball teams, and Athletes in Action, which places roughly half the NFL's team chaplains as a small part of its far-flung international ministry work—but McClanen's creation remains the pre-eminent ministry, the granddaddy of them all. The Kansas City–based FCA oversees more than eight thousand school groups or "huddles," with hundreds of thousands of young athletes participating in its programs, and it fields a paid staff of several hundred men and women across the United States.[6] Although it is not primarily dedicated to the professional leagues and players, it maintains a strong presence in major league sports via a network of prominent pros—FCA alumni, essentially—who support the organization by speaking at FCA camps and other events and by helping spread the Christian message to fellow players, youth, and the public.

At a very early juncture, FCA faced a fork in the road, and the direction it chose continues to define the faith-in-sports movement today. As McClanen set out with Rickey and a prominent Presbyterian minister named Louis Evans to win wider support, as they approached a widening circle of would-be advocates and supporters, the FCA founders were asked if they would consider a more inclusive name for the organization. Would they change the Fellowship of Christian Athletes to the Fellowship of *Religious* Athletes?

Evans, especially, was adamant, and McClanen had little choice but to follow the sponsor's lead lest he lose his support. The answer, crucially, was "no."[7]

*

The Fellowship of Christian Athletes, and with it the marriage of evangelical Christianity and big-time sports, was well established by the time Herbert Lusk was coming of age as a star tailback in the early 1970s. Lusk grew up in Monterey, California, where his father was the minister of a Baptist church and, as if to foreshadow his son's more storied career, the founder of a nonprofit organization that worked to help people in need. Herbert Lusk, according to his official biography, was saved at the age of sixteen.

Lusk left Monterey for Long Beach State to play college football. Overcoming a career-threatening injury, Lusk amassed 2,142 career rushing yards, which at the time of Justice Sunday III placed him third on the university's all-time list. He earned honorable mention All-American honors for his efforts in the 1975 season, in which he ranked second in the nation with a per-game rushing average of 145.1 yards. Long Beach is where Lusk began praying after touchdowns. As he later told a newspaper interviewer, "I started praying in the end zone in college. It was my way of being grateful to be able to play the game. My junior year I had a knee operation that could have been career-ending. After that, I came back and became the second leading ground-gainer in the country. I started praying to honor my Lord in scoring a touchdown." The end zone, he said, became his "pulpit."[8]

The NFL draft beckoned, and when the Philadelphia Eagles selected him in the tenth round, Lusk became a pro. Professional football may be a dream career for a great many American youths, but Lusk was adamant that he would devote no more than three years to the Eagles. He had a higher calling that he was not willing to defer for long. He wanted to become a minister.

"The Praying Tailback" had a pro football career as unremarkable, in most ways, as it was brief. He did indeed keep his promise to play just three seasons, retiring at the age of twenty-five and foregoing the pension he would have earned by playing one more season. "Who could take better care of me than God?" he would later say when asked about the squandered retirement benefits.[9] He scored just three touchdowns in his brief time in the NFL, but one was enough to leave a legacy. On October 9, 1977, he took a pitch from Eagles quarterback Ron Jaworski, broke through the New York Giants' defense, and dashed seventy yards to the Giants Stadium end zone. Upon arrival in that Promised Land, reprising a ritual from his days at Long Beach State, Lusk dropped to his left knee and bowed his head in prayer.

Reflecting on the moment twenty-five years later, Lusk spoke of the pride that wells in him when he watches today's NFL players honor God in the end zone—something that has become commonplace in the spectacle of a pro football game, whether it takes the form of a bended knee and bowed head or, more common today, a showy display of raised arms and an index finger pointed to the sky. "Sometimes," Lusk said wistfully, "when I see a player kneel down and pray, in my heart I think, 'there's one of my sons.'"

What awaited Lusk after pro football was seemingly no prize. Greater Exodus Baptist Church on Philadelphia's North Broad Street languished in bankruptcy. Collecting the water that leaked through the porous ceiling were fifteen buckets, by Lusk's telling—buckets that substantially outnumbered the congregation's active members, a grand total of nine.

What a contrast between that and the thriving religious, and nonprofit, enterprise encountered by those who visited Greater Exodus in more recent times, whose ranks included the forty-third president of the United States, George W. Bush. By the time Lusk hosted Justice Sunday III, the church had grown to some two thousand active members, primarily African American, who worshipped in a well-maintained sanctuary that had no need for rain-catching buckets. Lusk was overseeing more than a congregation in the midst of blighted north Philadelphia, and he accurately billed himself as "CEO" as well as "pastor." Flanking the formidable stone church were a constellation of Lusk-run businesses and services, many bearing the name of Lusk's nonprofit organization, People for People, Inc., and its confident motto: "We Change Lives!" Among the minister's going concerns: A well-appointed catering center and banquet hall, featuring views of the Philadelphia skyline; a child-care center; the People for People charter school; the "New H.O.P.E." pregnancy crisis center; a credit union; and a computer lab. Lusk, together with his church and nonprofit, was certainly contributing to the improvement of people's lives. And his work did not end at the Philadelphia border. The Greater Exodus congregation was giving 10 percent of its income to help relieve the suffering of AIDS victims in Africa.[10] Asked to explain the church's growth and success, Lusk gave credit to the same source to which he turned on his fateful visit to the Giants end zone in 1977. "God," he said, "blessed the work."

So did President Bush, who cited Lusk as a shining example of a "social entrepreneur who can make things happen . . . who believes, as I do, in the power of faith to touch every heart and change every life."[11] Bush not only brought national attention to Lusk, but his administration poured $1 million into the Praying Tailback's community work via the president's faith-based initiatives program. Then, in 2006, the president named Lusk to his President's Advisory Council on HIV/AIDS. The appointment caused Lusk's increasingly numerous liberal critics to charge that the minister's only "qualification" was his conviction that abstinence, and abstinence alone, was the remedy for the scourge of AIDS.[12]

Bush's support of Lusk, financial and otherwise, was not merely given, but earned. It was Lusk who had come to Bush's aid at the 2000 GOP National Convention, when the Bush candidate was in desperate need of help, any help at all, from an African American leader. Lusk delivered the invocation at the convention via a satellite link from Greater Exodus, declaring on behalf of the congregation, "We are supporting Governor Bush!"

Lusk spoke up for Bush again in 2004, praising the president for his stances against abortion and gay marriage, and for Bush's faith-based approach to urban revitalization, as he announced his support for Bush's re-election. On what basis did he continue to stand with the divisive president who enjoyed the support of only a small percentage of African Americans? In an opinion article in the *Philadelphia Inquirer* published just days before the election, Lusk made the claim—a claim incredible to many—that the president deserved support because of his compassionate commitment to "improve lives in our inner cities." Bush did not express that compassion through government programs, Lusk admitted, but by empowering churches and community organizations to perform the healing work.

By the middle of the decade, Lusk had a growing national reputation, not merely as a tailback-turned-minister, not merely as the man who first kneeled in prayer in an NFL end zone, but as a rising and polarizing figure in conservative politics. There could be little doubt of Lusk's arrival at a position of prominence when he received the seal of disapproval from a man who represented all that is wrong with America today to the minds of many conservative Americans. Barry Lynn, executive director of Americans United for Separation of Church and State, described Lusk this way on the occasion of Justice Sunday III: "I'm not at all surprised that Pastor Lusk would turn his pulpit over to the Religious Right for partisan purposes. Lusk long ago decided to play ball with the Bush administration in exchange for government grants."[13]

As Lusk noted in his bombastic speech that night, his associations with certain white political leaders known for their silence on racial injustices—including several standing with him at the pulpit that night—had prompted some to label him an "Uncle Tom." Lusk didn't reject the label. The other black man at the altar, Wellington Boone, might have welcomed the charge.

For it was Boone who had written ten years earlier that there was much to be said in favor of Uncle Tom. As Boone put it in his book *Breaking Through*, "I want to boldly affirm Uncle Tom. The black community must stop criticizing Uncle Tom. He is a role model." Boone had added that slavery was "redemptive," an apt metaphor and preparation, he explained, for a life of slave-like devotion to God.[14]

To be fair, Boone's pro–Uncle Tom and pro-slavery statements, seen in their fuller context, were about the imperative for Jesus' followers to be humble servants rather than seekers of power and wealth. But another of Boone's associations seemed to bespeak an opposite impulse. As the journalist Max Blumenthal pointed out, Boone was a member of the Coalition on Revival, a right-wing Christian group committed to rebuilding civilization, from government to education to the arts, in accordance with their literal reading of the Bible.[15] The coalition was committed to creating "the kingdom of God" not on a spiritual or symbolic plane, but in the here and now—and by force, if necessary, a concept at odds with nearly every form of serious Christian theology and America's founding ideals.[16] Ironic for a religious/political movement often associated with ultra-patriotism, the "revival" movement Boone supported would essentially throw out the U.S. Constitution and replace it with the Bible, or one dubious interpretation thereof, as the governing playbook for the United States.

Perhaps the biggest player of all on the altar of Greater Exodus that January night was James Dobson, the overseer of the vast media and political network of the Colorado-based Focus on the Family. One might not have guessed solely from Dobson's speech at Justice Sunday III—relative to the charismatic Lusk and King and the highly polished Perkins, Dobson was bland and halting during his turn at the microphone—but he had in the preceding years become a Republican kingmaker of sorts, wielding enough perceived clout over conservative Christian voters to convince GOP political aspirants of the need to seek his blessing. The 2004 election, one that clinched the popular (and since-discredited) idea that socially conservative Christian voters play the trump card on the new political landscape, had only heightened the perception that the road to Washington led through Focus on the Family headquarters in Colorado Springs.

Even those leery of Dobson's message and influence had to be impressed by the vastness of his empire. Owing to the deluge of mail generated by the outreach efforts of Focus on the Family, the U.S. Postal Service gave the organization's headquarters its own zip code. Helping generate all that mail were the numerous books Dobson had written—among them, *Straight Talk to Men* and *What Wives Wish Their Husbands Knew about Women*—and *Focus* magazine.

Enhancing his clout were the Focus on the Family radio program, reaching an audience of an estimated seven million Americans, and Dobson's newspaper column, syndicated to more than five hundred weekly newspapers around the country.[17]

From his late-1970s emergence on the public stage with the mega-selling book *Dare to Discipline*, through to the early 2000s, Dobson had exerted his political influence from the sidelines. He had largely limited himself to his true stocks in trade, his advice-giving about child-rearing and his passionate offensive against homosexuality (which, to Dobson and like-minded Christian Right leaders, is a deviant lifestyle choice that a gay man or woman can reverse through prayer and therapy.)

But Dobson's distaste for politics, with all its compromising and deal-making, eventually lost out to other impulses as the culture wars reached their crescendo. "The attack and assault on marriage," Dobson explained of his heightened political action, "is so distressing that I just feel like I can't remain silent."[18]

So Dobson became an all-out warrior for George Bush in the 2004 election and helped push to the forefront the so-called values issues—abortion, gay marriage, Christian prerogatives in American public life—that were credited with giving Bush his narrow re-election. Dobson not only plunged into politics, but he brought with him a hard-edged message that belied the mild-mannered appearance and grandfatherly voice that were so familiar to his audiences. Dobson railed in a hyperbolic speech just before the 2006 congressional elections, for example, that "homosexual activists and liberal media . . . are hoping to change the age-old definition [of marriage] to include not only same-sex marriage but polygamy and perhaps group marriage and who knows what else. If that becomes law, the family as we know it will die."[19]

As they stood together before the Greater Exodus congregation and the Christian TV audience at Justice Sunday III, Dobson and Lusk shared more than their combative rhetoric and their outspoken hostility to homosexuals and "liberal activist" judges. They were both linked to the Fellowship of Christian Athletes—as a onetime member of the FCA board in Lusk's case, and as a prime honoree and oft-invited speaker in Dobson's case.

His friendship with FCA was just one of Dobson's ties to evangelicalism in pro sports. When a Christian events promotion company called Third Coast Sports staged its first major league baseball "faith day" in 2006, there was Dobson's organization in the lineup of sponsors at Atlanta's Turner Field, hosting a table and dispensing its literature—including promotions for Internet resources that, among other teachings, portrayed homosexuality as an affliction akin to alcoholism, from which the sufferer needed to seek recovery and religious-based rescue.

In the run-up to the game, Third Coast president Brent High had proudly announced that his company was in partnership with Focus on the Family in staging that faith day, and two more faith events to come in Atlanta that season. "To have the opportunity to help Focus on the Family expand their reach," High had enthused, "is very rewarding."[20]

By describing the Braves' faith day as an opportunity to help James Dobson's organization "expand their reach," the faith day organizer had said it all in the view of those who see Christianity in sports as a front for the promotion of conservative politics and culture. Braves management insisted that Focus on the Family be excluded from the second and third faith events scheduled at Turner Field that season, and Dobson's organization was out. Yet those concerned about a Christian Right incursion into professional baseball could take scant comfort. Focus on the Family and Third Coast Sports were still partners for ten more faith days and faith nights scheduled across the country over the remainder of the season at minor league parks. Sounding more defiant than sorry, Focus on the Family's marketing director, Rich Bennett, issued a media statement declaring the Atlanta faith event a success. "For Focus on the Family, our involvement in Faith Days is all about being there to support the marriage and parenting needs of families," Bennett said. "The Braves game in July was a great experience for us, and we are looking forward to participating in other faith days and faith nights events with Third Coast Sports in the future."[21]

In 2006, when a group of evangelical NBA players decided to honor the league's Christian chaplains and their wives by bankrolling a three-day, expenses-paid retreat for them during the all-star break, Dobson was chosen to appear as a featured speaker. When recounting the retreat later that season in an interview, one of the chaplains articulated a philosophy about faith and politics that, to his mind, made the Dobson connection only natural. "I think it's the nature of religious faith . . . that you'll be drawn more to conservative views, pro-life positions, and those kinds of things," the chaplain said. "I would think people of strong faith are going to gravitate more toward the [political] party living up to conservative values."

Not only does the chaplain's observation help explain the affinity between Christian sports ministries and Dobson, but it reveals volumes about the under-recognized political dimension of a faith-in-sports movement that is publicly defended as purely innocuous and wholesome, as merely a resource for religious ballplayers. Set aside for a moment the emergence and rising profile of many progressive and beyond-partisan evangelicals in the years following the Bush re-election. (Clearly, being devoutly Christian is not synonymous with being unswervingly conservative in politics.) And set aside the dubiousness of Christian Right claims that the Bible makes a top-priority, slam-dunk case against abortion and homosexuality. (The matters are clearly far more complicated than that.) The basketball chaplain's observation nonetheless reveals important truth about religion in sports today: Going to bat for Jesus quite frequently means more than embracing Christianity and sharing the get-Jesus proposition with the public.

The faith being dispensed to our sports stars, and from them to the public, frequently comes with a set of conservative cultural and political views that are frequently one and the same as the agenda of the Christian Right movement—anti-abortion, anti-gay, and intent on publicly asserting the superiority of theologically conservative Christianity over other religious beliefs. The religion fed to athletes, and through them to sports-loving America, is the religion of the Praying Tailback, Herbert Hoover Lusk: well-intentioned and constructive in part—but often partisan and divisive, and generally aligned with a Christian Right political power structure that has become increasingly distasteful to many Americans and discredited in many circles as a legitimate public expression of the religion of Jesus.

Perhaps it is useful at this juncture, more than a half-century after the founding of the Fellowship of Christian Athletes, to revisit a proposition put to the ministry around the time of its formation, when some suggested that it consider calling itself not the Fellowship of Christian Athletes but, for the sake of greater inclusiveness, the Fellowship of *Religious* Athletes. What if the question, and all of its implications, were brought *today* to the men whose beliefs and behavior constitute religion in pro sports? Would they accept, even promote, a more open form of faith in the game?

Maybe someday. As later chapters will explore, promising possibilities and the impetus for change are emerging in these closing years of the decade. In the broader culture, we are in the midst of a changing of the guard. Notably, three of the Christian Right luminaries sharing the pulpit with Lusk at Justice Sunday III have moved on, Dobson resigning from his Focus on the Family leadership role in 2009, Falwell dying in 2007, and Santorum losing his 2006 re-election bid. In bottom-up fashion, some staff members of the leading ministries are voicing aspirations for a new model of religion in sports.

But for now, if one is to judge from its rhetoric, strategies, tactics, promoters, friends, and funders, sports world Christianity remains generally closed off to the possibility of religion in professional sports becoming more than a narrow form of evangelicalism in the game. To any suggestion that religion in the locker rooms, stadiums, and arenas might become more ecumenical, more open to the different faiths and worldviews that permeate the communities supporting major league franchises, the movement generally projects the same reply that was given by the Fellowship of Christian Athletes fifty years ago. The answer then, and the answer today for the most part, is "no."[22]

Even if we graciously concede a role for evangelical Christians and their beliefs in pro sports, as this book attempts to do, the time has come that we stop taking that "no" for an answer. The rest of us—we Jews, Muslims, Buddhists, Hindus, atheists, agnostics, progressive and moderate Catholics and Protestants—have a stake in this, too. Because professional sports—that messy, profane, and wonderful colossus that for all its faults and excesses can still lift us to our feet and bring us to our knees—don't belong to just one segment of the American public.

They belong to all of us.

Notes

1. "Football & Religion," NFL Films, 2004.

2. Andrew Knox, "Morgan Ensberg: Three Strikes . . . You're Saved," CBN News, Christian Broadcasting Network, June 20, 2005. (See http://www.cbn.com/entertainment/sports/700club_morganensberg-062005.aspx.)

3. Tom Krattenmaker, "Going Long for Jesus," *Salon*, May 10, 2006. (See http://www.salon.com/news/feature/2006/05/10/ministries/index.html.)

4. Tony Ladd and James A. Mathisen, *Muscular Christianity: Evangelical Protestants and the Development of American Sport* (Grand Rapids, MI: Baker Books, 1999), 129.

5. Murray Polner, *Branch Rickey: A Biography* (New York: Atheneum, 1982), 251.

6. Fellowship of Christian Athletes organization fact sheet; see http://image.teamfca.net/site-uploadfiles/FCA/59D89C1C-74BF-4C4F-978D811000467BC8/E19061F4-F7BC-4BE8-B55CB1CD9FE77B16.pdf

7. Ladd and Mathisen, 130.

8. Michelle Hiskey, "Q&A / HERB LUSK II: First prayer; Displays of faith on football field started 3 decades ago, when Herb Lusk II kneeled," *Atlanta Journal Constitution*, February 4, 2006.

9. "Football & Religion," NFL Films, 2004.

10. Stephen Evans, "America's Generous Aid to Africa," BBC News, June 15, 2005, http://news.bbc.co.uk/1/hi/business/4091528.stm.

11. George W. Bush, address on HIV/AIDS delivered in Philadelphia on June 23, 2004; for transcript see http://www.state.gov/s/gac/rl/rm/2004/33867.htm.

12. For examples of the anti-Lusk vitriol spurred by his appointment to the Advisory Council on HIV/AIDS, see "Bush names homophobe to federal AIDS council," *The Advocate*, March 10, 2006, and "Bush Abstains from Appointing HIV Experts," Act Up New York website, http://www.actupny.org/-reports/bush_lusk.html.

13. "Pastor of Church Hosting Alito Rally Received Financial Support from Bush Administration," Americans United for Separation of Church and State news release,

January 4, 2006. See http://www.au.org/site/News2?JServSessionIdr005=ambpvbtge1 .app1b&abbr=pr&page=NewsArticle&id=7775&security=1002&news_iv_ctrl=1241.

14. Wellington Boone, *Breaking Through: Taking the Kingdom into the Culture by Out-Serving Others*, (Nashville, TN: Broadman and Holman Publishers), 1996.

15. Max Blumenthal, "Who Are Justice Sunday's Ministers of Minstrelsy?" *The Huffington Post*, January 6, 2006, http://www.huffingtonpost.com/max-blumenthal/ who-are-justice-sundays-_b_13348.html.

16. For background on, and liberal critique of, the Coalition on Revival see http://65.175.91.69/Reformation_net/Pages/COR_About.htm, http://www.rapidnet .com/~jbeard/-bdm/Psychology/cor/general.htm, and http://www.talk2action.org/ story/2008/5/2/131557/1558.

17. Michael Crowley, "James Dobson: The Religious Right's New Kingmaker," *Slate*, November 12, 2004, http://www.slate.com/id/2109621.

18. Crowley, "James Dobson."

19. Bob Baysinger, "Upcoming Election Critical in 'Gay Marriage' Debate, Pro-Family Leaders Say during Rally," Baptist Press, October 16, 2006, http://www.bpnews.net/ bpnews.asp?ID=24172.

20. Dyana Bagby, "Braves Bench Focus on the Family," *Southern Voice*, August 4, 2006. Note that High explained in a subsequent interview for this book that his comment referred not to the political views espoused by Focus on the Family and its leader, but its teachings on parenting and family issues.

21. Associated Press, "Braves Give Boot to Conservative Group at 'Faith Day,' " ESPN .com, August 11, 2006, http://sports.espn.go.com/mlb/news/story?id=2547167.

22. Additional evidence on the virtual evangelical monopoly on religious practice in sports, and its inhospitable regard for other forms of faith, is furnished by an analysis of content in the two leading evangelical sports magazines, *Sharing the Victory* and *Sports Spectrum*. Despite the significant numbers of Catholic athletes in the major professional leagues, some of whom are profiled in the magazines, searches of the magazines' archives reveal an almost complete absence of mentions of Catholicism and other Catholic-specific terms such as "mass."

CHAPTER 2

∼

A Cross on the Logo

Representing for God in the High-Profile World of Major
League Sports

He was, the headline said, "on a mission from God."

So began the introduction of basketball prodigy Dwight Howard to the American public in the winter of 2004. Howard, an African American high school student from Georgia with a wholesome smile and prodigious talent, was emerging as the possible No. 1 pick in the upcoming National Basketball Association draft, and as ESPN and other media outlets came calling, they were hearing and seeing a lot about God.

On Howard's bedroom wall, sharing space with Michael Jordan and Julius Erving posters, was a simple wooden cross, and next to it a hand-scrawled list of the young man's "personal commandments." Among them: "And it shall come to pass that Dwight Howard II will surpass LeBron James for the best high school basketball player, college player, and NBA player. Amen. And it shall come to pass that Dwight Howard II would stand head and shoulders over 2004 prospects in the name of Jesus. Amen." Ending the young evangelist's list was a promise to change professional basketball itself. "It shall and will come to pass," read the commandment, "that the NBA will be [run] by the standards of God." To symbolize his mission to Christianize the NBA, Howard had drawn beneath his personal commandments a crude rendition of the NBA logo. Howard's version replicated the familiar silhouette figure of the player widely believed to be former Los Angeles Lakers great Jerry West. But it bore one addition, a cross on the silhouette player's chest. "One day, I was writing down my goals," the six-foot, eleven-inch Howard explained. "I closed my eyes, and I saw a cross in the middle of Jerry West's chest." The revised logo, he explained, represented his aim "to raise the name of God within the league and throughout the world."

Profiles of Howard by ESPN, both on its television channels and its ESPN .com website, along with a spate of coverage by other news outlets, were quickly transforming Howard from a prospect known only to insider basketball junkies to something approaching a household name, at least in those millions of American households obsessed with sports. He was, suddenly, the large ultratalented kid who wanted to affix the cross to the NBA logo, the one who wanted to use his sports fame to spread the Christian message. The idea turned heads. It puzzled some, thrilled others. It prompted at least one skeptical columnist to predict the young man would experience a "nightmare" as his dream ran into the cold reality of life in the hedonistic National Basketball Association.

But even non-Christian fans who did not appreciate Howard's zest for evangelizing had to admit there was a lot to like about the giant ballplayer with the choir-boy image. The previous year's high school phenom, LeBron James, had leveraged his NBA future during his senior year to buy a gaudy Hummer. Howard? He wore braces and still drove the 1984 Crown Victoria his father had bought him for $900. Whereas James was apparently following the maximum-marketing path blazed by Michael Jordan and Tiger Woods—sports figures often criticized for avoiding principled stands that might compromise their commercial viability as product endorsers—Howard was standing up boldly for what he believed, even though it would likely limit his marketing appeal. Offering none of the "street cred" of James or Allen Iverson, how could Howard pitch sneakers and soda to teenage males? In his usual fashion, Howard dismissed those concerns with an expression of his faith. "It will be up to God for that to happen," Howard said. "If he wants me to market myself, then I'll do it. I'm not trying to give glory for myself. I'm trying to give glory for him."[1]

The Internet and sports media buzzed about Howard's logo with the cross and all that it symbolized. Was there a place for Christianity in a pro sports world known as much for sex, greed, and self-glorification as virtue and Christ-like humility? Not if Howard was going to force his religion down fans' and teammates' throats, opined Jack Haley, a television analyst and former player. Howard's vision, Haley said, "is not something I can see the NBA embracing. Jerry West is the logo. Jerry West, for lack of a better expression, was God to the NBA. . . . [Howard] is going to be dealing with grown men who like to have a lot of fun and enjoy being massive celebrities. There are guys who drink. They like to go to strip clubs. There's partying. There are groupies. He's in for an eye-opening experience. The NBA is a man's world. He's very naïve if he thinks he's going to come into the league and change a lot of things quickly."

Haley, who played for the San Antonio Spurs in the mid-1990s, said Christianity had become a wedge between members of that team. Haley and the flamboyant Dennis Rodman were part of one camp; the newly converted Christian superstar center David Robinson was the leader of the other. On team flights and in the locker room, the Christian group would huddle for Bible study and prayer; the non-Christians, Haley said, felt pressured to join and judged for not participating. They resented it. "When you have that kind of pressure from your leaders, from your MVP David Robinson and the co-captains, guys tend to fall in line. There was definitely a rift," Haley said.[2]

Avery Johnson, a guard on the Spurs during that time and a member of the team's Christian circle, came to the defense of Dwight Howard as well as his Bible-believing teammates from the mid-1990s Spurs. Reprising the old team dynamic, Johnson suggested Haley could probably have benefited from some Bible study. If Robinson had come on too strong back then, Johnson said, it was because of the fervor that typically animates the recent convert. Dwight Howard, Johnson said, "has noble goals in line with his faith." Could his dream of a cross on the logo be realized? "Nothing is impossible," Johnson said.[3]

The problematic nature of Dwight Howard's vision was glaringly evident in another way. As the media were quick to remind, league commissioner David Stern is Jewish. The Christian magazine *Sports Spectrum* suggested that was hardly an impediment since Jesus, too, was a Jew. Stern himself was diplomatic but dismissive. "I admire [Howard's] fervor and won't disrespect his religious belief," Stern said. "But [the realization of his goal] would be imposing something on lots of other players who may not share his beliefs. So I think it's always a question of balance." The league's stance on religion, Stern explained, was to allow players to practice their faith but to draw a line at "someone trying to impose his beliefs on somebody else."[4]

In June came draft day, and with it all the hoopla—the breathless, live television coverage, the hard-core fans turning out in team gear to cheer, or boo, their team's decisions, and the draftees in their flashy suits gliding to the stage upon the calling of their names, towering over the diminutive commissioner as they shook his hand and posed for the customary photo. Howard did go first, to the Orlando Magic. He strode up to the stage at Madison Square Garden in his stylish blue suit, donned his "Magic" cap, took Stern's hand, and flashed his appealing smile for the cameras. Moments later, the media asked him how it felt to be the new crown prince of professional basketball. "I thank God just for allowing me to be the first person selected," Howard answered. "It just feels so good. . . . I just want to go out there and prove all the doubters wrong—just keep working hard and just keeping God first, and everything will fall in line."

As the summer went on, then training camp, then the opening of Howard's rookie season, the buzz around his cross-on-the-logo comments gradually faded, and the young player seemed intent on reassuring the league and the public that he wasn't going to step over David Stern's line. "People are thinking I'm trying to go in and get on the podium and make everybody a Christian," he told one newspaper. "That's not my goal. My goal is to let my actions speak louder than my words."[5]

As he ventured into the rough waters of the NBA, Howard had a buoy of sorts in the Magic's executive suite. Pat Williams, executive vice president of the team, had more than three decades' experience in pro basketball, and as a devout Christian who had authored several Christian-themed books, he had stature and credibility as a leader in the sports world Christian community. In an interview, Williams played down concerns about the evangelical enthusiasm of the choirboy player becoming an issue on the team. "If your biggest problem with a player is that he sings too loud at church, I think we'll take it," he said with a laugh.

(It would not continue to be the biggest problem with the boy-wonder big man as he progressed into manhood and his ball-playing career. Word leaked to the media in early 2008 that the young superstar had fathered a child out of wedlock with a former member of the Magic's dance team.[6])

As the 2004–2005 season began, attention fixed not on Howard's outspoken Christianity but on his play, which was remarkably good for a player straight out of high school. Through the early weeks of the season, Howard was among the league leaders in rebounding. He was playing like a man, and with a subtle change in his persona, his braces gone, his God-speak toned down, Howard was presenting an image more tempered than what the public had seen the previous spring. If the testimony of the team's biggest-name player was any indication, Howard was fitting in well with his teammates, too. "He's been pretty amazing. He's so professional and mature for his age," veteran Grant Hill said. "We're kind of like his big brothers." Hill added with a laugh: "I hope we don't corrupt him."[7]

So began the fading of the sensationalism around Dwight Howard's evangelical faith and his quest to Christianize pro basketball. But a bigger story continues to unfold, a story told in microcosm by Howard's entry into professional sports with his Christianity on his sleeve. For all the cheering and booing over Howard's stated aim of Christianizing the NBA, there is nothing shocking or new about a young man's evangelical Christianity infusing his professional athletic life. For all the wows and furrowed brows provoked by Howard's vision of a cross on the logo, his crude redrawing of the symbol of the NBA was a fairly accurate symbol of a state of affairs that already exists, not just in professional basketball but in football, baseball, and other professional sports as well. Truly, Dwight Howard has plenty of company, and these Christian athletes, as they take the field with their faithful words, gestures, and prayers, all wear the Christian cross. As Howard himself would say a few years after his entry into the league, he and his fellow Christian ballers *were* the cross. When fans "look at players around the league who are Christians like myself," he told the *Orlando Sentinel*, "they see the cross."[8]

*

If an avid pro sports fan from the 1950s, even the 1970s, were suddenly transported to the first decade of the twenty-first century, he would be confronted with huge, perhaps shocking, differences in the games our athletes play for pay. The rules of the games haven't changed much, or the dimensions of the fields. But the time-transported sports nut would probably be stunned by the enormity of the spectacle that pro sports have become—the huge, posh stadiums, the crazed fans with painted faces and bodies, the front-page coverage in daily newspapers, the nonstop chatter on television and sports-talk radio. He would be floored to learn the players' salaries. He would be stunned to observe the greatly elevated status of sports on the scale of cosmic significance. As to the latter, this wide-eyed fan from the past would be witnessing much more talk about God, gestures to God, pleas to God, and thanks to God from the athletes themselves. Lest today's jaded fans forget, the current state of affairs is relatively new. "It wasn't long ago that sports fields were the devil's playground," journalist David Plotz writes. "But today there are *Angels in the Outfield*, and God seems to be following pro sports more intently than ever."[9]

The transported fan might be surprised, too, to see all the professing and proselytizing heading in a single theological direction, unlike the 1970s when some of the highest profile pro athletes were changing their names and stances not in allegiance to Jesus but to Muhammad. Today, religion in sports correlates almost exactly with *Christianity* in sports, with the exception of an occasional Muslim in basketball and football and a handful of Jewish players in baseball.

How did this come to be? Suffice it to say that Christianity's strong presence in sports is no accident. It happened because a movement of athletic-minded evangelical Christians have been *making* it happen since setting out more than a half-century ago to reach and convert athletes and leverage their influence to spread the gospel to the wider sports-loving public. The growth of faith in sports is part of a bigger story, too, one in which evangelical Christianity has come to play a more visible role in American politics and public life than a generation or two ago. Sports reflect, at the same time that they reinforce and promote, the country's evangelical revival.

The sector of professional sports, like American society itself, is alive with fervent Christianity. Fans might appreciate it, or they might hate it, but it is unlikely that they have managed to avoid noticing the large and conspicuous role played by religion in today's game. Batters are crossing themselves as they step in for a plate appearance, summoning the Father, Son, and Holy Ghost in their bid for a hit. Baseball stars such as superstar slugger Albert Pujols are concluding their home run trots with a dramatic gesture to God, gazing skyward and pointing triumphantly to the heavens as they cross home plate. No one has brought this particular religious ritual to more fans—and with more baggage, given his eventual entanglement in steroids and legal scandals—than Barry Bonds. The since-retired San Francisco Giant broke the all-time single-season home run record in 2001 and six years later passed Henry Aaron as the all-time home run champion, meaning he had plenty of opportunities to perfect his display and have it seen by millions, over and over and over, on sports highlights shows. But it doesn't take a home run anymore to inspire a religion demonstration on the diamond. Hitters are acknowledging God after singles, too, and pitchers are gesturing to the Almighty after getting a big out.

Owing to the extensive network organized by the Pennsylvania-based Baseball Chapel, each of the thirty major league baseball teams has its own chaplain, a volunteer lay minister who holds chapel services at the ballpark on Sundays and ministers to players throughout the week. The network extends deep into the multitiered minor leagues of professional baseball, where Christian chaplains are provided for the more than one hundred minor league teams.

Football, like baseball, has a pace and rhythm that furnish isolated moments of triumph, and Christian players take full advantage. Growing since the 1990s are the frequency and drama of religious gestures on the field. The more common practice in the 1990s—one acted out with impressive regularity by touchdown-scoring machine Cris Carter of the Minnesota Vikings, in seeming homage to Herb Lusk—was to kneel prayerfully in the end zone, ball in hand, head bowed. But now players face and point a different direction after scoring, their gaze and index finger fixed skyward. The practice seems to mirror the larger trend in American society in the first decade of the new century, one in which evangelical Christians have become increasingly assertive in the public arena—even showy and arrogant at times, in the view of their critics—ushering in an era not of bowed heads, but of proud display. Any deconstruction of the sky-pointing ritual leads to the realization that, save for the back-tilted head and skyward gaze, it is quite similar to the standard "We're number one!" sports world gesture, both in form and, in the eyes of cynics, in meaning as well.

Because of its flow and constant scoring, basketball doesn't frame the singular moments conducive to sky-pointing. But the relative scarcity of religious displays on the court certainly does not mean professional basketball is any less charged with religious enthusiasm than baseball and football. Alongside and in competition with the hip-hop culture of pro basketball, NBA Christians, like their brethren in Major League Baseball and the NFL, are forming Bible circles and huddling with their team chaplains. And like the football players who congregate in prayer at midfield at the conclusion of games, some Bible-believing basketballers are circling on the court after the final horn, their heads bowed and hands clasped together.

Christian practice was becoming so prominent in the New York Knicks' locker room in the early 2000s that then-coach Jeff Van Gundy publicly protested, calling religion one of the two worst things to happen to the league's player culture (the other being golf). The fraternizing between Christian members of the opposing teams might douse his players' competitive fire, Van Gundy worried. Nor did he appreciate the unusually high level of access to players granted to team chaplains, which was bad for players' focus, according to the famously intense Van Gundy. It hardly helped when Knicks point guard and devout Christian Charlie Ward was quoted in the *New York Times* around the same time charging that Jews were "stubborn" and guilty of persecuting Christians, remarks that set off a controversy that reverberated in the New York media for weeks.

In objecting to the flourishing of Christianity in NBA locker rooms, however, Van Gundy was swimming upstream—and the current shows no sign of abating anytime soon. If journalist David Plotz is right in asserting that pro sports is the most heavily proselytized sector of American society—and he is probably not far off—the ranks of Christian players are not likely to dwindle.

As is true for the culture at large, the evangelical faith permeating sports takes numerous forms; the degree of controversy is in the eye of the beholder. It can be as simple as a player vocally appreciating his many blessings in ascending to the top of the sports world and reaping the substantial benefits. It can involve players turning to the supernatural for safety and success on the field. As to the latter, one recently retired pro football star explained it this way in an interview conducted during his playing time with the Philadelphia Eagles: "Every time I step onto the football field, I know it's not me. I need God to take total control of my body and mind. Everyone's big. Everyone's fast. Everyone can catch. Everyone can tackle. But those who really excel, there's something a little bit deeper . . . that you can't see in the natural [world]."[10]

At other times, athletes' talk of God veers in the direction of divine favoritism toward the player's victorious team, a practice typified by the comments of a member of the Pittsburgh Steelers after the team's narrow escape victory over the New York Jets in a 2005 playoff game. The day will live in infamy for New York fans. Their kicker, Doug Brien, missed not one, but two potential game-winning field goal attempts to give Pittsburgh the chance to win in overtime. "God had a hand in that game today," Antwaan Randle El of the Steelers declared.[11] "We had no chance. Who misses two field goals like that? It doesn't happen." Another Steeler, Jeff Hartings, said, "God gave us another chance."[12]

Quite common is the practice of using the high-profile moment of triumph—and the media microphones and cameras that invariably go with it—to glorify God. Michael Redd of the NBA Milwaukee Bucks, a minister's son, typified the practice when he stood up for the post-game interview following his team's one point victory over San Antonio in 2004. Asked whether he'd been through a game as dramatic as the one just finished, he said, "First of all I just want to give praise to the Lord for blessing us with another victory, in his glory." Jason Campbell, quarterback for the Washington Redskins, sounded remarkably similar to Redd in an ESPN interview following his team's victory in a Monday night game in 2007. When ESPN's Michelle Tafoya asked how he felt to earn the starting quarterback position and open the season with two wins, Campbell said, "It's a blessing. I give all the glory to God for giving me the opportunity to be in the position."

These are just two examples, but Christian athletes deliver the same line of reasoning countless times over the course of a season, their words so similar they begin to sound as though the players are reading from a script. That's because they are, in a sense. Statements like Redd's and Campbell's come almost verbatim from the rhetorical playbook of faith promoters in and around sports, who use as a foundational premise the notion that God has elevated these fortunate few men into their high-profile positions that they might proclaim his name and spread his gospel.

Players sometimes get the opportunity to express (and promote) their Christian belief in the highest profile situations imaginable. In the trophy presentation spectacle following the 2007 Super Bowl, in front of a television audience estimated at more than 140 million people in this country and millions more around the world, both the coach and owner of the champion Indianapolis Colts went big for God. As coach Tony Dungy declared, the Colts had not only won football's grandest prize, but they had done it "the Lord's way." Back in the locker room following the trophy-awarding, Dungy had his players interrupt their celebrating and media interviews to kneel and recite the Lord's Prayer ("Our Father, who art in heaven . . ."). All complied, reported ESPN the Magazine writer David Fleming, but some shot looks of disbelief at one another as they hit their knees. "To reporters in the room," Fleming wrote, "the moment appeared awkward and forced."[13]

To many Christian figures in sports, the high-achieving religious athlete has something of a deal with the Lord, the terms of which go like this: God has placed the player in his position of success and influence so that he may use the platform to celebrate and promote the faith. A vivid example was furnished by the college basketball world earlier this decade when Mike Davis, then the coach of Indiana University, explained to the Christian sports magazine *Sports Spectrum* how God had propelled his Hoosiers' run to the NCAA championship game. The feat, especially Indiana's upset win over heavily favored Duke, was considered especially impressive because of the circumstances under which Davis had become the school's first black basketball coach the previous season, following the hugely publicized and controversial firing of the legendary Bob Knight. As Davis told interviewer Dan Jackson:

> I knew God put me here for a reason. Who else would put me here? Who else would put a no-name guy in a high-profile position that everyone in the country is talking about? . . . As a Christian you know He's working all the time. Here we are in the same bracket as Duke, who everyone says is unbeatable. We haven't won a first-round game in a long time and we are facing them. The whole country saw that game. The whole country knew Indiana beat Duke. That platform was set for me because I gave God the credit. That's why I always felt positive. . . . On senior night I told the people we were going to [advance to the championship game] and we did. That was God's voice saying, "Give me the credit, and I'll bring you through it." There was no way on paper that Indiana should have beat Duke and Oklahoma and play for the national championship. . . . I knew we would be there. I knew God put me on the platform to share His Word.[14]

Sometimes, a franchise can take on the appearance of being God's team. So it was with the 2005 Houston Astros, who played their way to the World Series behind the leadership of a cadre of ballplayers known for their enthusiastic and outspoken Christianity. Given the rowdy, obscenity-hurling persona of their World Series opponents, the Chicago White Sox, and the relative scarcity of upfront Christians on the Sox' roster, that year's Fall Classic shaped up something of a battle between the Christians and the heathens. The heathens, the record will show, swept the series.

The "God's team" phenomenon rose to new heights of explicitness and visibility when the management of the Colorado Rockies went public in 2006 with their convictions about building the team in a Christian mold. Admitting they were nervous about their comments offending non-Christian fans, Rockies General Manager Dan O'Dowd and other team officials explained to *USA*

Today that they were cultivating a team culture of Christian character and clean living. The newspaper described a clubhouse atmosphere conspicuously free of cursing, sex magazines, and obscenity-laced rap music.

"Quotes from Scripture are posted in the weight room," *USA Today*'s Bob Nightengale reported. "Chapel service is packed on Sundays. Prayer and fellowship groups each Tuesday are well-attended. It's not unusual for the front office executives to pray together. . . . Behind the scenes, [the Rockies] quietly have become an organization guided by Christianity—open to other religious beliefs but embracing a Christian-based code of conduct they believe will bring them focus and success."

Complementing the religious words and gestures are the messages many Christian players inscribe on their uniform and equipment, even their skin. These, the athletes explain, can give them a boost on the field, a reminder of the divine "audience of one" for whom they play. The scrawled messages and tattoos can occasionally grab the attention of the cameras and reach audiences of millions, in ways that would surely bring a smile to the lips of the founder of the Fellowship of Christian Athletes, the man who dreamed of leveraging the visibility of sports stars to spread the Christian faith.

A prime example of ink on a faithful player's skin reached the reader of ESPN's magazine in a 2008 issue. Sprawled across a two-page spread was the long arm of a defender engaged in the unenviable task of guarding superstar LeBron James. The arm (belonging to the Chicago Bulls' Thabo Sefolosha, a Christian imported from Switzerland) bore a tattoo featuring the outlines of a bare foot and the word: "God guides my steps." In a similar fashion, major league pitcher Todd Jones had "JN 20:29" tattooed on his left hand, a reference to John 20:29, "Blessed are those who have not seen and yet have believed."[15]

Ink on cloth, not skin, was the medium employed by a college football champion in 2007. Dallas Baker, a star receiver for the University of Florida Gators, punctuated his team's national title game victory by standing for the live, nationally televised interview in a t-shirt bearing the scrawled words of Philippians 4:13, a go-to Bible verse among Christian athletes: "I can do all things through Christ." Florida quarterback Tim Tebow, throughout the 2008 college season, donned eye black referencing that same passage via a simple "Phil 4:13"; for the national championship game, Tebow switched his eye black verse to John 3:16: "For God so loved the world that he gave his one and only Son, that whoever believes in him shall not perish but have eternal life."

Baker and Tebow would not have been able to execute the feat in the professional game, where player garb is so tightly restricted that even the height of players' socks is specified and monitored by the league's uniforms police. Yet that does not stop players from expressing their faith on their gear. Ben

Roethlisberger, quarterback for the Pittsburgh Steelers, wore the letters "PFJ" —"playing for Jesus"—on his armbands for a time.[16] Provoking a controversy, then-Bengals quarterback Jon Kitna, one of the most fervent Christians in the league, began wearing a baseball cap with a cross logo to post-game news conferences several seasons ago. Here was a player taking Dwight Howard's cross-on-the-logo quest to its near-fulfillment—and provoking a crackdown by league management in the process. The NFL fined Kitna $5,000 (a paltry sum for an NFL quarterback), citing its rule that only official NFL apparel could be worn in interviews immediately following games. While agreeing to stop wearing the hat, Kitna appealed the fine, and with his fellow Christians rallying in Kitna's support, the NFL rescinded it.[17] On a feisty quarterback's head, Dwight Howard's dream of a cross on the logo had been realized, if only partially.

It was Kitna, by then with the Lions, who cited divine healing following a 2007 game in which he made a quicker-than-expected return from a first-half concussion and led Detroit to a 20-17 overtime victory over Minnesota. The boldness of Kitna's claim stirred considerable media attention, as did Terrell Owens' (supposedly) divine healing in the run-up to the 2005 Super Bowl. The Eagles' brash superstar receiver guaranteed that his surgically repaired ankle would be sufficiently healed for him to go to battle against the Patriots—this, despite the team doctor and management withholding any official determination of Owens' ability to play. "God has already cleared me," Owens told the media hordes. "It doesn't matter what the doctor said. I have the best doctor in God."[18]

Supernatural intervention so that Terrell Owens might play in the Super Bowl? It was a step too far for numerous media members, pundits, and skeptical fans. "I've heard of God is my co-pilot," NBCSports.com contributor Mike Celizic wrote. "But God is my orthopedist?"[19]

*

The "religion" of rabbit's feet and crossed fingers runs deep in the sport of baseball. Major league players are notoriously superstitious, enacting strange rituals to earn good fortune, ward off bad luck, and win a psychological edge. Some players go out of their way to avoid stepping on the foul line as they trot to and from the dugout between turns in the field. Some go through precise pre-game rituals dictating what they eat, the route they take driving to the ballpark, and how they put on their uniform. Others enact intricate multifaceted rituals between every pitch while batting. Baseball superstition broke onto the sports pages in a humorous way in 2006 when word surfaced that Justin Morneau, first baseman for the Minnesota Twins and a native of Canada, was vying for good fortune every game by wearing under his Twins uniform a Vancouver Canucks jersey t-shirt bearing bad-boy player Todd Bertuzzi's name and number. Never mind that Minnesota sports fans loathed Bertuzzi and the Canucks, who were arch-rivals of Minnesota's hockey team. Morneau was on his way to the league's Most Valuable Player award, and the Twins were riding an extended hot streak to a division championship.

Who can blame ballplayers like Morneau for wearing talismans? More than other sports, baseball is a game in which luck truly counts. Poorly hit balls frequently plop down between fielders for base hits, and hard-hit line drives find fielders' gloves regularly, leaving hitters with just another failed at-bat in the box score. Players get hot and cold, seemingly at the whim of unseen forces. Entire franchises can seem under the sway of ill winds. Baseball lore is full of stories of curses, omens, and mystical forces. There is the Curse of the Billy Goat that has afflicted the Chicago Cubs, who have not reached the World Series since 1945. And there is—make that *was*—the Curse of the Bambino.

Most fans know the legend well: The Boston Red Sox, prior to the 1920 season, traded a young star named Babe Ruth to the New York Yankees. What ensued were nearly nine decades of dramatically divergent fates for the two franchises. The Yankees went on to win twenty-six World Series championships over the next eighty-five years; the Red Sox, precisely zero. The disparity seemed almost cruel when one took into account the devotion with which New England fans followed the Sox, the loyalty they exhibited through year after year of disappointments and near-misses. It was enough to make even a purely rational thinker wonder if maybe there wasn't a measure of truth to the notion of something supernatural plaguing the Sox.

Enter the Red Sox of recent vintage, led by a collection of Bible-believing players who set out to vanquish the curse with something more powerful—the cross.

Despite representing a part of the country known for religious reticence, several of the highest profile members of the Boston Red Sox through the early and mid-2000s made much of their Christian beliefs, talking about God frequently, boldly, and, thanks to the bright national spotlight that tends to shine on the franchise, to a very large audience.

Rewind to the post-season of 2003. Boston's Trot Nixon has just hit a dramatic walk-off, extra-inning home run to win Game Three of the Red Sox' first-round playoff series with Oakland. After his teammates have finally finished mobbing Nixon at home plate and rubbing his freshly shorn head, ESPN's Gary Miller corrals the hero for a live interview. As the dejected Athletics shuffle off the field, the hyper-excited Boston outfielder collects himself for the live interview against a backdrop of delirious Sox fans waving "WE BELIEVE" signs. In the parlance of the Christian athlete, Nixon is about to use his platform for the Lord.

"I went to the plate asking the Lord to calm my nerves," explains Nixon, whose game-ending blast cleared the center field wall by barely a foot or two. "The last thing you want to do is [try to bat] with those nerves going crazy, so I told him to calm my nerves and allow me to honor him out there on the field. He came through for me today. It wasn't me swinging the bat. It was the Lord Jesus Christ. . . . I was [a] little tardy on [the swing], but that ball just carried out. Usually the ball doesn't carry in this cool weather here in Fenway, but the Lord blessed me right there." Why did the ball carry better than the meteorological conditions would normally allow on a chilly fall night in New England? As Nixon tells the newspaper reporters a few minutes later, the Lord provided "a gust of wind."[20]

Indicative of the disconnect between players who wax religious and their not-quite-buying-it interviewers, ESPN's Miller quickly changes the subject to Nixon's supposed good-luck haircut, administered that same day, and the riff that was running through the post-season about the Red Sox players' and their ultrashort hair. So it must have been the haircut that made the difference, Miller offers with a chuckle, seeming to have missed what Nixon had said a moment earlier about *God*, not superstition, coming to his aid. Nixon takes it with a smile, but Christian viewers warmed by the ballplayer's ringing statement of faith might well be feeling that Miller has trampled on something sacred.[21]

Boston followed up on Nixon's heroics with a win in Game Four, forcing the series to a fifth and deciding game. In the run-up to the series finale, Red Sox catcher Doug Mirabelli told the *Boston Globe* that God "does answer prayers. And I guarantee you there are millions of people out there who have been praying for the Red Sox to win the World Series, no doubt about it."[22] Boston indeed prevailed in the decisive game and advanced to the league championship series against New York.

As fans well know, God's blessings—or the good luck conjured through buzz-job haircuts?—did not last for the Boston Red Sox in 2003. Their age-old nemeses in pinstripes, the Yankees, eliminated them in the American League Championship Series, and in a most excruciating fashion, coming back from a three-run deficit to win the seventh and deciding game on an extra-inning home run. It was tempting to conclude, against all rational judgment, that maybe there *was* something to this Curse of the Bambino and its cruel hold on the Boston Red Sox. If there was, the 2004 edition of the Boston club was ready to explode it, ready to vanquish superstition with true Christian religion (and some good, gutsy baseball).

Twelve months after the heartbreaker in Yankee Stadium, the Red Sox found themselves in the same venue, once again meeting New York in the league championship series, once again needing to overcome the powerful

Yankees if they were to advance to the World Series and win the championship that had eluded the franchise since 1918. Ill omens seemed to hang over Game One. Curt Schilling–Boston's Game One starter, the star pitcher who had signed with Boston in the off-season for exactly this moment–came up lame. Plagued by an ankle injury suffered in the first-round series against the Angels, Schilling was unable to push off the rubber with his customary power, and he was no match for the New York hitters. Boston lost decisively, and it appeared that Schilling, the Sox' best hope, was finished for the series.

The Red Sox' other star pitcher, Pedro Martinez, lost in the second game as Boston fell behind two games to none. In his post-game remarks, the very religious Martinez seemed to be turning to God not for strength, but consolation. Yankee fans had tormented Martinez throughout the game with chants of "WHO'S YOUR DADDY?" a reference to an earlier remark by the pitcher that the Yankees had consistently got the better of him and that he was thusly obliged to call his rivals "my daddy." Martinez, who had grown up poor in the Dominican Republic, claimed that the Yankee fans' mocking chants did not make him feel bad, however. "It actually made me feel really, really good," Martinez claimed. "I actually realized that I was somebody important because I caught the attention of 60,000 people, plus the whole world. . . . Fifteen years ago, I was sitting under a mango tree without fifty cents to actually pay for a bus. And today, I was the center of attention in the whole city of New York. I thank God for that. . . . My biggest daddy is the one who put me out there and the one that brought me from the mango tree to the biggest stage in the world"–namely, God.[23]

The series moved to Boston, and the Red Sox lost again, leaving them with the almost impossible task of beating New York four straight times if they were to "reverse the curse," as their fans' signs pleaded. By eking out a narrow victory in Game Four, Boston avoided a sweep. Then the Red Sox won Game Five, forcing the series back to New York for the sixth and, if necessary, seventh game.

Schilling, surprisingly, was going to get another chance on the mound. Days earlier, he appeared to be finished for the season. The ankle was bad; post-season surgery was now a certainty. Team doctors attempted some stop-gap medical wizardry to fortify the ankle for one more game, and it appeared to work well enough to convince Schilling to give it a try. He bravely took the mound, but blood was seeping through his white sock before the first inning was over, the vivid red spot captured repeatedly by Fox's camera close-ups. Schilling, it appeared, was not long for the game.

Three hours later, he was not only a survivor but a hero. The Red Sox had won, forcing a seventh and deciding game. Schilling had braved the pain and pitched brilliantly, allowing just one run and four hits in seven innings. Fox's Kenny Albert stood with Schilling for the post-game interview, the hero wearing a t-shirt with "Why Not Us" stenciled across the front. Albert asked the obvious question: How is the ankle?

"It's all right," Schilling replied, sounding surprisingly solemn. He looked up and continued. "I gotta say, I became a Christian seven years ago, and I have never in my life been touched by God like I was tonight. I tried to go out and do it myself in Game One, and you saw what happened. Tonight, tonight was God's work when I went out to the mound, no question."

Schilling, fresh from a live-television faith proclamation that was stunning for its Christian explicitness, elaborated with the print reporters, his quotes appearing in newspapers across the country. "God did something amazing for me," he said. ". . . I knew that I wasn't going to be able to do this alone, and I prayed as hard as I could. I didn't pray to get a win or to make great pitches. I just prayed for the strength to go out there tonight and compete, and he gave me that."

Boston beat New York again the next night and advanced to the World Series against St. Louis. After Boston's victory over the Cardinals in Game One, Schilling and the Red Sox medical team—and God, if one took Schilling's view of things—repeated what they had accomplished in Game Six of the New York series. Schilling wasn't as sharp as he was against the Yankees, but he had more than enough to pitch Boston to a 6-2 victory and a two-game jump in the series.

"I promise you," Schilling said in the live television interview after the game, "that when I walked out of the dugout today and headed to the bullpen [to warm up before the game] the most shocked person in the stadium was my wife. When I woke up at seven this morning . . . I wasn't gonna pitch. I couldn't walk. I couldn't move. I don't [know] what had happened, but I knew when I woke up there was a problem [with my ankle]. . . . Honest to God, I did not think I was gonna take the ball today. Then everything starts happening. You start looking around at your teammates and understanding what you've been through over the last eight months. And I did what I did last time—I went to the Lord for help. Because I knew I wasn't gonna be able to do this myself. . . . Thank God for Dr. Morgan. . . . I went out there and, well, it happened."

There was no stopping the Red Sox now. Boston won the next two games to complete a four-game sweep and claim the championship, bringing relief and joy to the team's long-frustrated followers. After the final game, one overwhelmed fan celebrating in Boston's Kenmore Square summed things up for Red Sox fans everywhere as he got on his knees, tears welling in his eyes, and shouted repeatedly, "Thank you, God!"[24]

After the final game, appreciation for the Lord poured out of the Red Sox players' mouths like the contents of the dozens of champagne bottles uncorked in the delirious Boston clubhouse. Slugger Manny Ramirez, whom the Red Sox management had attempted to trade the previous off-season in a failed bid for Alex Rodriguez, was named the series Most Valuable Player. "God sent me back for a reason!" Ramirez exclaimed.[25]

The joy, and the religious overtones with which it was voiced, was hardly confined to the players. Former Red Sox outfielder Johnny Pesky—a man so large in Boston baseball lore that the right field foul pole at Fenway Park bears his name—was red-eyed as he joined the celebration. A member of the 1946 Boston club that lost the World Series to St. Louis, Pesky told reporters he had been praying for the Red Sox to finally win the championship; God had answered. Ministers and writers around New England philosophized on the religious significance of the Red Sox *finally* winning the World Series. Some called it a stirring testament to the power of perseverance, others a demonstration of the rewards that await those who keep faith through the long darkness. Some saw powerful symbolism in the bright red blood spot on Schilling's white sock. Perhaps the pitcher's blood was an emblem of the team's grit. Maybe it was blood atonement for transgressions of the distant past—selling Babe Ruth, perhaps, or resisting baseball's racial integration a half-century earlier.

Pedro Martinez turned talk away from superstition and back to where he felt it belonged—in the direction of his heavenly "Daddy." "I don't believe in curses," Martinez said, echoing what many of his teammates were saying. "I just believe in God, and he was the one who helped us today."[26]

*

The willingness of several of Boston's biggest stars to speak up for God during and after their run to the title was noted approvingly by the Religion News Service, which praised Martinez and other Christian players on the team for introducing New Englanders to the "divine source of their strength." The Red Sox faith talk was treated respectfully, reported evenhandedly, by the mainstream press, whose members tend to sneer at the statements of religious athletes. *Peoria Journal Star* columnist Kirk Wessler praised Schilling, in particular, for the clarity and maturity of his religious statements.

"Unlike some people—especially the majority of my jaded colleagues in the press corps—I don't have a problem with these public demonstrations [of faith], as long as they don't evolve into holy hootenannies at home plate," the columnist wrote. "I do wonder, however, for which players such actions come from the heart and which are for show. And I would love to know for sure which players return to the dugout after a strikeout, or after being hooked from the pitcher's mound after a shellacking, and thank God for the opportunity to play and try their best." By invoking God as a source of inner strength and courage—not some fickle heavenly arbiter who doles out wins and losses—Schilling "got it exactly right," Wessler wrote. "And nobody, not even the cynics in the press box, misunderstood."

Schilling's religious talk had evidently played well in Peoria. But as the columnist Wessler implied, God-invoking athletes often *fail* to "get it right," at least by the standards of most journalists and unconverted fans. At the very least, faithful players puzzle many fans when they talk of "God's blessing," cite God's help in making the big play or winning the game, or pay tribute to God through their frequent on-field gestures. As fans might wonder, what exactly do these Christian players mean? That God chooses favorites, intervening for one team or player at the expense of another? That the team that prays the hardest *plays* the hardest? Or are they merely modeling Christian humility and gratitude, eschewing the sports world's all-too-common narcissism and humbly giving credit to forces larger than themselves?

In some instances, religious players end up sounding downright silly, in the ears of many fans, with their public comments about God. Such was the case when football defensive lineman Sean Gilbert claimed it was God's will that he stage a holdout in a bid for a better contract, and when Cowboys wide receiver Michael Irvin said it was "a God thing" when a judge threw out cocaine charges he was facing. (The Lord, Irvin said, "stepped in and got it done before we even went to trial."[27]) So it was when Packers defensive end Kabeer Gbaja-Biamila told his ESPN interviewer that God did indeed have a deep interest in his football success—right down to his prodigious sacks total—and when Rams receiver Isaac Bruce said it was his increased tithing at church that elevated his performance and healed his persistent hamstring injury. And so it was when Steelers Super Bowl hero Santonio Holmes said on Pittsburgh television that it was "God's will" that he caught the game-winning touchdown pass in the 2009 Super Bowl. "He placed the ball where it needed to be," Holmes said at the jubilant championship celebration, "and it all came through for us."[28]

In many ways, however, the flourishing of Christianity in pro sports makes eminent sense. After all, religion offers players something they often need—a psychological boost, a way of making sense of their ascent to stardom and wealth, a measure of perspective and consolation in times of failure, strength to resist temptations from groupies and performance-enhancers to runaway egoism. Christian ministries' popular message about a personal relationship with God, one that pays off in the here and now as well as the hereafter, can be powerfully persuasive. Under intense pressure, and sensing all that is at stake in pro sports—games that can turn on the random bounce of a ball, untold amounts of money, public humiliation or adoration—athletes gravitate toward any source of strength and assistance they can find. Given the evangelical emphasis on God's abiding concern for the well-being of his followers, an athlete might naturally turn to Christianity and, in some cases, begin to perceive a divine role in his and his team's success.

As religious fans are wont to ask, what could be wrong with players connecting their religion with their trade? What could be problematic about making religious counselors available to meet athletes' understandable spiritual needs? The answer, at one level, is nothing. Of course players in the NFL, NBA, and Major League Baseball, like everyone in America, have a right to practice and speak about their religion. And, with games and travel making it difficult for players to attend church, it seems sensible that chaplains are invited to bring church to the players.

Yet religion, in the shape and form common in pro sports today, might not be the innocuous, purely wholesome force that its defenders say it is. Recall the comments of Orlando Magic executive Pat Williams about Dwight Howard, that "we'll take it" if the biggest problem was his rookie's tendency to "sing too loud" at church. Williams is probably being disingenuous with his glib dismissal of concerns about the rookie who would emblazon the cross on the NBA logo. Because it is obviously not just the volume of the Christian player's singing that matters, but the hymnal from which the song is being sung.

And so we arrive at the heart of the conundrum that is religion in sports.

One can think of evangelical Christianity as the ivy of religions. This is not to suggest that the religion flourishing in sports is poisonous, like some varieties of ivy, or that it must be pulled out by its roots. On the contrary, the metaphor acknowledges the positive aspects of evangelical religion in sports, including an aesthetic quality and a penchant for confident, robust growth. Ivy pleases the eye, and it is brought in to a particular environment—a yard, for example, or an outfield fence like the one in Wrigley Field—to improve it. Once planted, it grows with an impressive vigor. If left unchecked, however, decorative ivy can take over a yard and spread beyond its intended confines. Ivy can invade nearby woods and take over the forest floor, crowding out the other plants and climbing (and eventually killing) the trees.

Similarly, the evangelical faith infusing major league sports, for all that might recommend it, can overpower and subordinate other forms of religious belief (or nonbelief), whose adherents are entitled to equal standing in America's public venues. True enough—evangelicals are just being themselves, just living up to their Great Commission, when they share their religious message with the unconverted. After all, isn't it for the hearer's own good to learn the route to a godly life and eternal salvation? Yet even if good-hearted in its intent, evangelizing can take on less desirable forms. Implicit in evangelizing is the conviction that other forms of faith are deficient, inferior to the one exclusive truth of Christianity. "Evangelical Christianity is very exclusive in its claims," notes Shirl Hoffman, a leading scholar of evangelical engagement with sports and the author of a book on Christianity in sports due out in 2010. "And that doesn't go down well in a society where you're not supposed to make judgments about someone else."[29] As will be explored in later chapters, the effect is that nonbelievers and never-will-believers, as well as followers of other religions or other varieties of Christianity, can be overrun in an environment where evangelical faith has taken control.

NBA Commissioner Stern attempted to draw a line on the court when he said Dwight Howard was free to go about the enthusiastic practice of his faith as long as he wasn't "trying to impose his beliefs on somebody else." Stern made it sound simple. What he didn't acknowledge was that, for Howard and his many Christian fellows in pro sports, the sharing of his beliefs in the hope that others will adopt them is precisely the point. Call it sharing. Call it proselytizing. Or call it imposing one's religion on someone else. But understand that the Dwight Howards in professional sports are intent on affixing the cross to the logo, symbolically at least, even if the league commissioner himself happens to be Jewish. Is Stern's line a line that can be drawn, recognized, and enforced?

As stated earlier, sports reflect as well as reinforce the potent role of evangelical Christianity in American culture—and all the attendant complications. So as Stern and the other managers of our major sports leagues continue to navigate the difficult waters of religion, and encounter the numerous and inevitable shoals, perhaps they might take some comfort in knowing they have lots of company. In truth, American society as a whole is grappling with the same unresolved issue: What *is* the proper role of evangelical, one-truth Christianity in a religiously diverse society? How much latitude can evangelicals enjoy in the public sphere before the free exercise of *their* religion impinges on other people's free exercise? At what point does the quest of a young Dwight Howard and so many like him to bear the cross on the courts and fields of pro sports become an unacceptable infringement upon America's real, and growing, religious diversity?

In sports, as in the rest of the culture, we have seemingly just begun the difficult task of finding the answers.

Notes

1. Darren Rovell, "On a Mission from God," ESPN.com, May 25, 2004, http:// sports.espn.go.com/-nba/news/story?id=1769153.

2. "Outside the Lines," ESPN, April 15, 2003.

3. "Outside the Lines," ESPN.

4. "Outside the Lines," ESPN.

5. David A. Markiewicz, "Seeking an Amen from Admen," *Atlanta Journal Constitution*, May 9, 2004.

6. Chris Colston, "Howard Blossoms into Magic Force," *USA Today*, February 14, 2008.

7. Brian Schmitz, "'Everything We Thought He'd Be,'" *Daily Press* (Newport News, VA.), October 31, 2004.

8. Andrea Adelson, "Debate Continues: What Place Does Religion Have in Sports?" *Orlando Sentinel*, February 24, 2008.

9. David Plotz, "The God of the Gridiron," *Slate*, Feburary 4, 2000.

10. Interview conducted in person with an active National Football League player, May 2004; name withheld by request.

11. Jim Salisbury, "Steelers Lucky to be Alive," *Philadelphia Inquirer*, January 16, 2005.

12. "Reed's 19th Straight Made Field Goal Gives Pittsburgh Win," ESPN.com, January 15, 2005.

13. David Fleming, "Kitna Seeks Help From Above," *ESPN The Magazine*, September 16, 2007.

14. "Heart of the Hoosiers," interview with Mike Davis, *Sports Spectrum*, January–February 2003, 22–25.

15. Joanne C. Gerstner, "Prayer is a Key Player," *Detroit News*, December 18, 2007.

16. Art Stricklin, "Steelers QB Roethlisberger Aims Career Toward 'PFJ,'" Baptist Press, February 4, 2005.

17. Joe Kay, "NFL Rescinds Kitna Fine for Cross Cap," Associated Press, February 5, 2004.

18. Mike Celizic, "Is God Owens' Orthopedist, Too?" NBCSports.com, February 2, 2005, http://nbcsports.msnbc.com/id/6895597.

19. Celizic, NBCSports.com.

20. Pete Thamel, "Absorbing a Blow, and Delivering One, in Dramatic Fashion," *New York Times*, October 5, 2003.

21. Readers should note that ESPN's Miller is anything but hostile to Christian ministry in sports; in fact, Miller is the narrator of an Athletes in Action evangelism DVD pegged to the Red Sox' 2004 championship season.

22. Bob Hohler, "In Spirited Revival, It's One for All," *Boston Globe*, October 4, 2003.

23. Pedro Martinez, interview transcript, MLB.com, October 14, 2004, http://www.mlb.com/news/article.jsp?ymd=20041014&content_id=894097&vkey=ds2004news&fext=.jsp&c.

24. "At Last, Red Sox Fans See 'The Curse' Broken," Associated Press, October 28, 2004.

25. Manny Ramirez, interview transcript, MLB.com, October 28, 2004, http://www.mlb.com/news/article.jsp?ymd=20041028&content_id=907100&vkey=ds2004news&fext=.jsp&c.

26. G. Jeffrey MacDonald, "In World Series Win, Some Players and Fans See the Hand of a Higher Power," Religion News Service, October 29, 2004.

27. Steve Rushin, "It Came from the Sports Pages," *Sports Illustrated*, December 24, 2001.

28. KDKA television, Pittsburgh, February 3, 2009; video available on the Internet at http://video.aol.com/video-detail/santonio-holmes-catch-was-gods-will/2739988715.

29. Tom Krattenmaker, "Going Long for Jesus," *Salon*, May 10, 2006, http://www.salon.com/news/feature/2006/05/10/ministries/index.html.

CHAPTER 3

~

Faith Coach

Discipling Athletes for a Roster Spot on *God's* Team

I am a member of Team Jesus Christ. I wear the colors of the cross.

—The Fellowship of Christian Athletes "Competitors Creed"

Sharp-eyed fans of the NBA's Philadelphia 76ers began noticing a new team ritual during the 2005–2006 season. After the final buzzer, superstar Allen Iverson and several of his teammates—perhaps more if Philadelphia had just pulled out an exciting victory—would circle at midcourt in thankful prayer, the players' long arms draped around one another while a member of the circle praised God on behalf of the assembled. Although with fewer athletes involved, the Sixers' ritual mimicked one that was already common in professional football, whose bruised Christian combatants were known for joining hands on the 50-yard line after the fourth quarter and giving thanks to Jesus for the opportunity to represent him on the grand stage of the National Football League.

Today, with seemingly more pro players than ever using their respective fields of play as pulpits to express and promote their faith, fans are probably accustomed to the conspicuous religiosity in sports. What might not be as clear, however, is that the piety in sports is not entirely spontaneous. Often, there's a faith "coach" behind the post-game prayers and testimonies—in the Sixers' case, one Kevin Harvey, the team's volunteer Christian chaplain and, by day, a staff member of the Fellowship of Christian Athletes.

It was Harvey who first encouraged the players to have the post-game prayer huddles at mid-court. "I look for ways to challenge the guys all the time—everyday things they can do with the platform God has given them," Harvey explained in an interview later that season. "So I told them, 'Guys, I know God is doing good things on this team.' I brought up the way some teams in the NFL gather up after the game and give thanks to God for the opportunity to compete. The guys said they wanted to do it. So now, after all games, they circle up and pray."[1]

Evangelical Christian chaplains like Harvey are embedded, with very rare exception, inside each of the nearly one hundred teams in the "big three" major league sports: baseball, football and basketball. Generally coming from the conservative end of the religious and cultural spectrum, the chaplains and the ministries they represent are a driving force behind the powerful presence of evangelical Christianity in professional sports. Indeed, it's no accident that fans today so frequently witness players' public faith proclamations and their pious gestures during the action. The players are coached in faith and evangelism—not just when they reach the pros, but in many cases from their days in high school and college—by sports world missionaries like Kevin Harvey.

Several dozen Christian sports ministries are busy at work in sports-obsessed America today, filling niches from basketball and bowling to skateboarding and surfing. But none rivals the size, longevity, and clout of the Fellowship of Christian Athletes (FCA). Formed in the years following World War II, when America's love affair with spectator sports was coming into full bloom, FCA was founded on a simple marketing concept: Star players were being used to promote commercial products. So, as the ministry's founders asked, why not leverage sports' growing cache to promote something of even greater importance, Jesus? That foundational premise remains at the center of FCA's work, as expressed in the vision statement it uses today, more than a half-century later, on its website and literature: "To see the world impacted for Jesus Christ through the influence of athletes and coaches."

It is a vision expressed every day at many thousands of high schools and colleges around the United States, where young athletes come together in their FCA "huddles" to explore the Bible and its meaning for their lives on and off the field, and at major league sports venues from coast to coast, where highly paid athletic warriors, many of them active with FCA since their teenage years, live out ministry teachings by dedicating their careers to God and advancing the Christian gospel. Even though FCA concentrates its work on high schools and colleges, the organization maintains a strong presence in the pros through a web of relationships, many of them with campus huddle alumni who have made it big.

Turning young athletes into better people has always been an important part of FCA's mission. The ministry has a job for them, too—to take advantage of the public attention that follows athletes and use it to promote Christianity.

"Basically, we're target-marketing. We're trying to reach a certain segment of society," explained one FCA staff member in an interview. That "certain segment," of course, is the massive market of sports-playing and sports-watching Americans. "Through the influence of athletes and coaches, we have the opportunity to do that," said the staffer, who did not authorize the use of his name."[2]

*

Growing up in suburban Philadelphia in the 1970s and 1980s, watching the likes of Julius Erving and Bobby Jones leading the hometown 76ers, Kevin Harvey dreamed of a career in the National Basketball Association. "Basketball," he says, "was my passion, my obsession." Today, Harvey is living his dream, although not exactly the way he had imagined it. His annual FCA salary falls light years short of the seven and eight figures that players command, and for his volunteer work with the Philadelphia 76ers, he receives nothing except free tickets. Harvey is now at the age when many career jocks are well into their coaching careers. Such is the case with Harvey, although his coaching doesn't deal in x's and o's. His medium is the cross.

As the chaplain of the Philadelphia 76ers, Kevin Harvey is on the front line of the evangelical Christianity's outreach to a sector perhaps unparalleled for its high profile and influential status in American popular culture, and perhaps unmatched in the degree to which it is targeted for evangelizing: the world of the National Basketball Association, National Football League, and Major League Baseball. Teams in those three pre-eminent American professional sports leagues all have someone like Kevin Harvey organizing chapel services, ministering to Christian players, spreading the gospel message to nonbelievers and fence-sitters.

Harvey relishes his chaplain's role. Being around the game he once played, and still loves, is just part of why he can't imagine anyone having a better job than his. The real satisfaction, he says, comes from the knowledge that by influencing basketball players, he has a chance to reach the millions of people who will see the 76ers play, or who will hear and read about them in the media. In the lexicon of athletic Christianity, and true to the words used by FCA to describe its mission, Harvey is impacting the world for Christ.

What kind of influence can professional athletes have? Harvey sees that question answered every time he brings a professional athlete to a high school or middle school event. "Bringing a guy into a school, seeing two hundred, three hundred kids show up for a voluntary meeting after school, being able to hear a *pin drop* when the athlete is talking, that kind of lets you know how esteemed athletes are in this culture," says Harvey, who in his day job organizes southern New Jersey outreach for FCA. "They can have an extraordinary impact on people's lives."

Perhaps surprising for a man whose life work depends on the strong relationship between sports and faith, Harvey gave up playing the former when he found the latter.

"I was raised in a Catholic home, but it was a nonpracticing religious home. At times I felt very despondent, lacking in purpose. I just had a lot of questions that were unanswered. So I kind of drifted into what most seventeen-, eighteen-, nineteen-year-old boys in our culture drift into—girls, drinking, you know. Basketball at that point was my driving force."

Seated in a suburban Philadelphia diner that serves as his unofficial office and conference room, Harvey is reflecting on his own conversion experience. At six feet, two inches, he has the height and athletic bearing that testify to his background as a collegiate player at La Salle University. Nothing about his very casual clothes or rugged appearance suggests his religious line of work, save for the small, cross-bearing FCA logo on the chest of his gray t-shirt.

"I had about four or five years of just kind of drifting. I started feeling like something was missing in my life. I thought that once I got into college, things would fall into place. You know, they really didn't. I started asking myself the bigger questions: 'Is this really what life is all about?'

"I was visiting my mom and dad one spring night in 1982 when it happened. Basketball season was over. I just started praying, asking God, 'If you're real, and you have a purpose for me, show me.' And, you know, God definitely saw my heart and saw that I was sincere. I was literally, totally changed the next day. I was thinking differently. My behavior was different. . . .

"Two things drastically changed overnight. One was that I completely lost the desire to drink. I had been drinking like a fish, trying to escape. I lost that desire overnight and stopped drinking, cold turkey. And the other thing was the cursing. I always had a hard time controlling that on the court. I was always cursing, always feeling angry. I think the last time I cursed was 1982.

"So my desires drastically changed. And I remember looking in the Bible that week and, really, for the first time, understanding what Jesus was talking about when he said you must be born again. And that he offered a new way of life when he said, 'I am the way, the truth, and the life,' and no one comes to the Father except through him. I began to understand that. I turned my life over to Christ."

Harvey worked in the food management industry after college and performed voluntary Christian ministry in prisons and on the streets of Camden, a run-down city across the Delaware River from Philadelphia. He went to work for FCA in 1997. In 2001, he became the Sixers' chaplain. "I pinch myself every day," Harvey enthuses. "Nowadays, I tell people I made it to the NBA after all—just not as a player."

Like other chaplains in the major professional leagues, Kevin Harvey enjoys a rare level of access to the team. After practices, after the "shoot-arounds" that precede each of the 76ers' forty-one home games, Harvey can be found at courtside with a player or players. The discussion might revolve around the player's recent shooting slump, or maybe a family issue with which he is struggling. It could be the book Harvey has loaned him. It could be the fate of his soul. Often, it's about what it means to be a Christian and a player in "The Association."

When he deals with one of the nonbelievers, Harvey intentionally avoids coming on too strong.

"To me, it's about genuineness and sincerity, showing that I truly care about him as a person and that I'm not trying to convert him. I still remember what it was like to be on the other side. And I see a lot of Christians approach people as trophies. Subconsciously or consciously, they're trying to get someone to believe what they believe. But, you know, I can't force a person. I can share what God has done in my life. I can show love. I can show compassion and sincerity. But I cannot change a person's heart. That's God's job. . . . If they never come to chapel, then—praise God—I'm still going to be their friend. I'm not going to look down on them. I'm not going to judge them."

The rock star status of NBA players affords them copious opportunities for easy extramarital sex, especially on road trips; Harvey believes it's part of his job to help them resist that and the numerous other temptations laid at their feet. "I was listening to an interview on television last week with [former 76ers player] Darryl Dawkins," Harvey says. "He made the claim that he must have slept with a thousand women. He said anything goes on the road. As a chaplain, one of the desires of my heart is to challenge these guys to make sure they know that with each and every decision they make, they need to make it to please God. I want to make sure they understand that some day they're going to have to answer for all the things they've done."[3]

Harvey believes, too, that the Christian basketball player is called to please God by the way he performs *on* the court. Faith, he says, compels the Christian to play in a manner that is not always in his selfish interest—not always conducive to the accumulation of the statistics that pay off at contract negotiation time—but with a style that puts the team's need first. It is incumbent upon the Christian, Harvey believes, to forego his own shot and pass the ball if his teammate is open and in a better position to score. The Christian, in Harvey's view, is called to perform the other selfless and sometimes painful tasks that don't make one a star but that *do* help a team win, such as diving for loose balls and "taking a charge"—holding his ground and absorbing the impact of an offensive player hell-bent for the basket. This philosophy would seem to make chaplains the natural allies of basketball coaches, who are forever preaching team play in a sport that offers ample opportunities and rewards for individual freelancing.

To Harvey's mind, the religious commitment likewise obliges a player to serve as an exemplar of Christian character in his manner of dealing with teammates, the public, and adversity.

"Like all of us, they can have a bad day or bad performance. To me, the growth of a person is when you can recognize that God's in control and you're still loved by him even if you've just had your worst game of the season," Harvey says. "To me, that's the essence of character. All of us can smile, give teammates a pat on the back, when things are going great. But how do we react when you know things aren't going so well?

"With a couple of my guys with the Sixers, I've seen some growth in those areas. . . . They're reacting differently when they have a bad performance; you can see it on their face, the way they carry themselves. They're getting more rock-solid in their faith, and it doesn't matter as much now whether they shoot 10-for-15 or 2-for-15."[4]

*

Rock solid. No man fit the term quite like Tom Landry. Anyone who came of age as a professional football fan in the late 1960s or before probably holds a clear-picture memory of the late Hall of Fame coach of the Dallas Cowboys. Landry, with his frozen facial expression and rigid bearing, in his fedora and precise coat and tie, stood like carved granite on the Dallas Cowboys sideline through the first three decades of the storied franchise's existence.

Landry represented more than the competitive success of the Dallas franchise that came to be known as "America's team." If ever there existed a perfect human symbol of resistance to American liberalism—a symbol of restoring order after the wild, rebellious 1960s—it would be Landry. This icon, this Bible-professing, traditional values-promoting fixture on the sidelines of the National Football League, was also an emblem of the ultramasculine conservative Christianity that was making serious inroads to pro sports as the country migrated from the assassination-plagued, protest- and hippy-influenced heyday of the counterculture to the era of Ronald Reagan and George H. W. Bush.

Sportswriter Bill Minutaglio wrote persuasively about Landry's cultural meaning in an article for The Sporting News following the retired coach's death in 2000: "Well beyond his inflexibly conservative religion and politics," Minutaglio wrote, "well beyond his coldly calculating 4-3 defense and shotgun formation, he chose his life's work in a place blamed for the killing of a president . . . and then with each consistent Sunday, each eternal moment from Roger Staubach, Mel Renfro, Randy White, Tony Dorsett and Bob Lilly, he allowed his city to wear something other than grief on its sleeve."[5]

"Rock solid" also aptly describes Landry's relationship with the Fellowship of Christian Athletes. Landry, then early in his Cowboys tenure, committed to the young organization in 1962 and remained one of its strongest supporters for the rest of his life. Landry served as FCA board chair from 1973 to 1976, chaired the board of the Dallas branch for twenty years, and continued as a lifetime trustee of FCA right up to the time of his death in 2000.[6] His name lives on in one of the organization's best-known awards.

That FCA would adopt this symbol of bedrock cultural conservatism, this icon of a state (and state of mind) that became the country's political center of gravity over the legendary coach's career, reveals much about the ministry's cultural and political proclivities. FCA, like the other athletic ministries, unabashedly aligns itself with the nation's pro-business, pro-Republican, pro-Christian Right power establishment. As mentioned in the opening chapter, a mid-decade retreat for NBA chaplains and their wives featured James Dobson of Focus on the Family as a speaker—a natural choice, given Dobson's career of advice-giving on family issues, but certainly a highly political one, too, in view of Dobson's evolution into a hard-right presidential king-maker in the middle years of the decade and a polarizing force in American public life.

The Dobson and Landry connections are but small parts of the network of affiliations and mutual endorsements linking the Missouri-based FCA with leading carriers of the banner of the American right. Dal Shealy, who served as FCA president and CEO for thirteen years before retiring in 2005, was listed by Source Watch as a member of the board of the far-right Council for National Policy (CNP),[7] launched in part on the largesse of notorious right-wing magnate (and FCA supporter) Joseph Coors.[8] CNP's founder was Tim LaHaye, an anti-gay and anti-public education crusader best known today as the coauthor of the mega-selling "Left Behind" series.[9]

Shealy's name appears in numerous other contexts that bespeak his, and FCA's, affiliation with religious right political interests. The then-FCA president joined a veritable Christian Right "Who's Who?" in signing "The Chicago Declaration on Religious Freedom: Sharing Jesus Christ in a Pluralistic Society," in which the signatories agreed: "Misguided or false notions of pluralism must not be allowed to jeopardize anyone's constitutional right to evangelize or promote one's faith."[10] Among the other signers were LaHaye; Bill Bright, the since-deceased founder of Campus Crusade for Christ; David Brickner, executive director of Jews for Jesus; Jerry Falwell, the since-deceased chancellor of Liberty University and founder of the Moral Majority; Franklin Graham, the son of famed evangelist Billy Graham, the head of Samaritan's Purse, and the source of the infamous line "Islam is an evil religion"; and Donald Wildmon, president of the American Family Association.

The careers and political roles of some of FCA's board members reinforce the portrait of FCA as a bastion of political conservatism. A prime case in point is onetime FCA board member Kay Cole James, who has worked in such capacities as a senior fellow at the Heritage Foundation, the leading conservative think tank; as a professor at Regent University, the Christian institution founded by the famed Christian Right leader Pat Robertson; as secretary of health and human resources for former Virginia governor George Allen; as a director of public affairs for the National Right to Life Committee; and as senior vice president of the Washington-based political ally of Focus on the Family, the Family Research Council. James has also been in the administrations of two presidents, serving in the George H. W. Bush administration as associate director of the White House Office of National Drug Control Policy and in the Reagan administration's Health and Human Services Department.[11]

Leading Republican politicians and candidates frequently beat the path to FCA, speaking at the ministry's Kansas City headquarters or the numerous banquets and other events it organizes around the country. Among them: Dick Cheney, then a candidate for vice president, who made a campaign appearance at FCA in 2000, receiving his introduction and welcome to the stage from then-Kansas City Royals star Mike Sweeney.[12] To cite two more among numerous examples, Republican congressman Jim Ryun, a former track star, gave the keynote address at FCA's fall gala in 2004,[13] and Ken Wingate, a conservative (and unsuccessful) candidate for the South Carolina governorship in 2002, spoke to the FCA chapter at the University of South Carolina.[14]

Listed first among featured FCA sponsors on the organization's website is the Chick-Fil-A Corporation. If ever there were a "faith-based" corporation, and a conservative one at that, it would be this purveyor of fast-food chicken sandwiches. In its statement of corporate purpose, Chick-Fil-A proclaims a commitment "to glorify God by being a faithful steward of all that is entrusted to us." Christianity infuses the company's workplaces; in 2002, a Muslim man working at a Houston Chick-Fil-A sued the company after being fired—a termination he said was prompted by his refusal to participate in a group prayer that invoked Jesus.[15] Founder S. Truett Cathy and his corporation have promoted Focus on the Family and a good-parenting program called All-Pro Dads that is a spin-off of the group Family First, best known for its promotion of covenant marriage, a pet cause of the Christian far right.[16]

Democratic politicians, activists, and organizations with FCA affiliations and friendships are conspicuously few in number. One is Heath Shuler, a congressman from North Carolina who was active with FCA while playing quarterback for the University of Tennessee. But be clear: Shuler, one of a new wave of religious Democrats, is no liberal; he opposes abortion rights, gun control, and liberalized immigration policies. To search for a true liberal with FCA ties is to search in vain. Liberalism and the Fellowship of Christian Athletes, it turns out, mix about as well as New York and Boston roughnecks in the Fenway Park bleachers.

*

It would not be fair or accurate to say that FCA condones racism. On the other hand, the organization, in its public posture, website, and *Sharing the Victory* magazine, is largely mute on race issues in big-time sports, and on the persistent race problems in the United States that afflict the African American community from which most NBA and NFL players come, even as the ministry celebrates the community-service efforts of religious players to ameliorate some of racism's effects. FCA aligns with a conservative political movement in America that, by action and policy, shouts out the conviction that racism is a solved problem. Given the proclivities of the conservative evangelical world FCA inhabits, there is nothing surprising about the ministry's silence on race. Yet there is an unmistakable irony there, too. For FCA's founding history is inextricably bound up in the story of one famous Christian and his moral and religious crusade to cleanse the stain of racism from the nation's public life.

Branch Rickey is best remembered as the Brooklyn Dodgers executive who brought Jackie Robinson into major league baseball and thus integrated the game, changing not only the sport but American society in the process. Less known is the important role played by the famed baseball executive in nurturing the relationship between sports and Christianity, primarily by helping found the Fellowship of Christian Athletes. In both cases, Rickey drew his motivation from his strong Christian beliefs and his conviction that all good things were built on a foundation of character and morality. To some, Rickey was a sanctimonious moralizer; to others, something resembling a saint. "Basic honesty," the self-styled sage once said, "allows a man to go to the mirror, look himself in the face, and not be ashamed ever." Rickey was uncompromising, too, when it came to what he perceived as the moral imperative to integrate major league baseball. "A moderate," he once said of those favoring a more gradual approach to integration, "is a moral pickpocket."[17]

Christianity influenced the Rickey-Robinson saga in multiple ways. Girding Rickey's determination to integrate the game was his long-standing, religiously derived refusal to abide racism. Robinson's evident Christianity came into play, too, helping persuade Rickey that Robinson was the man on whom he would place his risky wager that America would accept an African American major leaguer. After learning that the gifted and highly skilled ballplayer Robinson was a church-going Christian, Rickey decided to give him a closer look and arranged a meeting, one that would turn into an emotional three-hour marathon. At one point during the discussion, the bespectacled baseball man read out loud from Giovanni Papini's *The Life of Christ*, a passage dealing with the practice of turning the other cheek—of resisting the temptation to respond violently to violence. These Christ-like principles and tactics, Rickey knew, would have to be employed by Robinson in the face of the abuse he was sure to encounter as the major leagues' first black player. Could Robinson, a man Rickey knew to be feisty by nature, practice Jesus-style nonviolence?

"Mr. Rickey, I've got two cheeks," Robinson whispered in response. "If you want to take this gamble, I promise you there will be no incidents."[18]

Another marathon Branch Rickey meeting would prove crucial to the founding of the Fellowship of Christian Athletes. By 1954, seven years after Robinson's debut with the Dodgers, Rickey was vice president and general manager of the Pittsburgh Pirates, a man in great demand, of great stature, who was continuing to work for racial integration through public appearances and service on a presidential committee striving to end discrimination in federal employment. His health shaky, his schedule tightly controlled by assistants, Rickey was not an easy man to see. But Don McClanen was determined to try.

The young football coach of Eastern Oklahoma A&M, McClanen was intent on enlisting Rickey in his quest to found an organization that would combine his two passions: sports and Christianity. Rickey, with his well-known Christian devotion and his obvious influence and resources, seemed the ideal man to join the cause. So McClanen camped out at his door and waited. "I was finally given five minutes," he later recalled. "It turned into five hours."[19] With Rickey's support and connections, McClanen was on his way to securing crucial funding and his first influential sports world endorsers. The Fellowship of Christian Athletes was under way.

Of course, what McClanen and Rickey created was not entirely new. The roots of the sports-religion relationship were already in the ground, established in the middle of the previous century in both England and America by the movement known as muscular Christianity. The original concept, however, had as much to do with improving and promoting *sports* as advancing religion. Sports, like other leisure pastimes in that era, were gradually overcoming a bad reputation, and their proponents were keen on demonstrating that athletics and Christianity were hardly incompatible; that, in truth, they were mutually supportive. By playing sports, advocates reasoned, boys and young men could develop their health, manliness, and morals; they could develop the strength of character that would make them better Christians and transfer to their pursuits beyond the athletic fields. To the mind of one English writer in 1874, "Games conduce not merely to physical but to moral health; that in the playing fields boys acquire virtues which no books can give them; not merely daring and endurance, but, better still, temper, self restraint, fairness, honour, unenvious approbation of another's success, and all that 'give and take' of life which stand a man in such good stead when he goes forth into the world."[20]

Leading the advance of muscular Christianity in American in the 1880s was a man named Luther Gulick and the organization over which he presided—the Young Men's Christian Association (YMCA). Gulick viewed the organization's gymnasiums as a means to attract young men; by participating in sports under the tutelage of the YMCA's teachers, Gulick believed, these men would become morally and physically fit, and Christian as well. "Christ's kingdom," Gulick declared, "should include the athletic world."[21]

Yet as Gulick and allies were working hard to bring Christianity and sports closer together, one of the era's most famous Christian athletic figures was doing what he could to draw them farther apart. Billy Sunday, a famous player for the Chicago White Sox, made the much-publicized decision in 1892 to end his playing career and work full time in Christian ministry. In an article he wrote to explain his decision, Sunday laid out a rationale that helped trigger a separation of Christianity and athletics in America, a disengagement that would generally hold through the first half of the twentieth century.

Sunday was no pacifist. He had no objections to the physical, aggressive behavior required by participation in sports, once expressing the desire to punch the nose of any man who lacked "the grit . . . to be a Christian." But his experience in professional baseball convinced him that a man could not serve Christ and play pro baseball at the same time. One objection was that ex-ballplayers tended not to pursue useful careers, many of them ending up in the saloon business. But his opposition ran much deeper. Playing baseball, Sunday said, "develops a spirit of jealousy and selfishness; one's whole desires are for personal success regardless of what befalls others." Moreover, baseball was an endeavor that did not prize morality. "One might be a consummate rogue," he claimed, "and a first-class ballplayer."[22] Other like-minded religious leaders would echo Sunday's sentiments, urging American Christians to devote their Sabbath days to pursuits more pious than playing or watching sports.

Evangelical Christianity's disengagement from sports paralleled a wider trend in American society at the time: Conservative Christians were generally pulling away from the popular culture through the first half of the twentieth century. The withdrawal from mainstream society was partly due to the public relations beatings they took in such episodes as the hugely publicized Scopes "monkey" trial of 1925, in which Clarence Darrow made William Jennings Bryan and fellow creationists look like benighted fools. More generally, the disengagement owed to conservative believers' mounting frustration over their inability to change the culture without compromising their core beliefs. Sports, meanwhile, were turning in directions anathema to strict Christians, with gambling and Sunday play becoming more deeply ingrained in athletic culture. The Christians' aversion to sports—and to American popular culture—would not last.

By the time Don McClanen came to see Branch Rickey in 1954, reengagement was well under way, thanks in large part to the outspoken evangelizing of a Christian track star named Gil Dodds. Since the 1940s, Dodds had been using his stature as a record-breaker in the mile to promote his faith to the sports-loving public. "Running is only a hobby," he once said. "My mission is teaching the gospel of Jesus Christ."[23] As Dodds demonstrated, the new communion of Christianity and sports would place less emphasis on young men's character development through playing sports, and more emphasis on leveraging sports to communicate the Christian message to an increasingly obsessed spectator culture. If pro ballplayers could convince people to buy a certain brand of shaving cream or cigarettes, couldn't religious athletes persuade them to accept Jesus? As scholar and former NFL player Michael Oriard has explained it, "The shift from justifying sport in the nineteenth century by appeals to religion, to promoting religion by appeals to sport, reveals much about the changing status of both sport and religion in America."[24]

FCA, buoyed by successful summer conferences in its early years and the favorable press coverage that followed, began a pattern of growth and formalization that has made it the best-known and largest sports ministry today. From the start, FCA has enjoyed the support of high-profile professional players—footballers Doak Walker and Otto Graham in the early days, for example, and the NFL's Shaun Alexander in this decade—as speakers and endorsers of its evangelical message. To be sure, numerous other organizations have appeared with variations on the theme, including Athletes in Action, the sports offshoot of the mammoth Campus Crusade for Christ, and Baseball Chapel, with its domination of ministry in professional baseball. Other niche or sports-specific ministries also mark today's landscape. Since the advent of Baseball Chapel have come ministries devoted to professional basketball, hockey, golf, and motor racing, as well as to youth-oriented sports like surfing, skateboarding, and snowboarding.

Although other ministries have followed it, FCA has a deep reach and high status that none can match. The organization hosts hundreds of camps every summer for boys and girls ages eight to eighteen, a record 46,562 attending in

2008.[25] Far fewer in number, but more important to the mass-marketing mission, are the prominent professionals who go to bat for FCA, agreeing to be featured in the ministry's magazine, to speak at school groups and camps, and to talk about Jesus every time a media opportunity presents itself.

FCA claims a dual purpose today: To minister to and bring together Christian athletes, and to use the influence of sports and its players to reach the wider culture. The FCA mission, as described in the ministry's literature, is to "present to athletes and coaches and all whom they influence the challenge and adventure of receiving Jesus Christ as Savior and Lord, serving Him in their relationships and in the fellowship of the church." The ministry also promotes its "Competitor's Creed," which found its way onto the wall of the locker room of the Air Force Academy football team earlier this decade before the academy administration forced the coach to remove it. The creed reads: "I am a Christian first and last. . . . I am a member of Team Jesus Christ. I wear the colors of the cross."[26]

"We've all seen athletes endorsing products on television," explains one FCA staffer who did not authorize the use of his name. "Here in Kansas City, when Marty Schottenheimer was coach of the [NFL] Chiefs, he was spokesman for Trane air conditioners. I remember him on television using sports analogies [to make his sales pitch]. This kind of thing is everywhere. With maybe the exception of Hollywood stars, athletes have probably more influence on society as people from any other walk of life. . . . If they have that influence and they have something to share, why not use it?

"I could walk into a restaurant somewhere in Kansas City and announce, 'Folks, I want to share my faith in Jesus Christ. I want to tell you what Christ has meant in my life.' Maybe two or three people would turn their heads and maybe a couple people would throw a tomato at me because I'm interrupting their lunch. Most people would say, 'Yeah, whatever.' If [then-Kansas City Royals star] Mike Sweeney were to walk into a restaurant and do the same, every head in the place would turn. Ninety percent of the people in there would know who he is. . . . Mike Sweeney could share his relationship with Christ and have an impact. Some people will listen just because he's able to hit a fastball 400 feet. That's the concept of influence. Rather than bemoaning the fact and questioning why someone should listen to a man just because he can hit a baseball, let's accept that Mike has something to share and equip him to share it."[27]

It's telling that FCA representatives and their fellow sports world faith promoters so frequently use the language and logic of marketing; it hints at the treatment of Christian faith as something akin to a product, something to be promoted by the most effective means possible. If the public will listen

to ballplayers, the reasoning goes, ministry by all means should use ballplayers to convey the message. Whatever one's opinion on the appropriateness of
the methodology, there can be little doubt that it is quintessentially American
to harness the forces of popular culture—in this case, love of sports—and the
tools of marketing to promote religion. The cultural landscape abounds with
examples of evangelical entrepreneurship and uses of pop culture: Christian
publishers reaching out to teenagers by repackaging the New Testament as
Seventeen- or *Cosmo Girl*-style magazines; Christian media outlets capitalizing on
the latest content-delivery technologies to make their programs downloadable
to MP3 players and cell phones; Christian musicians using the genres of rock,
rap, and punk to reach a youthful, music-loving audience. We have come a
long way, for better or worse, since the days when evangelicals withdrew from
culture lest they be compromised by it.

Orlando Magic executive Pat Williams contends that sports and Christianity work well together because "both speak the same language—the language
of victory."[28] A message based on "victory," however winning is defined, has
long resonated in America. One can readily understand the logic of marketing
faith to America on the culture's terms. Yet we must also ask: Might not the
vernacular also distort the "product" being promoted?

In the fullest meaning of the term, marketing is more than crafting and dis-
seminating promotional messages. Marketing is a two-way street, an enterprise
dependant upon the gathering of intelligence about the wants and needs of
prospective buyers and tailoring one's product and price—and certainly the
pitch—in such as way as to appeal to those prospects. Those practices make eminent sense in promoting a service or product. But one can legitimately question the appropriateness of the marketing model when the product in question
is religious faith, a "commodity" that, at its core, is not about convenience,
pleasure, or a better standard of living, but about the fate of one's soul and
the ultimate meaning of life. It is a "commodity" whose true observance might
compel believers to take unpopular, even painful action against the prevailing
cultural norms. In shaping their message for maximum appeal with athletes
and the fans who follow them, have the muscular Christians of FCA and its
fellow ministries at times inadvertently warped the product itself, inventing
something not entirely biblical? Is the faith of Jesus best spoken of in a tongue
other than "the language of victory"?

In the view of muscular Christianity experts Tony Ladd and James Mathisen, one historic failure of evangelical outreach to and through athletes is
its lack of theological heft. That, Ladd and Mathisen contend, is a predictable
outcome of a reality about evangelical Christianity itself: its commitment to
evangelism as its overriding organizing principle, which has made spreading

the faith a higher priority than upholding fidelity to sound theology. Chiding the muscular Christians for advancing a "folk theology," the scholars cite the telling example of one sports figure speaking to a college audience on the athlete's need for "focus" and then analogizing that with a supposed biblical imperative to "focus" on Jesus. Sophisticated theology it is not.

To Ladd's and Mathisen's example could be added the religious proclamations of many of the famous players quoted in FCA's magazine, *Sharing the Victory*. In one cover story, Shaun Alexander, the Seattle Seahawks star running back, cites as his favorite Bible verse Psalms 37:4, "Delight yourself in the Lord and He will give you the desires of your heart"—which, as Alexander makes clear, very much includes his own heart's desire to play football and score touchdowns.[29]

The appeal of such pitches by today's muscular Christianity to young sports-minded readers is clear enough—"accept Jesus and your athletic wishes will be fulfilled," the message seems to say—but the frequent emphasis on material striving and, in some cases, an almost magical belief in God-granted victories certainly leave the appeal lacking in theological depth. The youth and/or religious immaturity of the athletes quoted in FCA's magazine and other vehicles like it can hardly serve as an excuse for the promotion of these dubious ideas; after all, ministries grant them legitimacy by publishing them.

"In the absence of a sound biblical or theological background, muscular Christian heroes utilize the symbols they know best," Ladd and Mathisen write. "They then extrapolate to a theology that is grounded more in sports world rhetoric than orthodox Christian teaching. . . . Athletes and sports-related personnel are assumed to have adequate biblical and theological knowledge, based largely on the legitimation they enjoy as sports heroes. In public settings they talk about what they know best—the world of sport—and use the symbols and rhetoric of that world. Typically, they attempt to add some spiritual principle or theological insight which is often misguided, if not clearly incorrect, because that is why they were invited to speak in the first place."[30]

On the other hand, representatives of today's muscular Christianity, such as FCA staff member and 76ers chaplain Kevin Harvey, are making a stand against prevailing cultural norms in at least one area, the area of personal morality. A truly prophetic message might call for an end to Sunday games, for example—or even, hypothetically, emptying the stadiums and disbanding the teams to send the athletes out to feed the hungry and house the homeless. To state the obvious, sports ministries advocate nothing of the sort, and they would certainly regard such notions as preposterous. On the other hand, by taking a stand for individuals' moral behavior in a pro sports culture awash in greed, hedonism, and self-adulation, Harvey and his fellows in sports ministry maintain a Christian stance outside of, and against, at least one part of the prevailing pro sports norm.

Observers of the American religious landscape have long marveled at the seemingly endless capacity of its Christian believers for innovation and entrepreneurship. That ability is one reason why religion remains strong in this country while tending to wither in certain other parts of the developed world. Although the idea might seem anathema to evangelicals who consider faith to be the one aspect of life that is set in stone and never-changing, America's devoted keep Christianity vital by adapting it, reinventing it, finding ways to maintain its relevance and keep its practice not only tolerable but helpful in the culture with which they engage. If they don't tinker with the essential core of belief, they certainly innovate with its packaging and delivery. But what makes American-style evangelical Christianity strong can also make it weak. "In every aspect of religious life," religion scholar Alan Wolfe has written, "American faith has met American culture—and American culture has triumphed."[31]

Certainly, it has not been a complete rout for religion in the sphere of American life where sports and faith collide. Whatever one thinks of the FCA message and marketing model, credit is owed to it and its fellow sports ministries, to chaplains like Kevin Harvey, for consistently calling athletes to conscience on the level of personal morality. Numerous players are undoubtedly living cleaner, more moral, more purposeful lives than they would without the Christian faith exerting some hold on them.

Yet the truth of Wolfe's contention is quite evident in the shape of the athletic Christianity on display in America today. Promoters of the faith are, for the most part, speaking the language of sports—the language of victory—and, in so doing, unavoidably glossing over aspects of Christianity that would surely make it less appealing to athletes and those who watch them. What might those aspects be? Nonmaterialism, nonviolence, and the transformation of society for the benefit of the least powerful—all preached by Jesus—are but a challenging few.

To recall the words of the scholar and ex-player Oriard, it indeed does say much about popular evangelical Christianity and major league sports that the former continues its ardent pursuit of the latter. What it might say, above all, is that both are big and intent on getting bigger.

For the keepers of the faith inside and outside the game, the infusion of evangelical religion into pro sports may gladden the heart. But it should raise vexing questions as well. Because at what cost is this popularity being achieved? And with what pieces of Jesus left behind?

Notes

1. Kevin Harvey, interview held May 11, 2004, Marlton, New Jersey. Note that numerous follow-up conversations continued by e-mail and telephone in the five years following the formal interview.

2. FCA staff member, interview.

3. Dawkins indeed has made this claim in media interviews. For one example, see Dan McGraw, "Sports Stars, Sex, and Stalkers," Salon.com, August 6, 2003, http://dir .salon.com/story/news/feature/2003/08/06/sports_stars/index.html. Kevin Harvey, interview held May 11, 2004, Marlton, New Jersey.

4. Kevin Harvey, interview held May 11, 2004, Marlton, New Jersey.

5. Bill Minutaglio, "Landry: America's Coach," *Sporting News* retrospective on Landry's career, http://www.sportingnews.com/archives/landry/coach.html.

6. Cathy Harasta, "Tireless Fellow: Landry Preached with Actions, not Words," *Dallas Morning News* retrospective on Landry's career, http://www.dallasnews.com/s/dws/ spe/2000/landry-special/landryfea.htm.

7. Sourcewatch, produced by the Center for Media and Democracy, http:// www.sourcewatch.org. See in particular http://www.sourcewatch.org/index.php?title =Council_on_National_Policy#Board_of_directors.

8. Right Web, produced by Political Research Associates, http://rightweb.irc -online.org. See in particular http://rightweb.irc-online.org/gw/2806.html.

9. Sourcewatch, see http://www.sourcewatch.org/index.php?title=Council_on_ National_Policy.

10. "The Chicago Declaration on Religious Freedom: Sharing Jesus Christ in a Pluralistic Society," published by Unity World at http://www.unityworld.org/pages/ chicago.html.

11. National Academy of Public Administration information page, see http://www .marcomgroup.com/-napaperformance/gen_4.asp.

12. David Barstow, "The 2000 Campaign: The Running Mates," *New York Times*, August 31, 2000.

13. Legistorm, published by Storming Media at http://www.legistorm.com; see in particular http://www.legistorm.com/trip/approver/455/Rep_Jim_Ryun/all/full_ destination/asc.html.

14. Vanessa Poston, "Candidate for Governor Speaks to USC Students," *Daily Gamecock*, University of South Carolina, March 4, 2002.

15. Charisma News Service, "Muslim Sues Chick-Fil-A for Discrimination," Beliefnet, http://www.beliefnet.com/story/115/story_11581_1.html.

16. See the "What People Are Saying" endorsements page at the Family First website at http://www.familyfirst.net/page.php?id=17. For a liberal analysis and critique of Cathy's support of right-wing interests, see this Talk2Action critique, http://www .talk2action.org/story/2005/12/16/132516/73.

17. Branch Rickey and John J. Monteleone, *Branch Rickey's Little Blue Book* (New York: MacMillan, 1995), 7, 90.

18. Rickey, Monteleone, *Little Blue Book*, 81–82.

19. Murray Polner, *Branch Rickey: A Biography* (New York: Atheneum, 1982), 251.

20. Tony Ladd and James A. Mathisen, *Muscular Christianity: Evangelical Protestants and the Development of American Sport* (Grand Rapids, MI: Baker Books, 1999), 16.

21. Ladd and Mathisen, *Muscular Christianity*, 60.

22. Billy Sunday, "Why I Left Professional Baseball," *Young Men's Era* 19, no. 30 (July 27, 1983): 1.

23. Ladd and Mathisen, *Muscular Christianity*, 112.

24. Michael Oriard, *Sporting with the Gods: The Rhetoric of Play and Game in American Culture* (Cambridge: Cambridge University Press, 1991), 253.

25. "Camp Ministry" page at Fellowship of Christian Athletes website, http://www.fca.org/Camp.

26. Fellowship of Christian Athletes "Competitors Creed," which can be found on the FCA website, http://www.fca.org/TEAMFCA/CompetitorsCreed.lsp.

27. Telephone interview with Fellowship of Christian Athletes staff member, October 10, 2002.

28. Pat Williams interview, telephone.

29. John Dodderidge, "An Ambassador to (sic) the Kingdom," *Sharing the Victory*, December 2002, 6–9.

30. Ladd and Mathisen, *Muscular Christianity*, 221.

31. Alan Wolfe, *The Transformation of American Religion: How We Actually Live our Faith* (New York: Free Press, 2003), 3.

CHAPTER 4

~

Winning for Jesus (But Finding Him in the Loss Column)

The Tricky Relationship between Evangelism
and Sports Success

> It's important to win, not because God wants winners, but because Americans do.
>
> —a member of the Athletes in Action basketball team[1]

The first half of the 2007 season in the National Football League elevated a new star in the faith-in-sports firmament—and, for many of those dedicated to using the professional sports platform to promote Jesus, a shining new case study to hold up as evidence of the transformative difference that faith could make on a pro football team that could never seem to break out of the doldrums. But by the time the season's second half had played out, the sports public was left with a case study—a cautionary tale, actually—of an entirely different sort.

Gritty quarterback Jon Kitna and his Jesus-professing ways were not exactly strangers to NFL fans prior to the 2007 season. The former Central Washington University pass-slinger had been around the league for a decade and had held down the starting quarterback job with Cincinnati for five seasons before giving way to the up-and-coming star Carson Palmer, whom Kitna himself had helped groom. Kitna's bold—some said over-the-top—Christianity had been his calling card since he incurred the league's wrath, and a $5,000 fine, for insisting on wearing a cross-logo hat to post-game news conferences, all the better to use his place in the media spotlight to witness his faith.

But at some point in the early fall of 2007, Kitna crossed the line from "known" to "hot story." Probably because America loves rags-to-riches sagas—and Kitna's Detroit Lions had worn rags since forever, it seemed—the hot start to Detroit's campaign was getting people's attention. It wasn't just the Lions' 6-2 record at the halfway point—remarkable, given that the team had gone 3-13 the previous season—but the apparent mass Christian conversions happening in the locker room along with new infusions of character, unity, grit, confidence, and winning spirit behind the leadership of the team's Bible-preaching quarterback, Jon Kitna.

There is nothing like a stirring overtime victory to grab the attention of sports media and fans, especially when it's sparked by an injured team leader who makes a surprise return to action. Think Willis Reed, New York Knicks, Game Seven of the 1970 NBA finals. So it went on Week Two at Ford Field in Detroit, when the Lions met division rival Minnesota.

In the second quarter, with the score tied at 7-7, Kitna had to leave the game for what media sources later described as a "mild concussion." In the retelling by those moved by the story's inspirational qualities, the concussion was more than mild. Kitna called it the worst of the several he had suffered in his 11-year career. As he later told the Christian Broadcasting Network, "I was totally out of it." Lions Chaplain Dave Wilson testified, "He was out of it. He didn't know who I was. He didn't know who people were at halftime."[2]

By the third quarter, however, Kitna was feeling much better. "I was totally cognizant," he said, "no symptoms whatsoever." By the fourth quarter, with the score tied at 17-17, Kitna returned to the game, and with his usual guts and gusto, running the ball himself a handful of times as if to welcome more hard tackles and defy anyone worried about the lingering effects of his first-half head injury.

In overtime, after Minnesota fumbled on its opening drive, Kitna and the Lions gained possession at midfield. Kitna took matters into his own hands to get his team in position for an attempt at the game-winning field goal. On the first play, he accomplished another seemingly impossible feat, passing the ball to himself for a nine-yard gain. (The pass had deflected off another player to Kitna, who had the presence of mind to grab his own aerial and run for good yardage.) Two players later, facing a crucial third-down-and-two, Kitna took off running again, carrying the ball for six yards and a first down. A half-minute later, Lions kicker (and fellow Christian) Jason Hanson booted a 37-yard field goal for the sudden-death winner. The Lions were 2-0.

It was, to use the parlance of some Christian players, "a God moment"—a piece of thrilling good fortune and the resultant public attention that afford a Christian a chance to proclaim his faith. Never one to shy away from comments that might rankle the often-skeptical press or make himself a target of snickering, Kitna told everyone he could that his recovery from the concussion was a miracle. "I've never felt anything like that, and for it to clear up and go right back to as normal as I can be, is nothing short of a miracle," Kitna told the media after the game. "I just definitely feel the hand of God. That's all it was. You can't explain it. . . . I have no headaches, no symptoms, no lingering effects. But that was the worst my head had ever felt, and the worse my memory was. . . . Yet, after halftime there was nothing."[3]

It was a sensitive moment for the league, and not solely because of Kitna's claims about the hand of God. The NFL was facing worsening public relations around the prevalence of concussions and the perception that coaches and medical personnel had, for many years, been rushing players with head injuries back to action before they were ready, thus exposing them to the risk of even more serious head injury. Certainly aware of the issue, Kitna and coach Rod Marinelli—Marinelli being the man who made the decision to reinsert the quarterback—praised the team's medical staff for its responsible handling of the situation.

As it turned out, the medical issue wasn't what raised eyebrows the most as the days passed. As fans and media were asking, did the Lions quarterback really claim . . . a miracle?

Typical of one school of thought was this snarky observation from an Internet pundit at the "Adjusting the Cup" sports blog: "If I were a medical professional, and an athlete told me that his mild traumatic brain injury (MTBI) was miraculously cured by God (with the emphasis on *brain injury*), I would actually take that as proof that the player was not okay, and he still had lingering head trauma effects. (Read that as: he was still f***ed in the head)."[4]

Many, however, were surprisingly ready to honor Kitna's claim of a miracle, even in the mainstream, secular media. Among those coming to the defense of Kitna and his miracle claim was L. Z. Granderson, who, in an article published at ESPN.com, expressed puzzlement over all the cynicism about Kitna's hand-of-God talk. Granderson wondered why, in a country in which more than 90 percent of the people profess some form of belief in God, so many people were laughing at Kitna's claims. "Isn't that the kind of spiritual benevolence 91 percent of Americans say they also believe is possible?" Granderson asked. "And if that is the case, then why is Kitna saying what he said loony?"[5] Granderson's comments, initially published at ESPN.com, were promoted by numerous sympathetic bloggers and showcased in the newsroom area of the Athletes in Action website.

Kitna had captured the media's and public's attention, to put it lightly. After the Lions added several more wins to their record, ESPN turned over several pages in its magazine to the Lions' faith-fueled resurgence. The article, headlined "Kitna Seeks Help From Above," portrayed the Detroit quarterback as someone proud to be seen as a "fanatic for Christ." David Fleming reported that about 30 percent of the team was ending each practice by gathering for a group prayer and a chant of "One, Two, Three . . . JESUS." Fleming found a willingness on the part of even the nonreligious Lions—still the majority, he noted—to go along with the high-revved religiosity or at least stifle their concerns. And that, Fleming astutely noted, had everything to do with an ingredient that smoothes things out on a pro sports team the way oil keeps a car engine humming: The Lions were *winning*.

"Dissent of any kind is tantamount to blasphemy in the NFL, where nothing is more sacred than being considered a team player—especially when a team is winning," Fleming wrote. "The huge importance placed on unity in football creates a general intolerance of any kind of locker-room pluralism—something Christian athletes often mistake as tacit approval of their preaching."[6]

As Fleming correctly framed it, winning was the sugar that was helping the religion medicine go down. But, more important, it was winning that was suddenly drawing massive attention to the Lions and the faith that was flourishing in their locker room.

Winning in sports—or politics or business or any other worldly endeavor—may not be a central tenet of the Christian New Testament. But it *is* a central tenet of American culture. And judging from the enthusiasm with which Christian media and faith-in-sports promoters seized the Kitna story, competitive success is an irresistible hook for starting a discussion about the merits of faith and, to quote the revered Christian hymn, its "wonder-working power." With Kitna wearing his cross, literally and figuratively, and the once downtrodden Lions winning 75 percent of their games through the season's first half, it wasn't long before several Christian news outlets and ministries were touting the Kitna story.

Foremost among them was the Christian Broadcasting Network and its CBN News operation, part of the vast ministry and media empire of the evangelical icon Pat Robertson. CBN jumped on Kitna's and the Lions' success with a television feature and a print article on its website bearing the headline: "Christ Turns Kitna's Life, NFL Team Around." Sitting for an interview with the network, Kitna wore his customary red hat with the cross on the front, but had it turned around backward to display the message: "WASHED BY HIS BLOOD." After exploring Kitna's coming to Christ in college and his positive impact on his fellow Lions, CBN's print story concluded by once more sounding the "success" note: "Success in life. Jon Kitna knows the Source of that, and he's not ashamed to let the world know, leading others to victory as well."[7]

Also pouncing on the Kitna tale that fall was the magazine of the Fellowship of Christian Athletes (FCA), the aptly named *Sharing the Victory*. In an in-depth article headlined "Waking the Lions," FCA featured a large photo of dozens of Lions kneeling in the locker room, hands clasped, heads bowed in prayer. The article led with the conversion story of one team member, Dan Orlovsky, who had "bent his knee to Christ" the previous season under the influence of Kitna and his fellow evangelizing quarterback Josh McCown. As FCA writer Jill Ewert put it, "Men were saved. Broken marriages were mended. Christians deepened their faith. And a team that had for so long succumbed to the devastating effects of back-biting and selfishness congealed into a unified front."

Demonstrating the different layers of meaning attached to the concept of "victory"—winning on the field, building character, achieving salvation, and so on—the article dealt at length with the trying 3-13 season endured by the newly saved Orlovsky and his teammates in 2006, the season preceding the breakthrough campaign of 2007. Kitna was portrayed as a force for unity and the catalyst for the Lions' transformation, a transformation first taking place in the locker room and players' hearts and relationships before manifesting in the win column and division standings. While on-field losses mounted in 2006, the Lions were coming together as a group of men, according to FCA writer Ewert, with player after player accepting Jesus and joining the growing pride of Lions who would assemble at Kitna's house on Monday nights for Bible study and fellowship events led by team chaplain Wilson and his wife.

As FCA framed it, unity—unity around Jesus Christ and his chief proclaimer, Jon Kitna—was making all the difference as the Lions established a spiritual foundation, one that would make possible a different kind of success in 2007. As strange as it might sound to those who recognize the potential divisiveness of evangelism—and, indeed, Christian proselytizing is known to have divided as well as united professional sports teams over the years—FCA portrayed Kitna's hard-charging preaching as purely positive, as a force not for division but team harmony. (If unity were indeed the imperative, one has to ask about the wisdom of Kitna continuing to wear the baseball cap with the cross. Wouldn't it have been better to wear a hat with a *lion* on it?)

"One of the first things [Kitna] said to me," Orlovsky recounted in the FCA article, describing his quarterback's faith-first leadership style, "was, 'Are you going to heaven?'" As if anticipating objections from some readers, the FCA writer Ewart pointed out that Orlovsky did not find that or other discussions about religion "overbearing or forceful," almost making it sound as though it was nothing but friendly, everyday chatter to ask a teammate if he was bound for heaven or hell.[8]

Understandably, *Sharing the Victory* and other Christian media trumpeting the Lions story ignored some realities about the situation that might have lessened its value as a faith-promotion tool. Inconveniently, plenty of Lions—the majority, by all accounts—did not share the Christian faith advanced so boldly by Kitna and some of his fellow Christians on the roster. As became clear in Fleming's ESPN story and other media reports, many team members were going along with the pious practices to avoid the untenable position of being out of step with the team leader.

One player, however, was willing to publicly address the proverbial elephant in the room: the reality that, for some Lions, the quarterback's constant pushing of the Bible made them uncomfortable. Center Dominic Raiola, one of the Lions who was not joining the "One, Two, Three . . . JESUS" prayer circles, noted, "You can't bring religion up in most workplaces; you can't do a team prayer in the office. So this is something unique that we have to deal with. I don't think faith has a lot to do with football. Everyone in this locker room is a teammate, not a believer or a nonbeliever."⁹

Lions receiver Roy Williams—himself a participant in the team's religious activities—would later make clear that he, too, disagreed with at least one of Kitna's ideas about God's role with the team. Interviewed on an ESPN "Outside the Lines" program that aired later in the season, Williams said, "[Kitna] told me God took over his body. I'm like, 'Huh?' It's a weird take." Rolling his eyes, Williams added: "Out of 1,696 players [in the NFL], God chose Jon Kitna?"¹⁰

An even more inconvenient reality was coming.

"Victory" conveys many meanings in the parlance of evangelical ministry in sports, including the ultimate of all championships, the eternal salvation achieved by true believers in Christ. But even the *Sharing the Victory* writer, for all the attention she devoted to the team's spiritual victories, could not resist addressing the other kind of winning. As "Waking the Lions" author Jill Ewart put it, what could the spiritually transformed Lions "say to a world that was keeping score?"

"It would be unwise to bet against Detroit this season," Ewart wrote. "After a year of team-building and hard knocks, the Lions are turning a corner." She went on to detail the Lions' two season-opening wins, including the "gutsy" overtime victory over Minnesota, and quoted Kitna talking about the competitive success God was bringing to Detroit. "Talent," she wrote, "paired with team unity is an explosive combination."¹¹

Team chaplain Wilson and others emphasized in their media interactions that it was not their belief that God was intervening on the field to ensure Detroit victories. Yet from the way the coverage was framed, it was clear that the publicity blitz around the Lions was predicated on the team's winning— winning, in the view of some of those swept up in the religious aspects of the story, because of the power of Christian faith. The Lions were playing together because they were *praying* together. The point did not need to be made explicitly, but underlying all the coverage was the reality that few of the bandwagon-jumping media outlets, Christian or secular, would have beat the path to Detroit in 2007 but for the fact that the team was winning (for a while.)

For some, the faith-equals-wins equation was an unspoken assumption; others were willing to make the point quite explicitly. Lions receiver Mike Furrey—who had begun inviting area youths to his home for Christian fellowship—pinned the Lions' season-opening wins to the team's stronger Christian orientation. Surprisingly, a writer in the secular mainstream media one-upped even the Christian outlets in tying the Lions' material success to faith. *Orlando Sentinel* sports columnist Jemele Hill, in an article that appeared as a "Page Two" feature at ESPN.com, defended Kitna's outward religiosity and suggested that his and his Lions' religious faith was translating into wins. "Some pooh-pooh the Jesus talk," Hill wrote. "And while no one would dare say God is rooting for the Lions, it's hard not to note the impact spirituality has had on the team's incredible resurgence, which would be a far bigger story if not for those pesky New England Patriots."[12]

Hill seemed to be suggesting that those Patriots and their attention-grabbing winning streak were an unfortunate distraction from the stirring tale of the Detroit Lions. But something else happened in the second half of the season that had a far more ruinous effect on the perfect story line. The Lions—the team bursting with Christian-based character and unity, the team showing for all the world that religious faith could pave the way to football success—stopped winning.

After whipping Denver 44-7 in their eighth game, the Lions stood at 6-2. But then came a loss at Arizona, followed by home losses to the Giants and Packers. The Vikings, the losers in the concussion-recovery-miracle game back on Week Two, exacted revenge in the rematch, crushing the Lions 42-10. Next came a one-point home loss to Dallas and a 51-14 debacle at San Diego. The six-game losing streak dropped the Lions to a mediocre 6-8, leaving the team with no hope of making the playoffs or achieving the ten wins Kitna had predicted prior to the season. A victory over lowly Kansas City stopped the losing streak, but a one-sided loss to Green Bay closed out the season on the kind of low note that was all too familiar to pro football diehards in Detroit.

Kitna—the hero of the story when the wins were piling up, the veritable Christian crusader on the battlefields of the NFL—was not solely to blame. But nor had he distinguished himself with his play during the miserable second half of the season. Against Arizona: Two interceptions, three fumbles, four sacks. Against New York: Three interceptions, three sacks. Against Green Bay: Just nineteen completions in forty pass attempts, four more sacks. The shortcomings of the Detroit offensive line were being exposed, and with opposing pass-rushers breaking through with frightful ease, Kitna was absorbing a pounding. Earlier in the season, the snarky website "Deadspin" had made light of Kitna's religiosity by running a headline announcing, "Jon Kitna was sacked for your sins."[13] The hilariously cynical headline now seemed to be coming true. And while theologians might have found something redemptive and Christ-like in Kitna's suffering, one would have been hard pressed to find faith-in-sports advocates promoting *this* part of the story. Imagine it: "Getting sacked for Jesus!"

Obviously, victory—victory of the on-field, material variety—is a far more effective promotional tack, and the Lions were hardly the only success story of that type being touted by Christian ministries and media in 2007.

Around the same time that the Lions' season was coming to a sad end, Tim Tebow of the University of Florida won college football's Heisman Trophy and spoke up boldly about Jesus at his award-acceptance news conference. Said Tebow: "I just (want) to first start off by thanking my Lord and savior Jesus Christ, who gave me the ability to play football, gave me a great family and support group and great coaches and everything around me."[14] The Christian Broadcasting Network showcased the Heisman champ the way it had the Lions, running an article headlined: "Heisman winner holds strong faith in God." The Fellowship of Christian Athletes likewise found Tebow's ascent irresistible, naming his Heisman accomplishment one of the Top Ten Christian Sports Stories of 2007.

Tebow's profession of faith came against a steady drumbeat of claims like this by Indianapolis Colts defensive lineman Anthony McFarland following the Colts' Super Bowl win: "The way this thing went down, I couldn't have put it together or described it. It shows you how the good Lord works in my life and for this team." And like this by the Detroit Pistons' Chauncey Billups as he accepted, and kissed, the trophy for Most Valuable Player honors in the 2004 NBA Finals: "God is good. God is very good. He put me here for a reason, and *that*," he said, glancing at the trophy, "is the reason."

So it goes in a world of faith-promotion where status and evangelizing zeal usually count for more than theological accuracy, as the scholars Tony Ladd and James Mathisen have noted in their own trenchant analyses of Christianity in sports.

As it turned out, the true moral of the story of the 2007 Lions was that one ought to be careful, very careful, about holding up football wins as evidence of the merits of Christianity. Apart from the dubious theology, the problem with faith-based victory, and with victory-based faith, is that every winner eventually loses, and that every star that rises in the sports constellation eventually falls.

One season, Matt Hasselbeck emerges as the Jesus-loving hero of the conference champion Seattle Seahawks, eager to claim God as his ultimate teammate;
a few years later, an injury-plagued Hasselbeck and his team slide to the bottom
of the standings, Hasselbeck sporting a dismal 57.8 passer rating. One year,
the Houston Astros—a team with a large contingent of outspoken evangelical
players representing a city strongly associated with conservative Christianity—
reach the World Series to face the Chicago White Sox, a team with a heathen,
bad-boy reputation that no one would ever hold up as an advertisement for
Christian virtue; Chicago sweeps the series in four games. In one half-season,
Jon Kitna carries the cross and a resurgent Detroit Lions football team to the
top of the heap, seeming to show for all the world that faith *does* work; in the
season's second half, these same Detroit Lions go 1-7, and the next year, they
endure the first 0-16 season in league history.

Because of the calculus set up by winning-based evangelism, these riches-
to-rags stories beg a question: Do Hasselbeck's fall, the Astros' World Series
trouncing, and the Lions' collapse mean that faith doesn't work after all, or
that it only works for a little while?

The answer, of course, is that the rise and fall of these athletes' fortunes
prove nothing about the merits or truth of Christianity, which are exactly as
compelling or specious if the Detroit Lions lose as if they win. These stories
and the many like them do, however, demonstrate the perils of sports world
evangelizing on the coattails of victory. Because when God's team or player
flops, as he inevitably will, someone ends up with egg on his (or His) face.

Obviously, any embarrassment belongs not to God (who, according to
Christian teaching, is quite above that particular human experience) but solely
to the faith-promoters who hold up ephemeral on-field success as evidence of
the validity of the Christian religion. Even though the fault does not lie with
the religion or the object of it, the phenomenon ought to give pause to those
concerned about the well-being and advancement of Christianity. In a time
when the public behavior and rhetoric of some high-profile Christians give
their religion a bad reputation in many circles, these cautionary tales ought
to be carefully remembered by those singing the praises of faith-based athletic
successes. Do they really want to suggest that Jesus' viability in our culture is
dependent on something as insubstantial and fleeting as success on the football
field? And do they want to set up their fine religion for more jokes from the
cynical comedians, columnists, and bloggers who love to ask: Why don't players bring God into it when they lose?

*

For Ed Uszynski, issues of winning, losing, and evangelizing have special poignancy. Uszynski, former director of Athletes in Action's Ministry Training

Center, now its director of ministry resource development, played for the famed Athletes in Action (AIA) basketball team from 1992 to 1996. He recalled in an interview the dilemma often facing the AIA basketball team in making roster choices: Should the team opt for the better player, or the better Christian?

"We were unapologetically about evangelizing in the context of good basketball," recalls Uszynski, who knows something about good basketball, having starred in high school in his hometown of Elyria, Ohio, and having played for a time in Italy and Australia. Competitive excellence, he knew, bought credibility; losses, the opposite. "Do we put together a team of ministers who are maybe not as good on the court and lose more games," Uszynski asks, "or a team that plays better but has no heart for ministry?

"If your team is no good," Uszynski continues, "and can't put a decent product on the floor to compete against Carolina, Kentucky, Duke, then they won't want to play you, which essentially closes the door on ministry. So you can't just recruit missionary kids to play on your team; you've got to have guys who can play. . . . A lousy exhibition team has no ministry over time, but neither does a team of non-Christians. We're the basketball arm of an unapologetically evangelical ministry, but we still have to play by the secular rules of success to some degree. The question becomes, 'Where do we draw the line?'"

Uszynski knew from personal experience about the consequences of over-pursuit of competitive success. The son of a high school football coach, he grew up with a fanatical devotion to sports that he now views as borderline unhealthy. "I always had a ball in my hand or ball on my foot," he says. "Sports have been what I've lived and breathed since I was a little kid." And success in sports was often—*too* often—where he found his self-worth and self-definition, Uszynski says. When he found Jesus, in college at Kent State, the impact was so powerful, so transformative, that he decided to focus on his spiritual growth instead of competitive basketball.[15]

The AIA men's basketball teams, through a history stretching back more than forty years, have certainly achieved competitive excellence. According to the ministry's records, the fall touring squad had an all-time record of 1,076 wins and 613 losses through 2007 despite taking on many of the nation's top collegiate teams (until NCAA rule changes in 2004 forbade Division I colleges from playing noncollegiate opponents). As one top collegiate coach famously said after watching his team succumb to the AIA squad, "They beat you up in the first half, pray for you at halftime, then beat you up in the second half."[16]

The AIA men's basketball team, although certainly the most legendary of the ministry's traveling squads, is hardly its only highly competitive team. The lineup of sports, which has grown and changed over the years, today includes women's basketball, soccer (both men's and women's), baseball, strength and conditioning, tennis, track and field, volleyball, wrestling, and sports medicine.

Since the ministry first fielded its men's basketball team in the late 1960s, the formula for AIA's globe-trotting teams has remained essentially the same: Play highly competitive ball to capture the attention of the audience and opponent, and then use the opportunity to talk about the Christian faith. The ministry's motto spells it out like this: "One world to reach. One language of sport. One message of victory."

When AIA heralds its intention to reach "the world," it is not exaggerating. The ministry has operations in 75 countries in addition to some 125 American college campuses.[17] AIA has also penetrated the highest reaches of American major league sports; as of 2007, half of the 32 teams in the National Football League had AIA staff members operating as their official team chaplain, which, given the huge success and reach of the NFL, constitutes a major coup for the ministry. AIA has also installed its staffers as the chaplains of the two marquee teams in Major League Baseball, the Boston Red Sox and New York Yankees, with the NBA's Miami Heat (league champions in 2006), and with the majority of franchises in Major League Soccer.[18]

Uszynski is troubled by any notion that Christianity's proof lies in the pudding of victory on a field or court. Not that he and his AIA colleagues do not value competition; indeed, as they well understand, it's how people and organizations measure themselves, chart their progress, and give structure and meaning to our pursuits of excellence inside and outside the world of sports. And when it comes to ministry, AIA is definitely keeping score. Taking a page from the sports world, the ministry publishes evangelism statistics on its website that take the form of a baseball box score. With impressive precision, one statistical table neatly lays out year-to-date totals for such "key measurements" as evangelism (10,468,760), disciples (3,111), and "recruiting challenged" (8,829).[19]

The ministry's literature about its communications arm, AIA Media, announces the ambitious goal to reach 100 million people annually with the gospel message. How? In language that reveals much about the ministry's strategy, AIA pledges to do so by providing media resources that communicate the gospel message through both sports and athletes. "AIA's media tools and materials expose millions of sports fans to the good news each year. Countless volunteers, thousands of athletes, and more than 500 staff members stand together to share one message: Life's greatest victory is found in a relationship with Jesus Christ."[20]

How it works in practice in the pro sports setting is spelled out succinctly in an article in the magazine published by AIA's parent ministry, Campus Crusade for Christ. In a profile of AIA staffer and Boston Red Sox chaplain

Walt Day, the *Worldwide Challenge* publication states, "[Day] spends his days in the locker room, on the field and wherever players are, always looking for opportunities to tell them about Jesus Christ."[21]

The scope and depth of AIA's work no doubt testify to the ministry's success at speaking the "native tongue" of sports, as well as the native tongues of people in the many countries where AIA conducts outreach. It is Ed Uszynski's mission to transform its ability to speak the language of Jesus.

"Sometimes it bothers me—athletes sky-pointing, praising God for the win," Uszynski says. "What I'm surprised at is that when the loser gets interviewed he never gives the glory to God. It could be, 'I'm sad we lost, but thank God for the opportunity to play today.' To me, frankly, it's in the midst of losing that Christianity should speak loudest."[22]

Christianity that is more relevant to losing than winning? It is quite a statement coming, as it is, from a man who has been responsible for training Athletes in Action evangelists. Because AIA, from the time of its founding, has had competitive success embedded deep in its DNA.

The story of Athletes in Action starts with the late Bill Bright, whose Campus Crusade for Christ ministry, originally launched at the University of California–Los Angeles campus in the early 1950s, was well on its way to becoming a global colossus when a young football player named Dave Hannah founded AIA in 1966 as a Campus Crusade offshoot. That Campus Crusade would spawn a sports ministry was perhaps foreshadowed in Bright's and Crusade's early days on the UCLA campus; one of his first student converts was the famous track-and-field champion Rafer Johnson, and Bright's emphasis on attracting athletes to his flock yielded several players from the Bruins' football team as well.[23]

An Iowa native, Hannah had played collegiate football at Oklahoma State, and played it well enough to be drafted by the Los Angeles Rams. A training camp injury ended his professional football career before it even started, however, and Hannah redirected his energy and competitive nature to winning converts to the Lord. "Winning" is the appropriate word; in articulating AIA's founding philosophy and distinguishing it from the well-established Fellowship of Christian Athletes, Hannah revealed the hard-charging spirit of the football player he was.

"FCA is primarily a *fellowship* of Christian sports men and women," Hannah said at the time. "We're a fellowship, too, but our fellowship is grounded more in aggressive evangelism and discipleship training. We're activists, so to speak."

The founding philosophy articulated by Hannah holds up well today, four decades later, as a description of the central strategy of those promoting

Christianity through major league sports. "The purpose of this work," Hannah said, "is to introduce athletes to Christ, then to use the platform they have for evangelism. . . . This visibility is influential, because when spectators and athletes themselves hear the testimonies of our players and see the way they play, it makes an impression."

From the beginning, AIA fielded teams—in basketball, weight-lifting, wrestling, and track and field—and used them as the vessel for the religious message, a strategy that made quality of play and competitive success critical to the ministry's evangelism success. As one AIA athlete said in the early days, "It's important to win, not because God wants winners, but because Americans do." Even then, however, the approach had its critics. "Their effectiveness in converting teenagers," one skeptic said, "seemed dependent on their ability to deliver points."[24]

Ed Uszynski would agree—to a point.

"It is true that America pays attention to a winner," Uszynski reflects. "You want to ride a wave that's going to get attention. But you're on a slippery slope when you attach God to winning, as if it's God that is making us successful."

It's not that Uszynski imagines God as remote, as aloof from earthly affairs. "Make no mistake about it—God does care about winning and losing," Uszynski says, "but it's for his purposes, not ours. That confuses the issue for us because we'd like to think that a good life necessarily results in worldly victory, and that a sinful life will necessarily produce loss on the field. But that is a naïve view of both God and the world. Still, it is easy to fall into this thinking in every aspect of life."

Uszynski does not doubt the value of competitive success, including winning games, as an attention-grabber. The key, he says, is what happens after the door has opened and the conversation has begun. Perhaps surprising for a man in the forefront of the faith-promotion-through-sports movement, Uszynski agrees with one of the principal objections of the many people who are cynical about the shape and form of religion in sports.

"What's become so distasteful is this idea that God is only on the side of the winner," Uszynski says. "Winning players say they've been blessed, that God was in the details when it worked out in their favor. It's become almost a cliché among winners to go there. For [the faith expression] to be credible you have to go there in both cases—winning and losing.

"Which is why I have such respect for someone like Tony Dungy. When he loses a game . . . he doesn't change who he is. His faith still permeates every aspect of his life. Most athletes, when they start to walk with Christ, they have it in their minds that when things go right and things go well, it's obviously a sign that God was on his side. And when they don't, he wasn't."

The common saying "But for the grace of God go I" gives pause to Ed Uszynski. He understands that people are generally expressing gratitude when they utter those words. But he hears in it an implication that he does not abide. "I'm troubled by the suggestion that God's grace is *not* with a person whose life is falling apart, or that he's removed himself from the losing locker room. God may be *most* present in the losing locker room." Adds Uszynski, who stressed this wisdom to field staff during his years directing AIA's ministry training center: "If people in ministry are going to be wise and true, this is the moment to jump in and say nothing has changed."[25]

*

If the collapse of the awakened Lions confounded those keen on using football wins as a proof of Christianity's merits, so, too, might it disappoint cynics who want to demonstrate that religion is a joke and Christians are hypocrites. When Kitna and the Lions saw their season unravel, the usual punch lines were almost too easy to break out: "Where's his God now? What happened to all that faith? How come they're not talking about God *now*?" But, apparently, little changed with the Detroit Lions in the areas where faith matters, even when the losses piled up. Kitna and company kept on talking about God, kept on stressing the imperative to be virtuous men and trustworthy teammates. According to the accounts of those close to the team, the faith, character, and unity ballyhooed amidst the string of victories endured even when the winning did not.

The back-biting and dissension that had characterized pre-Kitna seasons did not return, insists Wilson, the team's longtime chaplain. "To have [the season] take a turn like that, whew, it was hard," Wilson recalled a month after the season's end, cringing at the still-fresh memory. "But the brotherhood, the team sense that we can figure this out—that held together."[26]

"It's interesting," said Wilson, a former AIA staff member, as he reflected on the flow and ebb of public and media attention to the Lions' season. "Before [the team started winning], few people in the city even knew there was ministry on the team. When we were 5-2, yeah, then the media start calling. They all wanted to talk about Jon Kitna and [the] faith aspect of the Lions. We're thinking, 'OK, if you want to talk about it, fine.' All we did—all Jon did—was answer questions, tell them what was going on, how it was no different when we were losing.

"Several writers asked if our strong faith element was the reason we were winning," Wilson recalls. "I said no. . . . As we started to fade, they stopped calling."

Wilson, a former college quarterback and a man who started his own congregation with the aim of reaching people who "hate church," exudes a straightforwardness and lack of pretension that characterizes the men in and around sports. Yet he becomes quite philosophical when reflecting on the Lions of 2007. Like AIA's Uszynski, he cautions against looking for Jesus in the win column.

"In lots of ways, it's the opposite," Wilson says. "The proof of Christianity is found in tough times. Can you stand strong? It's easy to glorify Jesus when things are going well. It's a whole different ballgame when the bottom falls out on your season, to find out if your faith is real."[27]

Kitna, the object of so much of the secular—and religious—media curiosity when the Lions were hot, addressed the season's lessons with remarkable honesty and a fair degree of pain when he and a handful of teammates came to speak at Wilson's Kensington Community Church shortly after the season's end. Listening to Kitna's brief sermon at Kensington's "Lions Night," one cannot help but understand why Kitna's teammates—Christian and non-Christian alike—praise him as the "real deal," as a man who pours out his heart without artifice, without regard for softening his edges or making himself look fashionable.

Kitna began his sermon that night with his characteristic exhortations to the congregants to "get saved" if they had not already done so. He then proceeded to lay out a remarkable no-holds-barred critique of purveyors of the health-and-wealth gospel, singling out Texas-based TV preacher superstar Joel Osteen in particular.

"Dave [Wilson] wanted me to share my heart," Kitna told the congregation. "Mine is like yours if you're a lifelong Lions fan. . . . There's frustration. I'm *mad*. Part of me wants to be mad at God. I'm mad because I'm listening to these people on TV, these preachers on TV like Joel Osteen, who say, 'Hey, if you live this way, God will bless you. . . . If you do good to others, God will overflow blessings upon you.'"

Kitna recounted the charitable work he and his Christian teammates had undertaken during the season, their intense and sustained Bible study, their praying together on the practice field, their using media opportunities to testify to their faith and praise God. "Every time guys put microphone in our face," he said, "we were pointing people to Christ!"

Sounding a little like Job from the Old Testament, that poster boy for faith in the face of undeserved adversity, Kitna began working up a rhetorical sweat. "We're taught to be obedient and give, and God will give back. Man, I've seen guys on this team take their giving to whole different levels. It was amazing to watch the way guys were loosening their hearts and giving. . . . So certainly we were going to the Super Bowl! We were *prayerful*. We were glorifying God. [According to what] Joel Osteen is telling me, we will be successful.

"Well, guess what. Things didn't quite go the way I was led to believe they should go if I really believed in all that. To be honest . . . I don't really listen to that teaching. There's a certain part of you that says, 'Yeah, that seems right. Six-and-two.' You start to think Super Bowl. It's natural.

"But as season went on . . . you know what our No. 1 prayer at Bible study was? If God doesn't give us another win he's done too much. The fact we're going to heaven—he's already done too much. How can that [gratitude] be manifested in our life? *That* was our prayer."

Kitna was far from finished. What of the apostle Paul, the biblical giant who did so much to spread Christianity in its crucial formative years? "He was in and out of jail, beaten and stoned," Kitna said. The disciples? They were killed for their beliefs.

"What does the word say?" Kitna asked. "Not *if* you face trials. It says *when* you face trials.

"We are frustrated as a team. We hate losing. Our desire is to win every single game. But ultimately, we want to know Christ. And through our lives we want other people to know. We started 6-2, and people were listening. But guess what. Can you do the same testimony when [you] go 1-7? No question. As a ministry we're closer to God today than we ever were when we were 6-2."[28]

Imagine a marketing pitch that suggests, "Heed our message, buy our product, and join us in a cause that finds its fullest expression in frustration and loss!" It is not the stuff of which winning promotional campaigns are made. So it is easy to understand why Dave Hannah, in founding Athletes in Action forty years ago, devised an evangelizing strategy built on competitive success and excellence, and why Ed Uszynski, whatever his qualms about an over-fixation on winning, is not about to press his organization to field incompetent basketball, baseball, and soccer teams and approach would-be converts with a message emphasizing the virtues of losing. America, obviously, would not listen.

Evangelical ministries are sometimes accused of the old "bait-and-switch" approach to outreach (a charge that is not entirely fair). The not-so-complimentary term describes a process of attracting new people with an appealing message that meets them on their terms—winning in sports, getting ahead in life, meeting friendly people, becoming a more effective person—and holding off on the challenging parts until they've been reeled onto the boat. Only later does the new convert learn about the complex and challenging aspects of the faith product: Commitments of time and money, giving up one's hard-partying or women-chasing ways, speaking up boldly about one's faith at the risk of being judged a fool. And the kicker, a product attribute shared by nothing else being promoted in America's marketing-saturated culture: Your new way will find perhaps its noblest manifestation in *suffering*.

What are Jesus' marketers to do?

The tale of Kitna and the Lions calls to mind the late great Reggie White, a quarterback-sacking and evangelizing superstar in the NFL in the 1980s and 1990s who did much to usher in the conspicuous religiosity of today's sports world, and who later disavowed most of what he did, and stood for, as the avatar of jock evangelism. Shortly before his sudden death in late 2004, White went public with claims of being exploited—"prostituted" as he put it—by pastors and ministries eager to use him as a marketing vehicle.

The men leading Christian ministry on the Lions—Jon Kitna, Dave Wilson, and others—might sympathize with White's point. It was they who were left high and dry when the winning stopped and the spotlight turned away. In the final analysis, the Lions' story did much to advertise Christianity: They kept the faith through tough times. They found Jesus in the loss column.

But by then, the Christian Broadcasting Network and other religion-promoting media and ministries had turned their sights elsewhere. January, and the NFL playoffs, furnished another opportunity to direct attention to Christian athletes on a hot streak. As it happened, the Green Bay Packers had advanced to the National Football Conference championship game. They were one victory away from the Super Bowl, and like virtually every team in pro football, the Packers had their share of pious players. One could see the CBN headline coming from a mile away: "Super Faith Taking Packers to Super Bowl?"

The Packers, alas, lost the game.

Notes

1. Carol Flake, *Redemptorama: Culture, Politics, and the New Evangelicalism* (New York: Penguin, 1984), 100.

2. Mark Martin, "Christ Turns Kitna's Life, NFL Team Around," *CBN News*, Christian Broadcasting Network, http://www.cbn.com/cbnnews/273516.aspx.

3. Associated Press, "Kitna Calls His Return a Miracle," *New York Times*, September 18, 2007.

4. "Adjusting the Cup," sports blog, http://adjustingthecup.blogspot.com/2007_09_01_archive.html.

5. L. Z. Granderson, "Why So Skeptical of Kitna's Miracle," ESPN.com, September 21, 2007, http://sports.espn.go.com/espn/page2/story?page=granderson/070921.

6. David Fleming, "Kitna Seeks Help from Above," *ESPN Magazine*, September 26, 2007, http://sports.espn.go.com/nfl/news/story?id=3036235.

7. Mark Martin, "Christ Turns Kitna's Life, NFL Team Around," *CBN News*, Christian Broadcasting Network, http://www.cbn.com/cbnnews/273516.aspx.

8. Jill Ewart, "Waking the Lions," *Sharing the Victory*, Fellowship of Christian Athletes, http://www.sharingthevictory.com/vsItemDisplay.lsp&objectID=D5C73473-97BD -484A-8AEBFDC539C2150E&method=display.

9. Fleming, "Kitna Seeks," ESPN.

10. "Outside the Lines," ESPN, December 2, 2007.

11. Ewart, "Waking the Lions."

12. Jemele Hill, "God's Quarterback Turning Everyone into Believers," *ESPN.com*, November 7, 2007, http://sports.espn.go.com/espn/page2/story?page=hill/071107& sportCat=nfl.

13. "Jon Kitna Was Sacked for Your Sins," Deadspin, September 18, 2007, http:// deadspin.com/300887/jon-kitna-was-sacked-for-your-sins.

14. Joni B. Hannigan, "Heisman Winner Has Priorities in Order," *Baptist Press*, December 10, 2007, http://www.baptistpress.org/bpnews.asp?id=27001.

15. Ed Uszynski, Athletes in Action, extended interview conducted via telephone, e-mail, and face-to-face between the fall of 2007 and summer of 2008.

16. Josh Levin, "Crossed Off: They're God's Favorite Team . . . Of Course Nobody Wants to Play Them," *Slate*, December 3, 2004, http://www.slate.com/id/2110667.

17. Athletes in Action, "Vision & Direction for the Future: Annual Report 2006," http://www.aia.com/-about/Annual%20Report%202006.pdf.

18. Athletes in Action, Pro Ministries web page, http://www.aia.com/pro.

19. The statistics appear beneath a profile of Ed Uszynski in the online AIA newsletter, "Get in the Game." See http://athletesinaction.org/about/newsletter/september06/ fruitfulness.aspx.

20. "About" page, Athletes in Action website, http://www.athletesinaction.org/about.

21. Jessica Cline, "Backing up Boston's Best: Walt Day Helps Boston's World-Champion Athletes Look to Jesus," Worldwide Challenge (September–October 2005), on line at http://www.worldwidechallenge.org/2005/sepoct056.html. Published by Campus Crusade for Christ International.

22. Ed Uszynski, Athletes in Action, interview 2007–2008.

23. Tony Ladd and James A. Mathisen, *Muscular Christianity: Evangelical Protestants and the Development of American Sport* (Grand Rapids, Michigan: Baker Books, 1999), 132–33.

24. Ladd, Mathisen, *Muscular Christianity*, 134.

25. Ed Uszynski, Athletes in Action, interview 2007–2008.

26. Dave Wilson, telephone interview, January 29, 2008. A review of media coverage and blogosphere commentary generally corroborates Wilson's point; one finds few incidents of recriminations, finger-pointing, and the like during the team's collapse. The point is also verified by Nick Cotsonika, a *Detroit Free Press* reporter who covered the Lions' season for the newspaper.

27. Dave Wilson, telephone interview, January 29, 2008.

28. Jon Kitna, remarks at "Lion's Night" at Kensington Church, January 9, 2008, as captured in podcast recording posted on the church's website.

CHAPTER 5

~

Church at the Ballpark

Baseball Chapel and Its Exclusive Theology in an Age of
Growing Religious Diversity

Our purpose is to glorify Jesus Christ.

—Baseball Chapel website

At long last, major league baseball had returned to Washington, D.C. A
contingent from Ohev Shalom, better known as the National Synagogue, was
quick to organize a group outing to RFK Stadium to watch the new hometown
team, the Washington Nationals, in its inaugural season. The members of the
fast-growing Orthodox congregation in the northwest corner of the District of
Columbia were all excited smiles on the early-season evening in 2005 as they
posed for a ballpark photo in "Hebrew Nationals" t-shirts, the hot dog brand
serving as an apt moniker for this crew of Jewish baseball fans. So Jewish-
friendly was Nationals management that its food service was serving kosher
meals at RFK.

By late September of that season, the baseball smiles had been wiped off
the faces of the synagogue's curly-haired young leader, Rabbi Shmuel Herzfeld,
and many other Nationals supporters in D.C.'s Jewish community—and not
primarily because of the sour finish to the Nationals' once-promising season.
Something had happened with the team that hurt worse than a loss. A story
had seeped from the team clubhouse, one involving an exchange between the
team's Christian chaplain and a young outfielder with the apt surname of
Church, that to Herzfeld and his congregants sounded anything but a welcoming tone.

The controversy started with the appearance of a *Washington Post* sports section feature about the work of the team's chaplain, Jon Moeller. An FBI agent by day, Moeller was serving as the team's religious adviser under the auspices of Baseball Chapel, a Pennsylvania-based evangelical Christian ministry that has been providing chaplains for all major and minor league teams for more than thirty years. The story was innocuous for the most part, evenhandedly describing Moeller's philosophy about God and baseball and his good-natured efforts to encourage players to attend chapel service. The problem was a brief vignette near the end of the story in which 26-year-old outfielder Ryan Church opened his mouth and stuck his foot deep inside.

As *Post* reporter Laura Blumenfeld wrote:

> The players not only pray, but they also discuss personal matters—marital tension, addiction issues, family illnesses, financial stress—drawing sometimes surprising lessons. Church was concerned because his former girlfriend was Jewish. He turned to Moeller, "I said, like, Jewish people, they don't believe in Jesus. Does that mean they're doomed? Jon nodded, like, that's what it meant. My ex-girlfriend! I was like, man, if they only knew. Other religions don't know any better. It's up to us to spread the word."[1]

To Herzfeld and his fellow baseball-lovers at the National Synagogue, the words felt like a line drive in the teeth.

"We were so excited about the Nationals; we have a lot of diehard baseball fans in our congregation," Herzfeld recalled in an interview. "We felt so hurt."[2]

Two days after the appearance of the *Post* story, the rabbi held a news conference at the stadium to denounce Church's remarks and the apparent content of Moeller's teachings. It appeared, Herzfeld said, that "the locker room of the Nationals is being used to preach hatred."[3] The rabbi met with Nationals president Tony Tavares, who on the same day suspended Moeller pending the results of a team investigation into his work with the team. The Nationals issued an apology on Church's behalf.

Church himself issued an "apology" several days later. "Those who know me on a personal level understand that I am not the type of person who would call into question the religious beliefs of others," he said in a statement distributed by the team and reported in the *Post*. "I sincerely regret if the quote attributed to me in Sunday's *Washington Post* article offended anyone."[4] (Several weeks after that, Church elaborated in a featured letter to the editor in *USA Today* following an opinion piece by this writer on the incident. Said Church: "My biggest mistake, in retrospect, was believing that I was attending a chapel meeting where asking questions, learning, expressing, and sharing thoughts on religion were not only appropriate, but also encouraged and private. On the day of the Bible discussion with team chaplain Jon Moeller, I simply asked a question to clarify the direction of the conversation. I absolutely said nothing that could have ever been construed as condemning another group. . . . I am a Christian, and I believe Jesus Christ is our savior; yet I have no problem with any other religion, ethnicity, race or culture."⁵)

There was more fallout to come. In something of a first—never in recent years had a commissioner of a major sports league publicly questioned the evangelical Christian network in pro sports—Selig said baseball would review the arrangement by which Baseball Chapel operated as the lone religious organization with access to all pro baseball clubhouses and the players who populate them. "I was deeply offended by what happened with Ryan Church and Jon Moeller," Selig said in a letter to a North Carolina rabbi, Ari Sunshine, who had written the commissioner to voice his objections.⁶

In some conservative quarters, the suspension of Moeller amounted to one more example of American culture supposedly ganging up against Christianity. Richard Land of the Southern Baptist Convention jumped to the suspended chaplain's defense, saying to the *Washington Post*, "Just how many ways can you interpret the words of Jesus in John 14:5-6, 'I am the way and the truth and the life; no one comes to the father but by me'? The worst this chaplain could be convicted of is ascribing to orthodox Christian historic faith, which is what I would think you would want from a Christian chaplain."⁷

Robert Knight, director of the Culture and Family Institute, juxtaposed baseball's quick action to suspend Moeller with its slow response to its mounting steroids problem. "As [doping] suspicions mounted," Knight wrote in an article on the conservative news site *World Net Daily*, "Major League Baseball's front office sat on its hands, finally roused to action when it was no longer possible to ignore the Pillsbury Doughboys knocking the ball around. Contrast that with the lightning speed with which the baseball gods bought into a *Washington Post* smear of a Christian chaplain and upcoming star outfielder Ryan Church of the Washington Nationals."

Picking up on Herzfeld's charge about the locker room being used "to preach hatred," Knight added: "Newsflash to Mr. Herzfeld: Christians don't hate you. We're talking here about the 2,000-year-old Great Commission stated by Jesus in Matthew 28:19. Christians—out of love—are told to share with everyone the Good News that Jesus came to die for their sins and give them eternal life."⁸

During an interview conducted later that fall, Herzfeld said he was encouraged by Selig's attention to the matter and the commissioner's promised review of the baseball's relationship with the evangelical ministry. Yet he also voiced skepticism about the commissioner's sincerity—skepticism that would prove well-founded. "If they do nothing, they're going to hear from me," Herzfeld said. "That I promise."[9]

The rabbi's doubts were justified. Whatever action was taken by Selig and his surrogates to review Baseball Chapel's work—if any—remains unknown. In the three years that ensued, the commissioner and his spokespeople said nothing publicly about the Ryan Church incident and the larger issues it raised. Repeated requests for comment for this book and related articles were ignored. The only tangible result of the incident: Moeller's permanent removal as the Nationals' chaplain, with a new chaplain installed by Baseball Chapel by the following season.

*

As the story is often told, Baseball Chapel is principally a solution to a logistical problem. Religious players, because of their hectic travel and game-playing schedules, rarely have the opportunity to attend church services on Sunday. So, beginning in the 1970s, Baseball Chapel has been taking church to them.

For all the one-on-one counseling and informal interactions that happen between the team chaplain and players, the pre-game chapel service remains the ministry's stock-in-trade. In no professional team sport is the chapel service as ingrained and long-standing as in baseball. On every Sunday in every major (and minor) league park where a professional baseball game is going to be played, a volunteer chaplain representing the 35-year-old Baseball Chapel organization presides over brief Christian services for the players.

Fitting for a ministry that serves the most history-rich of America's major professional sports, Baseball Chapel promotes its own history as the stuff of legend. As the literature of the Springfield, Pennsylvania-based organization tells it, the tale began with the Cubs and Twins in the early 1960s. Christian players were finding it difficult to attend church services on Sunday mornings during road trips. So, in the true entrepreneurial spirit of American-style Christianity, they began organizing their own chapel services at the team hotel. The practice began spreading to other teams.

In an unlikely turn of events given the media's general skepticism about players' religiosity today, it was a sportswriter, of all people, who spurred the next stage of the baseball ministry's evolution. In 1973, Warren Spoelstra, a Detroit writer and a Christian, approached then-Commissioner Bowie Kuhn with a novel idea: a program that would provide a Christian chapel service for every major league team on every Sunday during the season. Kuhn approved, and thus was born Baseball Chapel.[10]

Apparently no longer feeling a need to keep the organization and its activities at arm's length, baseball in 1974 allowed Baseball Chapel to switch venues and begin holding Sunday services at the ballparks rather than the visiting team's hotel. By 1975, the baseball ministry had achieved another impressive milestone: Every major league team had a Christian chaplain operating under Baseball Chapel's auspices. Over the ensuing years, the program grew down into the minor leagues and south into the professional baseball leagues of Puerto Rico, Venezuela, and the Dominican Republic—countries that today supply numerous players to America's major leagues. Baseball Chapel's work migrated to younger ballplayers, with outreach to youth in Latin America. Also, the ministry has expanded into Japan's major leagues, and as its next frontier, the organization has identified Japan's neighbor: South Korean professional baseball.[11]

Baseball Chapel's executive director, Vince Nauss, today sits at the head of a network with impressive reach and resources. The ministry's six-person full-time staff oversees about five hundred volunteer chaplains and operations around the world. According to financial records filed with the Internal Revenue Service, the ministry possessed some $2 million in assets in 2006. Fundraising, the ministry's chief revenue source, had advanced strongly through the decade, with donations growing by 25 percent from 2002 to 2006. The organization raised more than $1 million in contributions, gifts, and grants in 2006, mostly via donations from individuals associated with professional baseball.[12]

Nondenominational but distinctly evangelical in tone and philosophy, Baseball Chapel has a credo that succinctly captures the essence of today's sports-flavored Christianity—and that exposes the incompleteness of its claim (one similar to other pro sports ministries') that it exists merely to provide religious service to pro players: "Our purpose," the group declares in large-font form on its website, "is to glorify Jesus Christ." The organization's website also gives prominent display to a verse from Colossians 1:28 that speaks to its evangelical commitment: "We proclaim Him, admonishing and teaching everyone with all wisdom, so that we may present everyone perfect in Christ."[13]

On what biblical imperative does Baseball Chapel base the notion of glorifying God through a game played with bat and ball? Like many in sports ministry, Rich Sparling, Baseball Chapel's director for Hispanic outreach and the volunteer chaplain for the Philadelphia Phillies, finds answers in Colossians 3:23 and 3:24: "Whatever you do, work at it with all your heart, as working for the Lord, not for men, since you know that you will receive an inheritance from the Lord as a reward. It is the Lord Christ you are serving."

Sparling believes the Christian baseball player fulfills the obligation, or not, through his conduct on and off the field. According to the creed of athletic Christianity, as articulated by Sparling, a Christian player should be a hard worker and exemplary teammate; his play should be tough but clean. He must set a good example in the way he carries himself in public and navigates the at-times trying personal life of a sports celebrity. For a superstar, a player whose every move is under a media microscope, it means conduct beyond reproach, life without newsworthy scandals. For a marginal team member, a bench player who might go for days without appearing in a game, it means accepting his role without complaint. "If you're on the bench, you should be the *best* bench player," Sparling says. "You should be the one shouting encouragement, paying close attention, always ready to step in."[14]

Sparling, a spry middle-aged man, talks about his ministry while sipping a beverage in the snack bar at Philadelphia Biblical University, a small Christian college in the Philadelphia suburbs. A volunteer, fill-in baseball coach that season, he has just run the young collegiate Christians through an early-spring practice in the gymnasium, concluded by a prayer. He'll soon be heading to Florida to spend time with Phillies players at spring training. A former collegiate ballplayer who turned down a chance to try out for the pros, Sparling spent a decade in the Dominican Republic doing missionary work, running Bible-and-baseball clinics for Dominican youths, before returning to the United States and joining the Baseball Chapel staff.

On Sunday mornings when the Phillies are playing a home game, several hours before fans start filling up the seats, Sparling presides over a series of 15- to 20-minute chapel services—"mini-church services," as he calls them—at Citizens Bank Park in south Philadelphia. First comes a service for stadium personnel; next are separate services for the home team, visiting team, and umpires. His wife, meanwhile, presides over a service for the Phillies' wives and then a Sunday school-style session for the children. "We're there," Sparling says, "because these people can't get to church."[15]

To one longtime advocate for Christianity in pro sports, that idea of mega-millionaire ballplayers cramming into improvised ballpark spaces—storage rooms, trainers' facilities, even shower rooms—to worship Jesus before a game is nothing short of miraculous. "I was recently at a chapel service before a Yankees–Red Sox game at Fenway Park," Pat Williams, executive vice president of basketball's Orlando Magic and a longtime supporter of the Fellowship of Christian Athletes and Baseball Chapel, said in a 2004 interview. "The players put folding chairs into the showers, right off the main locker room, and had the chapel right in the shower room. I thought, 'Lord, this is amazing.' To me, it's something supernatural that chapel services are taking place in those kinds of settings."[16]

Sparling certainly has strong views on what it means to be Christian between the lines on the diamond, but in his religious counseling work with the Phillies he concentrates on a side of the ballplayer's life that is largely out of fans' view.

Much of it deals with the stresses unique to the players' line of work—travel that keeps them away from their families for long periods, pressure to perform, trades that can uproot their lives at just a moment's notice. "For a lot of guys in the majors, there is a constant fear of getting sent back down to the minors," Sparling says. "Being a major league baseball player seems glamorous to most of us who aren't players. But as these guys learn, it's a business. You could show up at two o'clock on the day of the game and be told, 'Head out to the airport. You're pitching for Kansas City tonight.' You have to call your wife on the way to the airport because there's no time to go home first."

Ballplayers face enormous pressure. Failure is witnessed by tens of thousands in attendance, many more on television; it is captured in statistics and game accounts that appear in newspapers across the country and on proliferating sports websites. The threat of injury looms, with the potential to end a career and cost a man millions of dollars in potential earnings. "The guys who learn to deal with it are successful," Sparling says. "The guys who don't? They won't last long.

"When you're a kid, baseball is a game. For these guys, it's not a game; it's a job. For the Christian player, it's a *calling*. This is what God has called them to do. God has placed them in their position to be a light. We're not there for the kingdom of baseball," Sparling adds, "but for the kingdom of the Lord."[17]

As demonstrated by the experience of Hall of Fame third baseman Mike Schmidt, Baseball Chapel's product can serve as the perfect balm for all that ails a ballplayer's troubled psyche. Pressure is an experience with which Schmidt was well familiar, playing as he did in Philadelphia, where the fans and media are notorious for negativity and ganging up on even their highest-performing hometown players if their performance dips. Schmidt, who wore the Phillies' maroon from 1972 to 1989, told biographer William C. Kashatus that participating in Baseball Chapel and accepting Jesus brought him much-needed perspective and comfort early in his career.

The mid- and late-1970s Phillies were not only a winning ball club, capturing three straight division titles, but a team pulsing with Christian belief and practice. Of the twenty-five players on the roster, Kashatus reports, some fifteen to twenty in that era participated in chapel service and/or Bible study and fellowship meetings. Catcher Bob Boone coaxed Schmidt into the fold and, along with outfielder Garry Maddox and veteran pitcher Jim Kaat, served as the new convert's religious guide.

"The idea that a spiritual entity could take the pressure off of my life . . . was extremely appealing to me," Schmidt recalled. "So my original desire for a spiritual relationship with the Lord was more selfish than anything else. I looked at it as an opportunity to take all the pressures out of my life and put them on the shoulders of Jesus Christ, allowing the outcome to be what he wanted it to be. That included everything, ranging from a dilemma in my personal life to going to bat with the bases loaded in the bottom of the ninth."[18]

Legions of professional baseball players, from Schmidt's era to the present, attest to similar experiences with, and benefits from, their embrace of the religion of and about Jesus Christ. In addition to the mental strength derived from faith—a cushion for the bumpy ride of a long baseball season—players cite the benefits of religion in binding Bible-believing teammates together. Prayer, Bible study, fellowship—in Schmidt's era as today—bolster players against the pressure, materialism, and runaway egoism that often attach to the fortune and fame of major league success, and they help them remain true to their wives and girlfriends during long road trips that afford numerous opportunities for extramarital sex.

Albert Pujols, an even bigger superstar today than Schmidt was in his time, describes his faith as more meaningful to him than his incredible success on the field—quite a statement, given that his success has included two National League Most Valuable Player Awards and two trips to the World Series with his St. Louis Cardinals. "People ask me if I believe how quickly my career has taken off," says Pujols, a Dominican Republic native who emerged suddenly on the baseball scene with a record-breaking rookie year in 2001. "I just tell them that Jesus Christ is my strength. God has blessed me, and I will continue to do my best for him. That is more important than anything I could ever do in baseball."[19]

Pitcher Jeremy Affeldt describes his Christian faith as essential to his navigating the adjustment from high school to professional baseball as a young man. "The things I saw, the things that were expected of me, the things that it took to live in the world as a professional man—the challenges were too great for me to handle on my own," he says. "I needed someone to lean on, someone to give me the strength that I didn't have. That was Jesus, that was my savior and that is who I love deeply."[20]

Such reliance on faith is hardly unique to baseball. Kurt Warner, whose sudden emergence as a Jesus-praising, championship-winning quarterback in the late 1990s brought new visibility to Christianity in sports, describes an experience in which God's presence settled his nerves and steeled his determination as he came under center to begin a crucial late-game possession in Super Bowl XXXIV—a possession that led to the game-winning touchdown and Warner's opportunity to witness his faith on the post-game victory podium before the massive television audience.

Although invocations of faith invariably accompany moments of victory, prompting comedians and cynics to ask why losing players so rarely attribute the result to God, star defensive back Troy Polamalu speaks of his faith as a source of consolation in moments of worry and struggle. "Jesus brings peace to my life," Polamalu said in the run-up to the 2006 Super Bowl. "Whether I have a major injury that ends my career tomorrow, or I make a bad play and get criticized by everybody, that faith brings peace."[21]

In an interview conducted during his playing days with the National Football League, one high-profile player, since retired, spoke of his Christian faith as the one constant he could rely on in a profession, and world, of highs and lows, successes and setbacks. "The word of God never leaves you or forsakes you. It doesn't change—unlike a parent, unlike a friend, unlike a business associate," Vincent said. "The word of God . . . is constant. It's full of life and prosperity and power."[22]

As the Phillies' Hall of Famer Schmidt put it, his acceptance of Christianity was, at first, "selfish," something that met his needs and wishes. It stands to reason that as a young Christian grows and matures in his faith, this selfishness will wane, and he will experience a deepening commitment to acting so that others, too, may possess the prize. And that, depending on how a player goes about this sharing of the faith, is often when the trouble begins.

More often that not, evangelizing amounts to nothing more and nothing less than a player encouraging a teammate to attend chapel or describing what faith has meant to him. At other times, however, "sharing" begins to resemble a religious bludgeoning.

Bob Tufts was a Princeton University graduate who had a run as a major league relief pitcher with San Francisco and Kansas City from 1981 to 1983. It wasn't just his Ivy League pedigree that made Tufts unusual. He converted to Judaism while in the minor leagues, which led to some uncomfortable moments with Christian teammates during the long stretches of relative inactivity in the bullpen that are central to the relief pitcher's existence. The experience that stands out for Tufts took place in a conversation with a Christian bullpen mate in Tucson when he was pitching for Phoenix, the Giants' triple-A affiliate at the time.

"We were sitting in the bullpen, and [the teammate] asked me if I accepted Jesus Christ as my savior," recalled Tufts in an interview. "I said, 'no,' and explained that I was going through the process of converting to Judaism. He looked at me—his eyes just blazed—and he said, 'Well, you're going to hell.' Then he turned away and started watching the game."[23]

Tufts' encounter with an intolerant strain of Christianity, while far from the norm in major league sports, is no isolated incident either. Mark Gilbert, a Jew who pitched in professional ball in the 1970s and 1980s, including a brief stint with the White Sox, told *Moment* magazine in 2007 that, as a player, he faced constant peer pressure to attend Christian worship services and accept Jesus.[24]

More recently, multiple non-Christians endured difficult interactions with Chad Curtis, a proselytizing outfielder who played for a half-dozen major league teams from 1992 to 2001. Among them was the Jewish outfielder Gabe Kapler, who was Curtis' teammate with Texas for two years. As recounted in an article in the *Jewish Press*, Kapler grew weary of Curtis' persistent questions and preaching, so he developed an innovative solution: He invited Curtis to join him, his Orthodox Jewish agent, and a rabbi for a meeting at a kosher restaurant. Curtis, the newspaper reported, took the hint and finally dropped his pursuit of his Jewish teammate.[25]

At least one Jewish umpire in professional baseball has endured numerous uncomfortable moments in which Baseball Chapel representatives have prayed in Jesus' name in his presence—even directly to him and for him—in situations where he had no feasible means of removing himself. As the umpire, Josh Miller, explained to the *New York Times*, the umpire locker rooms are typically small at minor league parks. "It's not like I could hide. . . . They preach to you. Some are more overbearing than others. At the end they ask if you have anything 'you want me to pray for.' The other guys would say 'our families, safe travel.' I'd say nothing. Then they would pray. It was very uncomfortable. They'd say Jesus this and Jesus that. At the end they'd say 'in Jesus' name.'"[26]

In contemplating the experiences of religious minorities in Christianity-infused clubhouses, it is important to remember that evangelizing ballplayers and chaplains come in contact with a wider circle of people than just their fellow players. There are clubhouse and stadium personnel, team support staff members, and the ever-present media. In the case of Curtis, Jewish sportswriters were often on the receiving end of his hard-edged preaching. Allan Wolper, a columnist for *Editor and Publisher*, wrote that Jewish journalists generally kept their many "unhappy encounters" with Christian athletes to themselves.[27] But one Jewish writer was unwilling to maintain the silence; in an article published in 2000, *Newsday* writer Jon Heyman wrote that "Curtis tried to convince some Jewish writers that they were making a big mistake and needed to rethink their beliefs."[28]

(New York—a huge sports market with a particularly large press corps, one including numerous Jewish writers—was also the site of a notorious anti-Semitism flare-up involving a Jewish writer and a Christian contingent from the NBA's New York Knicks. Eric Konigsberg, while researching an article on the Knicks for the *New York Times Magazine*, was subjected to point guard Charlie Ward's claims that Jews had the blood of Jesus on their hands and that they persecuted Christians "every day." Christian teammate Kurt Thomas jumped in with his teammate, pointing out to Konigsberg, "You know, there's Jews for Jesus, man."[29])

Journalist Steve Walz, in a 2001 article, described a wider pattern of religious disrespect. "During the past three years I have interviewed several Jewish players who spoke of uncomfortable incidents in locker rooms with small-town 'born-again' teammates who would make off-base comments about Jews and Judaism," Walz wrote. "These Jewish players chose not to respond to the abuse either from fear of causing a commotion and possibly being released or because they didn't know enough about historical Judaism to intelligently answer their detractors."[30]

To be fair, some Jewish major leaguers have attested to an atmosphere of religious tolerance and harmony prevailing in their own clubhouses—even clubhouses of teams known for their large and enthusiastic Christian contingents. Such was the message from Colorado Rockies relief pitcher Jason Hirsch in the 2007 post-season, when the media were exploring the pious ways of a Rockies team that featured not only numerous Christian players but an evangelical general manager and manager as well. Hirsch, a Jew, told the *New York Times* that he was never made to feel uncomfortable by his Christian teammates or bosses. "These guys are religious, sure, but . . . it's not like they hung a cross in my locker or anything," Hirsch said. "They've accepted me for who I am and what I believe in." Kevin Youkalis, a Jewish player for the Red Sox, has voiced similar sentiments about his experience with a Red Sox team that has featured numerous outspoken Christian believers.[31]

When religion goes wrong—when a player speaks of Jews and other non-Christians being destined for hell, for example—does Baseball Chapel bear responsibility? An examination of the ministry's public rhetoric reveals a mixed message about its regard for non-Christians, a theological stance that seems, in theory and in practice, to be open to use or misuse as a device to judge and condemn non-Christians.

On its website, the ministry uses ecumenical-sounding language to describe itself, saying, "Baseball Chapel is a nondenominational Christian ministry committed to the spiritual development of people throughout baseball." The organization's site includes a for-the-media background briefing that, among other points, denies any attempt to exclude or divide. "Although we hold to Christian beliefs, we seek to minister to baseball players regardless of their religious beliefs," the briefing says. Later, it adds: "The track record Baseball Chapel has demonstrated over four decades of service shows that the organization has never sought to be divisive, intrusive, or to exclude anyone of another faith."[32]

Vince Nauss, Baseball Chapel's executive director, echoes that theme in his rare comments to the media. Nauss declined several interview requests for this book, but in comments made to *Moment* magazine in 2007, he called the Ryan Church incident "unfortunate" and not representative of the ministry's work. "Players are never pressured to attend and there has never been any opposition to holding chapel," Nauss told the magazine. "There are definitely players who don't want any part of the chapel service. Our people know that they are guests and that only some people want what they have to offer. They're told not to be intrusive or condemning."[33]

Yet Nauss' statements and the inclusive-sounding pledge on Baseball Chapel's website contrast with other language used by the ministry. In addition to its emphatic pledge to "glorify Jesus Christ," Baseball Chapel's website further describes the ministry's mission as "bring[ing] encouragement to people in the world of professional baseball through the Gospel so that some become discipled followers of Jesus Christ," and its vision as one of seeing "deeply committed players use their platform to influence people around the world to become followers of Jesus Christ."[34]

It is even harder to square Baseball Chapel's pledges of tolerance and inclusiveness with its published creedal beliefs. "Our statement of faith," the ministry says, "is intended to accurately reflect the truths of Scripture we believe have been accepted by followers of Jesus Christ from the time He walked the earth. It includes the dogmatic beliefs of the church, specifically centering on the Triune God and salvation through faith in Jesus Christ alone." Nonbelievers, the ministry says, face "judgment and everlasting punishment separated from God."[35]

It is not the prerogative of players, fans, or writers to question the right of an organization like Baseball Chapel to have and promote its theology. Language about salvation through Jesus alone and "everlasting punishment" for those who believe otherwise may sound exclusive and alarming to nonevangelicals, but it must be acknowledged that such beliefs are hardly fringe or half-baked. On the contrary, they are quite consistent with the long tradition of conservative evangelicalism in America and the beliefs that more or less define the religious lives of millions of churchgoing Americans. What needs to be clearly recognized, however, is the tension between the ministry's public story about itself—that it mounts a purely innocuous and practical effort to provide faith resources for people who cannot conveniently make it to church—and the unavoidable fact that it promotes a message about ultimate truth—salvation through Jesus Christ and *only* Jesus Christ—that is inherently divisive and dismissive of other forms of belief.

Put another way, if a Chad Curtis struts around a major league clubhouse warning non-Christian players and reporters to accept Jesus or else, it cannot simply be shrugged off as the anomalous behavior of a misguided zealot. His tactics may be ill-advised and extreme, but a player in the Curtis mold is, after all, telling Baseball Chapel's truth, albeit in a particularly unsubtle way. If a Ryan Church asks his Baseball Chapel-appointed chaplain whether Church's Jewish ex-girlfriend is hell-bound, and the chaplain nods in the affirmative, the incident cannot be casually written off as one young ballplayer and his chaplain making a rookie mistake.

Which is why Shmuel Herzfeld, while waiting for an apology from Baseball Chapel that has yet to come, has not let go of the incident that marred the Nationals' inaugural season in the nation's capital in 2005.

*

Growing up in New York, Herzfeld attended a conservative religious school that frowned on most television. Sports were a different story. "Sports were kosher," Herzfeld recalled in an interview, "clean and pure. We were allowed to watch sports." And so he did, growing to love the Knicks, Jets, and Mets and becoming an avid reader of the sports pages.

Herzfeld worries that pro sports today are no longer "safe" for young Jewish fans, with sports heroes so frequently promoting one-truth Christianity. The rabbi is a leader of a group called Amcha: The Coalition for Jewish Concerns, which speaks out for "endangered" Jews around the world, and he has become a leading critic of many aspects of evangelical Christian engagement with pro sports, including the increasingly popular faith days and faith nights in major league baseball. While those ballpark faith events are large public gatherings designed, in part, to help churches attract new members, Herzfeld also worries about what goes on every day behind the scenes in major league clubhouses, where Baseball Chapel's representatives live out the ministry's mission in the chapel services and Bible studies they lead, and in their one-on-one interaction with players. A key part of sports ministry's teaching, the rabbi knows, is encouraging players to use their fame to promote Christianity.

"One of the major concerns," Herzfeld says, "is people using their personal and social capital as a player to evangelize for their particular faith. And they're doing it with the imprimatur of their team. That's problematic. As the father of children who love sports, I'm concerned about that. I don't think it's kosher."

Herzfeld was "uncomfortable" witnessing the Christian statements made by Indianapolis Colts owner Jim Irsay and coach Tony Dungy while they accepted the Super Bowl trophy in 2007—a moment Dungy used to brush aside questions about his being the first black coach to win a Super Bowl and to proclaim his pride at winning "the Lord's way" as a Christian coach, and in a roller-coaster of a game that he suggested was somehow controlled by God's hand from on high.

"Not that I don't think [Dungy] is a nice man," Herzfeld says, "but you can be a proud Christian without saying the Christian way is the only right way, and without suggesting that others ways are somehow defective. . . . What Dungy is doing is taking an opportunity to unite people and turning it into a divisive moment. He should know better. When you're in the stadium, and they're giving you the Super Bowl trophy, that's a captive audience. That's not the time to push your faith."

Herzfeld, an Orthodox Jewish rabbi with deep religious convictions and a conservative theology of his own, finds it odd that he would be in the position of seeming to speak out against religion. That, he says, is not what he is trying to do.

"Players have a right to pray," he is quick to point out. "I'm an evangelical, too, in a sense—I believe in spreading my faith. But I don't believe in spreading my faith to those who are captive. I don't believe in locking the train doors, so to speak, and proselytizing to everyone in the car. . . . I want to spread my faith, but not in that way. Because my faith teaches me it's not appropriate."[36]

Joining Herzfeld in his role as a critic of evangelical practices in baseball has been Ari Sunshine, the rabbi of a conservative synagogue in Maryland. Following the *Post* report about Baseball Chapel and the Nationals, Sunshine, then based in North Carolina, shot off a three-page letter to Bud Selig, who, like his NBA counterpart David Stern, is Jewish. Like Herzfeld, Sunshine raised as his principal objection the unfairness of a ministry with a Jesus-only message enjoying privileged access to major league clubhouses and players.

Sunshine wrote: "How many of the 3,000 personnel who go each week to Baseball Chapel realize that they are going to an evangelical Christian service? Is that truly what each of those people is seeking—to better understand one right-wing view of Christianity, which teaches . . . that faith in Jesus is the *only* key to salvation, and that, accordingly, their Jewish ex-girlfriends are 'doomed?' Yet as I understand it, this is the only style of Christian worship service made available to Major League Baseball personnel. That is unfortunate, since not all mainstream Christian denominations emphasize 'faith-based' salvation to a degree that denigrates legitimate religious alternatives and thus makes it difficult to have meaningful dialogue and healthy working relationships between people of different faiths."[37]

The pair of rabbis found an ally in a Christian leader who likewise recoiled from the Nationals incident. The Reverend Christopher M. Leighton, a Presbyterian minister and executive director of the Institute for Christian and Jewish Studies in Baltimore, pointed out in press statements that the Roman

Catholic Church and many Protestant denominations had migrated away from the once-dominant tradition in Christianity that taught that Christians alone could achieve salvation. There was growing understanding, Leighton said, of God's continuing covenant with Jews. Leighton called it "a real shame" that Jewish leaders like Herzfeld and Sunshine had to bear the brunt of the work in challenging the exclusive religious teachings in the Nationals clubhouse. "This is the work that really belonged to other Christians," the minister said, "to say this is an unacceptable understanding of our faith."[38]

Herzfeld has repeatedly stressed that he is not opposed to evangelical Christianity being practiced in the Nationals clubhouse or, for that matter, the presence of evangelical chaplains to support those in, or in the process of joining, the Christian flock.

"I don't object to players getting the spiritual nourishment they need," he says. "And I don't think representatives of every religion need to be in the clubhouse. But because the team plays a public role, the religious message ought to be an inclusive one." Herzfeld believes there is even a proper role for Christian evangelizing in clubhouses, as long as it's done with "extraordinary sensitivity." As demonstrated by the Jews-are-doomed incident with the Nationals, he said, Baseball Chapel's representative had clearly "crossed the line."[39]

The rabbi's line of reasoning about the team's public mission, and its attendant responsibility to respect the Washington area's burgeoning religious diversity, became substantially more relevant—and concrete—in the years immediately following the Ryan Church controversy. About ten miles south of Herzfeld's synagogue, a new Nationals' ballpark has opened near the confluence of the Anacostia and Potomac rivers on the city's south side. Making its debut in April 2008, the stadium has been a boon to Nationals fans keen on an upgrade from faded old RFK Stadium, where the team had played after moving to the capital from Montreal. As is invariably the case with new ballparks, city officials have been touting the transformative effect it will have in revitalizing the city's new "ballpark district." Not incidentally, one of the first events at the new stadium was a mass conducted by none other than Pope Benedict XVI, who was in the midst of a much-publicized U.S. visit.

The new stadium, dubbed "Nationals Park" pending the sale of naming rights to a corporate entity, seats approximately 41,000 people. Perhaps the more relevant figure is 611 million—the number of dollars committed by the city for development of the park. Another highly relevant number is zero. That is the amount of the projected stadium costs that the Nationals' owners, a group led by real estate developer Theodore Lerner, were required to cover in the financing agreement between the owners and city. A proviso in the stadium deal did hold the owners responsible for cost overruns, a factor that came into play when Lerner and his associates decided to sink approximately $30 million (an amount equaling about five percent of the city's share) into upgrading the scoreboards, the outfield restaurant, the video screen, and the club-level suites.[40]

So, while the new park has no doubt been a pleasant development for Nationals' supporters who attend games (apart from the roughly 43 percent jump in season-ticket prices from the final season in RFK), it has been anything but a boon for the city's taxpayers—and, for example, disadvantaged parents and children in the nation's capital. As the progressive sportswriter Dave Zirin has pointed out, the District funneled hundreds of millions of public funds into the ballpark at a time when it was laying off public school workers, closing its lone public hospital, and watching its infant-mortality rate rise to a level surpassed by only one country in the western hemisphere, Haiti.[41]

Given the baseball team's ability to command scarce public funds for its new stadium (trumping, for example, public health and schools), it stands to reason that it plays an important public mission. Alongside that apparent reality, contemplate this: The Washington metropolitan area has become the site of significant religious diversity, as have numerous other cities that host major league franchises in an America that has become the world's most religiously diverse country.[42]

According to the American Religious Identification Survey (ARIS), the percentage of Americans claiming no religious affiliation rose from 8.2 percent in 1990, to 14.2 in 2001, and to 15 percent by 2008.[43] Of those with a religious affiliation, the number of adults classifying themselves as Christian dropped from 86 percent in 1990 to 76 percent by 2008, and of those self-identified Christians, Roman Catholics—who tend to have significant theological differences with evangelicals—were the largest denominational plurality, at 25.1 percent of the U.S. total.[44] Including churchgoers from a range of denominations, the evangelical, or "born-again," category comprised 34 percent of the adult population in the ARIS survey.

The religious identification survey documented large percentage increases between 1990 and 2008 by several non-Christian religions, especially Muslims, Buddhists, and Hindus, although the overall figures remain small. "No religion" was the category with the most robust growth, from 8 percent to 15 percent in the 18-year interval.

Jews are a small population in the United States in absolute numbers, between 6 million and 7 million, but they are dispersed in such a way as to compose a critical mass in certain metropolitan areas. According to statistics from the international Jewish organization Ner LeElef, the Washington metropolitan area is home to approximately 165,000 Jews, making it one of the ten most "Jewish" metro areas in the United States.[45] The greater Washington area ranks even higher on the list of U.S. cities with the largest "Muslim-origin" populations, with an estimated 114,000 residents tracing their ancestral roots to predominantly Muslim countries. Overall, an estimated quarter-million Muslims reside in the D.C. area.[46]

As Herzfeld asks: Why, given the very real religious diversity of the Washington, D.C. area, are the civic resources known as the Washington Nationals and Nationals Park being used to promote an exclusive religious cause intent on advancing one-truth evangelical Christianity? Put another way, why should the tax dollars of Catholic and Jewish residents of Washington, D.C., not to mention the Muslims, Buddhists, Sikhs, Hindus, agnostics, and atheists, be used to facilitate an evangelical Christian mission intent on convincing players and the public that only a personal relationship with Jesus Christ will save their souls, that God will condemn all who do not become evangelical Christians? In the rabbi's view, Baseball Chapel and its cousin ministries in other major league sports should lose access to clubhouses unless they denounce "the theology of exclusion."[47]

It is unrealistic, not to mention inappropriate, to expect an evangelical Christian organization to alter its theology to appease critics and maintain its relationship with Major League Baseball. Baseball Chapel will believe as it believes. But that does not mean that those managing the league and its teams cannot take action to respect the rights of the many nonevangelicals in Washington and baseball's other markets—in the clubhouse, the stadium, and the community. Those who run Major League Baseball would do well to insist that the ministry's chaplains approach evangelizing with appropriate sensitivity, that they refrain from pronouncing other beliefs insufficient. So, too, should the league make provisions to meet the needs of non-Christian players (and moderate and progressive Christians) who are desirous of religious resources but do not subscribe to the conservative Christian teachings and praying styles of Baseball Chapel.

In addition, Baseball Chapel should continue to re-examine and refine its training regimen to ensure that its chaplains consistently exhibit the skill known as "discernment" in the evangelical vernacular—the ability, in particular, to sense what is appropriate and inappropriate in a given setting, how to share the faith in a manner that does not condemn or repel, and when to exhibit the obligatory humility that allows one to acknowledge uncertainty and shades of gray.

The latter is not merely the seat-of-his-pants recommendations of a skeptical, progressive writer, but of a former major league athlete with a doctorate from a theologically conservative divinity school and a long tenure in pro sports ministry.

The former pro athlete, who commented on the condition of anonymity, believes Baseball Chapel's volunteer chaplains sometimes lack the training to provide thoughtful religious instruction. "I fear that some of those who minister are not properly trained to handle some of the 'big' theological questions, such as the one Ryan Church asked," said the retired player. "The clubhouse should never be a place for disparaging other religions."[48]

I don't know. Those three humble words, the retired player says, are precisely what someone in Jon Moeller's situation might best have used to respond to Ryan Church's question about the eternal fate of Jewish souls.[48] Such a demonstration of humility might not come naturally to evangelicals in sports, who tend to project their faith with a vigor, confidence, and conviction that befit the straight-ahead personalities of successful athletes. But there is clearly a large measure of wisdom in the ex-player's suggestion, and it points the way toward possible accommodation between evangelical ministry in pro sports and the reality of the nation's religious diversity. Humility need not imply lukewarm faith or limp-wristed weakness; an authority none other than the Bible teaches the virtue of humbleness.

"I don't know"—and, with it, appropriately humble sentiments like "It's not mine to say" and "That's for God to sort out"—can go a long way toward coexistence, not just in baseball but the country at large. May sports ministry grow the wisdom to consistently use those words and model the humility they imply when excessive certainty is not only damaging, but entirely undue. And may league and team managements protect the rights of their stakeholders by insisting on it.

Notes

1. Laura Blumenfeld, "In Baseball Now, More Teams Pray Before They Play," *Washington Post*, September 18, 2005.

2. Shmuel Herzfeld, from a series of interviews held from 2005 to 2007, the first of which took place face-to-face at Ohev Shalom synagogue, Washington, D.C., November 2005.

3. Alan Cooperman, "Nats' Church Apologizes for Remarks about Jews," *Washington Post*, September 21, 2005.

4. Cooperman, "Church Apologizes," *Washington Post*.

5. Ryan Church, "No Intent to Disparage Others' Religions," *USA Today* letter to the editor, November 18, 2005.

6. Cooperman, "MLB is Reviewing Baseball Chapel," *Washington Post*, October 1, 2005.

7. Cooperman, "Church Apologizes," *Washington Post*.

8. Robert Knight, "Baseball's Latest Scandal: Going after Church," *WorldNetDaily*, October 5, 2005, http://www.wnd.com/news/article.asp?ARTICLE_ID=46668.

9. Shmuel Herzfeld, interviews 2005–2007.

10. Baseball Chapel, "Media Information" page at organization website, http://www.baseballchapel.org/-index.cfm?FuseAction=MediaInformation&CFID=17862337&CFToken=57740459.

11. Baseball Chapel, "Scope of Ministry" page at organization website, http://www.baseballchapel.org/-index.cfm?FuseAction=ScopeOfMinistry&CFID=17862392&CFToken=47922629.

12. Karin Tanabe, "Is the Nation's Favorite Pastime Pitching Jesus?" *Moment* magazine, October/November 2007.

13. Baseball Chapel website, http://www.baseballchapel.org.

14. Rich Sparling, interview, March 2004, Philadelphia Biblical University, Langhorne, Pennsylvania.

15. Pat Williams interview, telephone.

16. Rich Sparling, interview, March 2004.

17. William C. Kashatus, *Mike Schmidt: Philadelphia's Hall of Fame Third Baseman* (Jefferson, N.C.: McFarland & Company, 1999), 43–44.

18. "About Our Faith," Pujols Family Foundation website, http://www.pujolsfamilyfoundation.com/-faith.htm.

19. "Jeremy's Testimony," Jeremy Affeldt Foundation website, http://www.jaffeldt.com/content/jeremy-testimony.

20. Tom Krattenmaker, "Going Long for Jesus," *Salon*, May 10, 2006, http://www.salon.com/news/feature/2006/05/10/ministries/index.html.

21. Interview conducted in person with an active National Football League player, May 2004; name withheld by request.

22. Bob Tufts, telephone interview conducted November 17, 2005.

23. Tanabe, "Pitching Jesus?" *Moment*.

24. Steve K. Walz, "Anti-Semitism in Pro Sports: Malicious Hate or Simple Ignorance?" *Jewish Press*, May 30, 2001, http://www.jewishpress.com/displayContent_new.cfm?mode=a&sectionid=1&contentid=12802-&contentName=Anti-Semitism%20In%20Pro%20Sports:%20Malicious%20Hate%20Or%20Simple-%20Ignorance?

25. Murray Chass, "Should a Clubhouse be a Chapel?" *New York Times*, February 2, 2008.

26. Allan Wolper, "Ethics Corner: Off the Record," *Editor & Publisher*, July 10, 2000, 32.

27. Walz, "Anti-Semitism," *Jewish Press*, May 30, 2001.

28. Eric Konigsberg, "Marcus Camby Has Nobody to Play With," *New York Times*, April 22, 2001.

29. Walz, "Anti-Semitism," *Jewish Press*, May 30, 2001.

30. For example, see Bruce Feiler, "Jews and the World Series," Beliefnet, October 25, 2007, http://blog.beliefnet.com/feilerfaster/sports.

31. Baseball Chapel "Media Information" page, http://www.baseballchapel.org/index.cfm?FuseAction=MediaInformation&CFID=18158170&CFToken=66975404.

32. Tanabe, "Pitching Jesus?" *Moment*.

33. Baseball Chapel, "About Us" page, http://www.baseballchapel.org/index.cfm?FuseAction=AboutUs

34. Baseball Chapel, "Statement of Faith" page, http://www.baseballchapel.org/index.cfm?FuseAction=Doctrinal&CFID=20086087&CFToken=98793685.

35. Shmuel Herzfeld, interviews 2005–2007.

36. Tanabe, "Pitching Jesus?" *Moment*.

37. Cooperman, "Church Apologizes," *Washington Post*.

38. Shmuel Herzfeld, interviews 2005–2007.

39. Thomas Boswell, "Nationals Owners to Dig Even Deeper," *Washington Post*, December 23, 2006.

40. Dave Zirin, *What's My Name, Fool?* (Chicago: Haymarket Books, 2005), 223.

41. Diane L. Eck, *A New Religious America: How a "Christian Country" Has Become the World's Most Religiously Diverse Nation* (New York: Harper One, 2002), 4. Reprint edition.

42. Barry A. Kosmin and Ariela Keysar, "American Religious Identification Survey 2008," Trinity College; the survey can be accessed at http://b27.cc.trincoll.edu/weblogs/AmericanReligionSurvey-ARIS/reports/ARIS_Report_2008.pdf. Readers should note that "no affiliation" does not necessarily equate with being an atheist or agnostic.

43. Barry A. Kosmin and Ariela Keysar, "American Religious Identification Survey 2008," Trinity College.

44. "World Jewish Population," published by Ner LeElef, http://www.simpletoremember.com/vitals/world-jewish-population.htm.

45. "The Muslim Population," *Washington Post* web feature, http://www.washingtonpost.com/wp-dyn/content/graphic/2006/09/03/GR2006090300990.html

46. Shmuel Herzfeld, interviews 2005–2007.

47. Personal interview with a sports ministry staff member who is an ex-professional athlete. Name withheld by request.

48. Personal interview with a sports ministry staff member who is an ex-professional athlete. Name withheld by request.

CHAPTER 6

~

From Coors Field to Eternity
Faith Days in Major League Baseball

We are here because we believe Jesus is the son of God, died on the cross, and rose. We believe he is our Lord. We can celebrate that without putting people down in the process.

—Brent High, creator and promoter of professional baseball "faith days"

It's "Faith Day 2008" at Coors Field, and the Colorado Rockies ballpark is in the process of becoming a very large megachurch.

Religion has kept a low profile through most of this long, pitching-challenged August afternoon, one on which the hometown Rockies have absorbed a 16-7 beating from the last place San Diego Padres. No, faith has not been completely hushed. An ensemble called "Marked Men for Christ" performed an up-tempo rendition of the "Star Spangled Banner" some three and a half hours earlier, the crowd had sung "God Bless America" during the seventh-inning stretch, and the long list of church groups in attendance had scrolled on the huge scoreboard screen looming over left field. But the estimated 20,000 faith day participants in attendance, scattered in different sections around the stadium, have generally blended in with the rest of the crowd to this point, save for the ones wearing their faith on their t-shirts. (Jesus, declared one such shirt, leads the league in "saves.") Now, though, the just-another-afternoon-at-the-ballpark spirit is about to give way to something completely different.

Workers have quickly rigged a stage near third base, with microphones, a drum kit, and keyboards—as yet unmanned—facing the packed third base-side stands. Having stayed and rearranged themselves after the final out, those fans interested in the *faith* part of faith day have nearly filled the seats from home plate to the left-field corner on all three decks. People from Colorado Christian University, the event's main sponsor, are busy dispensing the university's promotional literature and a pamphlet version of the Gospel of John at its well-attended information table in the concourse nearby. Since the end of the seemingly interminable game, the huge scoreboard has been flashing a message urging fans to "Join us for Faith Day 2008!" and plugging the key performers who are about to hit the stage, Christian motivational speaker and ex-major league pitcher Dave Dravecky, and Christian music star Steven Curtis Chapman.

Rain clouds loom closer, but the skies remain dry, for now. The Christian rock that's been blaring on the house speakers fades, and the massive scoreboard video screen plays commercials for two Christian movies, one called "The List," just out on DVD, and the other, "Fireproof," scheduled to hit theaters the following month. The stage microphones go live, and up to the "plate" bounces Rockies chairman and chief executive officer Charlie Monfort. Faith day is officially under way.

"You're the greatest fans in baseball!" shouts Monfort, who is known for his enthusiastic Christian faith and his keenness on Christian character permeating the Rockies clubhouse and team culture. Noting that event organizers are declaring this the largest throng ever for a major league baseball faith event since this phenomenon started three years ago, the shorts-clad owner hollers out an even bigger compliment. "And you're the greatest fans in faith!"

Monfort gives a brief rendition of his own faith story—"I welcomed the Lord and Savior into my life seven years ago, and my life has never been the same"[1]—and then turns his attention to the friend on the stage with him, the ex-pitcher known for his battle with cancer, for his devout Christian faith, and, among progressives who keep up with sports, for his one-time associations with far-right politics. Ladies and gentlemen—Dave Dravecky!

Attention turns again to the scoreboard screen in left field, where a video presents the tale of Dravecky's trials and tribulations in stirring form: His rise to the top echelon of major league pitchers in the 1980s, the discovery of cancer in his pitching shoulder, the grim prognosis for his return to baseball, his recovery and against-all-odds return to the big leagues, and, finally, the tragedy that befell him just two games into his comeback—a devastating arm fracture and the discovery of the cancer's return. All fans can see what drastic measures had to be taken to save him from cancer the second time. The left sleeve of Dravecky's loose-fitting shirt dangles empty, his arm and part of his shoulder gone.

"We will all come face to face with adversity at some point in our lives," Dravecky says live from the stage, taking over where the video clips have left off.

The former all-star is sharing the figurative spotlight with a marginal member of the Rockies who, for reasons unexplained, is giving his testimonial today while a more obvious choice for the job, the Christ-professing superstar outfielder Matt Holliday, watches from the dugout. By way of introducing Seth Smith, Dravecky talks more about adversity—the adversity being experienced by Smith as he struggles to achieve a permanent promotion from the minor leagues, where he's toiled for the better part of five seasons. It's a situation that has proven most frustrating to the 25-year-old Mississippi native.

"The adversity I'm going through can't compare to what Dave went through," Smith begins, holding a Bible, now changed out of his uniform into an ultracasual sweater and pair of blue jeans. No, he hasn't had to cope with career-ending cancer, yet he admits that shuttling between Triple-A Colorado Springs and the major-league Rockies the past two seasons, after three full seasons in the lower-level minors, has tested him. Through it all, he says, his Christian faith has buoyed him. "The one word I'm going to leave you with is 'faith,'" Smith says. "I'm in God's hands. Wherever I am—the major leagues, Triple A, out of baseball—God has a purpose. Wherever I am it's my job to fulfill that purpose." Smith concludes by paraphrasing a revered line from Paul's letter to the Galatians: "I have been crucified with Christ and I no longer live, but Christ lives in me."

Dravecky takes back the speaking role now, and it quickly becomes clear that it's a role at which he is well practiced and well skilled. The dark, neat hair that fans might recall from his playing days is now gray and a little shaggy, and his once-trim physique has gone slightly paunchy. As the scoreboard has already advertised, Dravecky runs an organization called Outreach of Hope founded by him and his wife. Based in Colorado Springs, that home of seemingly all things evangelical, Dravecky's nonprofit provides gospel-based resources and inspiration to people bearing the burdens that ended Dravecky's professional sports career—cancer and amputation.

Dravecky's message on this day is impressively short on the prosperity-gospel themes that have flourished in many Christian circles while becoming the object of much secular ridicule, and it's conspicuously free of the popular framing of the get-Jesus message as a form of salvation insurance (as in, "Believe in Jesus, lest you miss out on your one shot at eternal life!").

Instead, Christian hope in the midst of darkness is the thrust of the testimonial that follows. It's a hope, Dravecky explains, that flows from the "powerful stories of the God we can trust in, who will be there in the midst of adversity, who will help us endure."[2]

The retired pitcher holds up an old Dave Dravecky baseball card to make his point about the rather unhealthy manner in which he once defined his self-worth: his pitching statistics, those small-font digits printed on the back of the card he's clutching. As Dravecky waves that piece of his history for all the crowd to see, another part of his story comes to this observer's mind. Not that many of the exultant fans hanging on his words are aware that Dravecky once was part of the notoriously far-right John Birch Society[3]—or that they would hold it against him if they knew. Not that Dravecky, despite his Colorado Springs address and friendship with James Dobson's Focus on the Family, has been known in recent times as a polarizing political figure. But why, as the unconverted progressive inevitably asks at moments like these, is center stage of sports world religion never occupied by a liberal?

If Dravecky's dubious political associations are faded now, obscured by his inspiring story of more recent times, the hard-edged politics of faith day's chief sponsor stand out fresh and stark. A hint of Colorado Christian University's role in the culture wars can be found in the university promotional brochures that a small crew of students, staff members, and alumni are enthusiastically passing out on the concourse, along with information cards and Gospel of John tracts for anyone who might take Jesus into his or her heart by the time the proceedings have finished. In the brochure, in between the pumped-up text and exciting photos of students in high-octane pursuit of ministry and mountain adventures, runs a list of major student organizations at Colorado Christian, among them a literary magazine, a dance club, the Omicron Delta Kappa honor society, and College Republicans. College Democrats? No mention.

That hardly comes as a surprise to those who follow the news from the nation's higher education sector. For despite the fine liberal arts education it promises in its marketing material, Colorado Christian University is best known to many in academia for firing an instructor who had the temerity to include, on a course syllabus, readings that allegedly undermined the Christian institution's commitment to free enterprise. The offending authors included on Andrew Paquin's reading list were Jim Wallis, a progressive evangelical activist and author, and Peter Singer, an atheist and animal rights activist. As explained by Paquin, who is the founder of a gospel-based nonprofit providing micro-loans to help poor Africans start businesses, he wanted his global studies course to expose students to the tensions between capitalism and Jesus' teachings about justice for the poor—tensions that Paquin felt himself as a believer in both.[4]

That was going too far for university president and former Republican senator William Armstrong, who, in explaining the 2007 firing to the *Rocky Mountain News*, said that Paquin's teaching strayed too far from the university's recently established strategic objectives. Those objectives, as Armstrong described them, could have been pulled straight from the missions of Christian Right political groups like the Family Research Council. Colorado Christian, the university president said, existed to "impact our culture in support of traditional family values, sanctity of life, compassion for the poor, biblical view of human nature, limited government, personal freedom, free markets, natural law, original intent of the Constitution and Western civilization." Above all, added Armstrong, "We teach Jesus is Lord."[5]

A similar message, without all that heavy political baggage, is being driven home by Dravecky now as he works toward his ringing conclusion. He's holding up a baseball card again, but this one is torn.

"Even as a Christian, my worth was wrapped up in what I did," Dravecky says. "Then my left arms snaps, I fall to the ground, and my career is over." As he struggled to find his post-baseball calling, depression fell over him. "I was in a deep, dark place," he says. "Many times, I felt I would have been better off ending it all."

He waves the tattered baseball card now. "If your baseball card looks like this," he asks, "what are you worth?"

The answer, he goes on to explain, is *everything*. The fans all possess worth, worth beyond compare, he says, thanks to the love of God and the sacrifice of Jesus on the cross. "How great is the love the Father has lavished on us. It's what Jesus did on the cross! My worth is not what I do but who I am. I'm a child of God."

Dravecky encourages those listeners who are wavering, or those who might be hearing the message for the first time, to pick up the gospel booklets at the sponsor's table in the concourse. "It's the greatest journey you'll ever discover," he promises. "Remember this: You can discover God in the darkness. He is always there."[6]

Strength in times of darkness—it's a perfect segue to the musical act that now takes over the stage. The performer is Steven Curtis Chapman, a multiple Grammy Award–winning Christian music superstar, and a man who is still bearing a fresh grief that most of the assembled fans know about. His adopted five-year-old daughter is less than three months dead from a tragic accident at the family's home outside of Nashville.[7]

Alternating between piano and guitar, backed by a rocking band that includes two of his own sons, Chapman sings and preaches his way through the sadness of recent heartbreaking experience and the joy of his faith. As his melodies and praise soar, audience members lift their arms to the rain-threatening skies. Fate and luck—or God, no doubt, in the view of many of the believers on hand—have been keeping the imminent rains at bay. The showers finally come halfway through Chapman's show, forcing a brief intermission. But nothing, seemingly, can dampen the earnestness and passion flowing between audience, stage, and heaven. The rain stops, and Chapman and his band rock on for another half-hour. Faith day—faith *evening* by this point—is finally over.

Down on the field, watching keenly from the wings, is a thirty-something Tennessean in a dark golf shirt bearing a "Third Coast Sports" logo. Excessive pride is something that Christians are taught to avoid, but if Brent High is feeling any, it would be understandable. Because this whole thing is a massive success. And, in a very real sense, it's *his* baby.

*

Speaking in his slight Tennessee twang, High tells his life's story with a boyish enthusiasm and innocence. Its theme, as announced on his BrentHigh.com website: "To Help Make an Eternal Difference."

Unlike Jon Kitna, the Jesus-preaching quarterback who chased alcohol and women before turning to the cross, and Josh Hamilton, the new-on-the-scene baseball superstar whose faith helped save him from debilitating drug addictions, High followed a relatively direct and wholesome road to his place in sports world Christianity. Baptized by his father as a boy, nurtured in his family's Church of Christ congregation and the churchy Nashville community, the young Brent High had but one distraction from his ardent pursuit of the eternal. It was a rather big one, actually: baseball.

High became a devout Atlanta Braves fan in his boyhood years, and as his own pitching career progressed at Nashville's Overton High School and Lipscomb University, he dedicated himself to pitching one day for his beloved Braves.

"As I got better and better, baseball became my god," High says, riffing on the testimonial he has given countless times. "I replaced *the* God on the throne of my life with baseball. And I left everything else behind."[8]

He could already see it in his mind's eye, the back of his Braves' jersey bearing the catchy combination of his surname and his favored uniform number. "HIGH 5," it would say. The vision seemed tantalizingly real one summer day following his freshman year in college, when he caught the scouts' eyes at a Braves tryout camp. High recalls his fastball hitting ninety miles per hour on the radar gun that day and his curveball breaking in particularly nasty fashion. Impressed, one of the scouts had High stay overtime at the tryout to show him more. He promised to follow the young gun's progress at college.

High was now more motivated than ever. Prior to his sophomore season at Lipscomb, he worked himself into the best condition of his life. In his first start that season, he pitched a complete game, striking out 13 batters and giving up just three hits.[9] Like his Braves, who had broken out of their 1980s doldrums to become one of the dominant franchises in baseball at the time, High was on the way up—which made his fall that much harder to bear.

In his second start that sophomore season, High again threw hard, and *a lot.* As he discovered later, his pitch count reached a ridiculous total of 180 that day.[10] It was well beyond what a young arm could normally endure, especially so early in a season, and especially given High's pitching form—his "horrible mechanics," as he put it—and the extra strain it placed on his shoulder.

The day after the game, High was in excruciating pain. Doctors diagnosed the problem as a torn labrum muscle. Surgery followed, as did rehabilitation and an attempted comeback. What did not come back was his fastball. High was cut from the Lipscomb team the following fall. His baseball god had abandoned him.

In an entry on his website, High reflects on God's role in his career-ending injury. He cites the Book of Hebrews in the New Testament/Jewish Scripture, which speaks of how the Lord "disciplines" those he loves and "punishes" all who would be his son.

"Whether He caused my labrum muscle to tear or not, I don't know," High writes. "That's one of those questions I'll save for heaven. While selfishly I'd like to have continued chasing my baseball dreams, it causes me to shiver when I think of where I'd probably be spiritually if baseball hadn't been taken away from me."[11]

Like many religiously inclined athletes and ex-athletes of his generation, High had numerous contacts with Christian sports ministry while playing sports in school and college. It was these, he says, that would eventually show him how he could "marry" his two passions—sports and faith—and place the former in the service of the latter. He attended Fellowship of Christian Athletes camps, once hearing the evangelizing NFL superstar Reggie White speak, and participated in the FCA huddles at his middle school and high school. Through these experiences, he says, "it became OK for me to have a Christian walk and be a competitive athlete."[12]

The other pre-eminent Christian sports ministry, Athletes in Action (AIA), also made an impression on the young High—by coming right to his doorstep. When High was fourteen years old, his family hosted two AIA baseball players who were in Nashville with their AIA team for a series of games. High and his two younger brothers reveled in the attention from the Christian players briefly under their roof, a pitcher from Georgia Southern and a catcher from Texas

Christian University. The collegians played Wiffle ball with the High boys and attended the brothers' baseball games. Brent and his brothers came out for the AIA players' games in turn, Brent watching with admiration as they gave their Christian testimonials to the spectators and opposing players. It was something of a revelation for the teenage High to see sports used so directly, so unabashedly, to introduce unconverted athletes and fans to the gospel. He absorbed the lesson. Fifteen years later, he would introduce to the world his own adaptation of that AIA model.

As Brent High completed his college education at Lipscomb and launched his career, his pitching aspirations all behind him now, he naturally gravitated toward sports promotions. Buoyed by his seemingly infinite supply of enthusiasm and affability, and by his keen instincts for generating publicity, High worked as sports information director for his alma mater and then the TranSouth Athletic Conference. He did radio play-by-play for Lipscomb basketball and baseball games and started a boosters club. At the same time, he was also shepherding the school's first FCA group, which High himself had founded the year after his graduation.[13]

High's affinity for sports promotion led him to professional baseball, to positions with the Nashville Sounds as church and youth programs manager and, after that, as vice president of sales. His biography cites a pair of key accomplishments during his two-and-a-half years with his hometown minor league team: His successful lobbying efforts for legislation allowing the construction of a new downtown ballpark, and the launch of a model for Christian-themed ballpark promotions that is now literally trademarked. "Faith nights" and "faith days" were born.

Not that the Nashville Sounds were ignoring the surrounding church community before High came on the scene. Like many other minor league teams across the country, the Sounds, with 3,000 Christian churches within a two-hour radius, had been doing low-key faith events already. The concept, High recalls, was "bring your church bulletin, and get a dollar off your ticket."

Typifying the growing sophistication and boldness with which American evangelicals have engaged American culture in this generation, High presented a grander vision.

"Back in January 2004," High remembers, "I went to talk to the director of marketing with the Sounds. I said, 'I've been here a year. I need you to give me some rope.' I said, 'There are two things I'd like to do this year. I want us to be first sports team in history to do a biblical bobblehead doll giveaway. I want us to have a night where we give Moses bobbleheads to the first 2,000 fans. Second, I want us to be the first team in sports history to do Bible giveaways.'"

High knew controversy was coming. He welcomed it. As he told his Sounds' boss, High pictured the venture leading to coverage by ESPN's Bob Ley on his much-respected program about issues in sports. "I want to be on 'Outside the Lines,'" High told the marketing director, "debating with Bob Ley whether religion has a place in sports."

The pair of Nashville faith nights were a hit in that 2004 season, attracting two of the team's biggest crowds of the year. The following two seasons brought rapid growth to High's faith night program as he carried the model to more and more teams across minor league America. He had his Bible giveaways. He had his religious bobblehead giveaways. And in July of 2004, High fulfilled another part of his vision: He appeared on ESPN to discuss his faith days and the role of religion in sports.

High had definitely stirred a debate. It wasn't primarily the Bibles and bobbleheads that had many nonevangelicals questioning the appropriateness of High's creation (although few things can arouse a secularist's cynicism like a bobblehead Moses doll). Nor was it the Christian rock concerts that High worked into the mix to give the events special appeal to younger fans. It was the players' Christian testimonials—which to critics seemed to put the imprimatur of the team behind the salvation-through-Christ-alone message—that seemed to raise eyebrows and hackles the most. Yet to High the Christian, those testimonials were precisely the point. It was the Athletes in Action model, but adapted and brought to a larger, professional venue. He and his colleagues, High says, were helping church leaders "use sporting events as a chance to reach out to those that don't have a church home." To see previously unconverted fans "standing up and making first-time decisions for Christ—that's the core of what we're trying to do."[14]

With his faith day creation well on its way to becoming a franchise, High quit his job with the Sounds to focus his attention on the company he co-founded to run the events, Third Coast Sports. The company name refers to Nashville's status as the alternative to New York and Los Angeles—East Coast and West Coast—as music-industry hubs. Befitting a company that keyed its name to a music concept, High and his Third Coast partners made music an essential part of the faith day formula. Over the years that followed, High's ballpark events featured some of the biggest names in Christian rock music: Mercy Me, Hawk Nelson, Casting Crowns, and Steven Curtis Chapman, among others.

Propelled by waves of publicity and ticket-sellers' thirst for anything that will lure a bigger gate, Third Coast Sports found itself very busy over the next three years. By High's count, the company staged more than 150 events from 2005 to 2007, more than fifty professional baseball teams taking part. His company made the events simple "turnkey" operations for franchises: All they had to do was give High's company the go-ahead, and High and his colleagues did the rest—conducting outreach to evangelical churches in the given market, lining up the music act and Bible-themed giveaways (the latter often paid for by corporate sponsors), and managing the logistics.

Those logistics, of course, had to be executed just right for the events to live up to High's stated commitment to ensuring a measure of separation between the regular ballgame experience and the Christian activity built around it. An opponent of what he terms "ambush evangelism"—picture a preacher striding out to home plate to address the stadium crowd with the get-Jesus pitch between innings—High devised a system whereby the church crowd would experience the religious programming separate from the rest of the audience and apart from the actual ballgame. The church fans would pay extra for a special ticket that would give them access to the *faith* part of faith night, which was staged before or after the game and typically in a fenced off part of the parking lot or a section of the stadium. The Christian rockers and ballplayers were "preaching" only to those who wanted to hear it.

With his formula refined and his faith nights thoroughly established in the minor leagues, Brent High and his partners were ready for the next step.

High, as a high school and college athlete, had dreamed of making it to the major leagues, of pitching for the Atlanta Braves. In the summer of 2006, he did just that, although not exactly in the manner he'd imagined while perfecting his twelve-to-six curve ball on the diamonds of Overton High School and Lipscomb University. It was his ability to pitch not a baseball, but Jesus, that propelled him to Atlanta's Turner Field for a Braves-Marlins game in July 2006, for Third Coast's first major league faith day.

"What sealed the deal for my mid-season call-up," High wrote on his website, likening his experience to that of a minor league ballplayer being promoted to the majors, "was my God-given ability to help create events at games that simultaneously accomplish the goals of teams, churches, and corporate sponsors. . . . It occurred to me that God was in fact allowing me to realize my boyhood dream, just in a much different way than I had planned. As I sat in that chair [waiting for the start of an interview with the Gospel Music Channel], I was at the perfect intersection of passion, vocation, purpose, and ministry."[15]

High describes the experience of that first Braves' faith day in the kind of vivid detail with which people typically recall the moments that form the highlight reels of their lives. What memories: the national media that swooped in, including CBS, NBC, CNN, ESPN, and Pat Robertson's 700 Club; his moments sitting in the Braves dugout before the game, waiting to be interviewed; his sighting the stacks of batting gloves belonging to Braves outfielder Jeff Francoeur, all with Joshua 1:9 ("Be strong and courageous") printed on the straps; the quick exchange and handshake with Braves pitcher John Smoltz, who would later serve as the featured speaker at the post-game Christian program; his stepping out before 3,000 fans after the game to serve as master of faith day ceremonies. High—the one-time athlete, the ballpark promotions whiz, the publicity genera-tor, the can't-wait-to-tell-the-world-about-Jesus faith enthusiast—had reached his Promised Land.

John Smoltz was a starting pitcher for the Braves that season, the eighteenth campaign in his Hall of Fame–caliber career, but "closer" was the role he played for High as he stepped on the stage to deliver what High would playfully call his "sermon on the mound."

Changed out of his Braves uniform and into a golf shirt, the bald, bearded Smoltz labored through his story in the sweltering late afternoon heat, dispens-ing the mix of self-deprecation, jock analogies, and exclusive theology that typify pro athletes' testimonials. He had come to Jesus in 1995 with the assis-tance of Baseball Chapel, Smoltz explained. He'd learned to trust in something bigger and more permanent than his baseball ability. "One thing I learned was that if baseball had been taken from me, I would have been a wreck. It was everything I was holding onto." What he was missing, he continued, was faith in the eternal, a relationship with God. "If this faith is put in man, it doesn't work for you. . . . I was missing what God had for me."

As Smoltz groped for the words to reach his over-heated listeners, he found refuge in the rhetorical device of evangelizing athletes everywhere: the sports analogy. Smoltz suggested that a failure to commit completely to Christ was analogous to a starting pitcher getting a "no-decision," a most unsatisfying sta-tistic that accrues to a starting pitcher's totals when the outcome of a particular game is determined after he has exited.

"On the pitching mound," Smoltz explained, "you get a win, or a loss, or a no-decision. You can be out there for eight innings and get a no-decision. . . . Do I want to live my life with a no-decision?

"I've heard, 'Just believe in anything. There are many paths.' [But] I want to trust the Bible to be absolutely true. On my death bed, do I want to be faced with that no-decision, that 'what if?' Those are the . . . most dangerous words as far as I'm concerned. 'What if?' and 'I'll take care of that decision later.' My challenge to you . . . is don't be caught in the no-decision."

Living a decent, ethically sound life—doing good—will not bring salvation, Smoltz warned. Nor, he suggested, will believing in God in the more open, generic sense. Reciting the standard creed of theological conservatives—the notion that faith is principally about achieving one's passage to heaven via belief in Jesus Christ—the Braves pitcher recounted a discussion he'd had with the team chaplain at a restaurant during his conversion process. Don't wait to make your decision for Christ, the chaplain urged. You might think there's time, he warned, "but you may not get to your target date. You are not in control of your next breath." Smoltz found the thought chilling, and highly motivating. What if he died that night? "I no longer wanted to take a chance," he told the crowd, "and just *assume* I was good enough to get in heaven."

Faith in God might not always come easy, Smoltz added, working toward his conclusion (and seeming to make an awkward pitch for creationism in the process). But he now knew, through his good seasons and bad, that something remained rock steady: his standing before God. "We are gonna have bad days. We are gonna mess up. [But] you're not too bad. You're not insignificant. Everyone is special. You were created to worship God. You know, it takes a whole lot more faith to believe in an explosion that happened—that we just evolved—than something we can't see. . . .

"So you've learned about the no-decision. I currently have ten this season, but it doesn't bother me. Because I know the decision I made in 1995 is the greatest decision. . . . I know where I'm gonna be [for eternity]. I only hope and wish that everybody else can experience that in their own way." The crowd rose and applauded.

As High reflected on his website, "My major league debut was complete. 'High, P' didn't show up in the box score, but the name of Jesus was lifted up as media outlets representing as many as forty million viewers and readers took note. . . . I got called up to the big leagues. Lord willing, I'll be here for a while."[16]

*

Brent High's "call-up" to the major leagues, it turns out, was no one-and-done deal. Two more faith events were staged in Atlanta that season. High and Third Coast Sports would maintain and strengthen their berth in the majors the next season, too, with faith events in Los Angeles; Washington, D.C.; Atlanta; Cincinnati; Houston and Arlington, Texas; St. Louis; and Minneapolis. A similar roster of cities would have faith events yet again in 2008, with the Colorado Rockies and Kansas City Royals added to the mix.

But for one of Third Coast's partner organizations at High's "major league debut," the stay in the big leagues would turn out to be nothing more than the proverbial cup of coffee. Focus on the Family was out. And that was only part of the controversy that has continued to bubble around faith days, the newest chapter in the evolving story of Christianity in sports.

In the run-up to the first faith day in Atlanta, High proudly announced that James Dobson's Focus on the Family organization was in his lineup of sponsors, entitling the group to host a table and distribute its literature.[17] While

High was enthusing about the long-term partnership he envisioned between the two Christian organizations—about helping Focus "expand their reach," as he put it in his news release—word of Focus' presence at Atlanta's faith day was provoking a much different response in progressive and gay circles. Whereas High associated Focus on the Family with the good-parenting and healthy-families advice for which Dobson's empire had long been known, and which High grew up hearing in his Christian home, Focus on the Family conjured something quite different for others—divisive, conservative political postures and a harsh intolerance of gay people.

Among the materials promoted by Focus representatives at that inaugural major league faith day were the "Focus on your Child" area of its website, which included information about gay activists supposedly targeting public schools to promote homosexuality,[18] and its TroubledWith.com website, which describes homosexuality as an affliction akin to alcoholism or depression, from which recovery must be attempted.[19]

Leaders of Atlanta's gay community—which had appreciated the team's relative gay-friendliness—were dismayed to learn of the involvement of Focus on the Family and the dissemination of its promotional materials at Turner Field. "People come to see a baseball game, not be exposed to politics or religion," protested Reverend Paul Graetz, senior pastor of a gay congregation in Atlanta, the First Metropolitan Community Church. "A baseball game is a neutral place for the purpose of watching a game."[20]

It would turn out to be the first and last time that Focus on the Family and Third Coast Sports were partners for a major league faith event. Still, the removal of Dobson's movement and message has hardly quelled the resistance to High's faith days from some secularists and religious minorities. For reasons beyond the homosexuality issue, the very idea of Christian faith events at major league ballparks has troubled those leery of the seemingly deeper and deeper penetration of evangelical religion into the nation's public venues. And High's chief motivation for organizing faith events at ballparks from coast to coast— proclaiming the Christian gospel—has continued to be as alienating to some as it is inspiring to others.

"Just what baseball needs," *New York Times* sports columnist Murray Chass groused in a piece objecting to faith days and faith nights. "Peanuts, popcorn, and proselytizing."[21] Adding Jesus to such standard ballpark fare as peanuts and Cracker Jack made for "an unsavory mix," declared a *Washington Post* headline.[22]

In comments to the media, a Washington, D.C., Jewish leader voiced objections to the name "faith night." Didn't *faith* night imply something more ecumenical? "These are called 'faith nights,' but they're really evangelical Christianity nights,'" said Rabbi Shmuel Herzfeld, the head of a large Orthodox congregation in Washington and a leader of the Coalition for Jewish Concerns. "They're not 'faith' nights," Herzfeld said. "They're not nights celebrating the greatness of different faiths. I'm a man of faith, the rabbi of a synagogue, and I respect all faiths. But this is really just a night for proselytizing, bringing people closer to their specific form of Christianity. They're taking one of the great neutral settings of our society—a setting where people of all faiths, colors, and ethnicities can come together, share a common bond—and they're turning it into a denominational setting, and they're making it an evangelical Christian event."[23]

It might take but a moment in the shoes of the veteran pundit Chass (who attends an Orthodox synagogue in New Jersey[24]) or the sports-loving rabbi Herzfeld to grasp the many ways in which baseball faith nights can be off-putting, even threatening, to religious minorities—and even to nonevangelical Christians who do not subscribe to the conservative, exclusive theology that is typically espoused at one of these events, a la John Smoltz and his "sermon on the mound."

Consider the tenor of Smoltz's faith pitch on that sultry afternoon at Turner Field (a pitch consistent with the message conveyed over and over by the dominant ministry organizations in sports and the many evangelical athletes who speak publicly about their beliefs). There may be "many paths," as Smoltz acknowledged, but just one passageway to truth and salvation—the "absolutely true" Christian Bible. Mere doers of good deeds, whether operating from a theological base of Judaism, Islam, moderate or progressive Christianity, or a simple belief in humanity, will not find their names written in "the book of life." Judging from the message delivered by Smoltz and many of his evangelical fellows in sports, it is, in the final analysis, salvation—one's fate after physical death—that should principally concern the person considering a faith commitment. The fate of those who do not subscribe? It is not, to be sure, a happy one.

As often happens when athlete evangelists mount the soapbox, Smoltz (a man already on the record with harsh condemnations of homosexuality) wasn't satisfied merely to call listeners to Jesus. As he suggested at Atlanta's faith day, the would-be Christian must choose between faith in God and faith in scientific explanations for the origins of the universe and the human race—an "explosion" and the notion that "we just evolved," as Smoltz dismissively phrased it. This, in an age when many Christians have found ways to accommodate faith and reason, belief and science.

So it goes with sports world evangelicalism, where it's not merely "faith" that's promoted on faith day, but often a dose of Christian fundamentalism sprinkled with right-wing politics. Is it any wonder that many nonevangelical sports lovers wish we could return to the days when the only religion in the game was, as the character in the classic movie *Bull Durham* put it, "the Church of Baseball"?

*

Should faith days and nights be demoted from the major leagues? In the view of critics like *Washington Post* columnist Marc Fisher, the answer is an emphatic "yes," whatever measures Brent High might take to avoid offending the non-evangelical fans. Baseball, Fisher wrote in advance of the Nationals' 2007 faith night, "is a secular church, an elaborate belief system with its own symbols, martyrs and gods. . . . Putting two kinds of religion on the same field is a sure way to lose the game."[25]

As a solution to the problem of the clashing values and freedoms created by faith nights, and by Christianity in sports more generally, Fisher and many like-minded critics suggest secularity. Given the excesses of sports world evangelicalism, the solution is certainly tempting. But while a clean separation of church and sport would meet the needs of nonreligious fans (and probably would not offend the many religious fans who approach their faith in quieter, more private ways), would it be fair to evangelical players and fans—people whose faith compels them to bring their God, and their Jesus, with them *wherever* they go?

If a neutral and fair playing field is the objective, pure secularity cannot be the solution, for it creates an environment that offends the evangelical sensibility as surely as the Jesus-or-else proposition alienates those outside the evangelical camp. On this and other fronts in the ongoing struggle over religion in the public square, pluralism, not secularity, promises the fairest, most sustainable solutions. Surely, the ultimate accommodation lies in pluralism, the model wherein followers of different faiths, or none, share the territory—if not always comfortably, at least in a fashion where all views are allowed, and no one camp drives out the rest.

So what are the offended, alienated, and threatened to do about those "evangelical Christianity nights" taking place at major league ballparks across the land?

Certainly, a measure of "protection" is already in place. Aware of the sensitivities surrounding the promotion of the Christian gospel in public settings, Brent High has taken care to separate the hard-core Jesus part of the events from the regular baseball game. As High puts it, "We are there because we believe Jesus is the son of God, that he died on the cross and rose, and that he is our Lord. [Yet] we can celebrate that without putting people down in the process."[26] As can be attested by anyone who has attended High's faith day events, those who stand to be offended and marginalized by the Jesus-only message are probably not going to be subjected to it. (The same, unfortunately, cannot be said about many other forms of evangelical expression in sports, in which Christian athletes frequently trumpet the message without warning, and without regard for those who do not appreciate witnessing it.)

What about the appropriateness of leveraging the popularity and influence of the community's baseball franchise to plug Christianity? On this score, the observations of a group-sales manager for one major league team—a Jewish one at that—point the way toward the clearest understanding of the issue and the best remedy for the out-of-balance situation that exists today at the intersection of religion and big-time sports.

In an interview conducted during the 2008 baseball season, the group sales manager expressed wonderment that anyone would have a problem with what High and Third Coast Sports have been undertaking. High and his partners can enthuse all they want about faith day being primarily about celebrating Jesus Christ. To teams, the ticket official said, faith day is about one thing, and one thing alone: selling tickets.

"That's what everything is about," said the sales manager, who did not authorize the use of his or his team's name. "There's no hidden agenda. Faith day to us is simply a great way to sell tickets. Everything we do as an organization is geared to that."

Giveaways of player bobbleheads and team backpacks, a night when dog owners parade their pets around the field, a day when parents run their kids around the bases, dollar hotdog nights, ladies night, teen night, "Fireworks Friday"—these were just some of the promotions the sales manager's employer was using to entice fans to its ballpark that season.

To team management, the sales manager explained, faith day isn't about promoting one form of religion. It's not about religion at all. The team also has Shriners nights and Masons nights, he said, and nights celebrating and accommodating numerous other groups and interests. "For us," he pronounced, "there's no difference."[27]

Obviously, the ticket official is glossing over some important details to make his point; to community members concerned about Christian evangelism that marginalizes other forms of belief, there clearly is a difference. Special ballpark nights for Hispanics, Shriners, or employees of a given corporation, for example, are not promoting an exclusive message concerning eternal salvation, and they do not typically mount endorsement testimonials from representatives of the home team in the fashion of Third Coast Sports' events. But the ticket manager has a point, too. It is not as though team management is favoring the evangelical Christians who throng to faith day. Faith days have become big because the evangelicals have *made* them big, demonstrating the enthusiasm, creativity, organizational acumen, and sheer audacity that have characterized their engagement with sports and numerous other public venues this generation.

What does evangelical faith day mean personally to the group sales manager who also happens to be Jewish?

"It doesn't mean anything to me. It doesn't impact me at all," he said. "If anything, it impresses me sometimes, how [the evangelicals] have gotten their message out, how creative they've been. From a selfish standpoint, it makes me think, 'I wish I could organize a Jewish heritage day that could sell half as many tickets as faith day.'"[28]

Third Coast Sports and its ballpark faith events appear more likely to flourish than fade in the foreseeable future. If anything, a series of organizational moves by Brent High and his supporters during the 2008 baseball season have laid a foundation for evangelical faith days to continue, and probably grow, in the years ahead. In time for the Colorado faith day in August 2008, High had phased out the for-profit iteration of Third Coast Sports and morphed it into the new nonprofit Third Coast Sports Foundation. Via the new model, wealthy Christian businesspeople buy and donate blocs of tickets to give away to church members and their guests, as well as to disadvantaged youths. (One donor for the Rockies faith day, High explained, donated a large bloc for churches' use, with the caveat that at least half the tickets go to guests who did not yet have church homes.) In the old model, attendees needed a special ticket, for which they paid a surcharge, to be admitted to the religious programming following the game. In the new model, *all* fans in attendance on faith day are welcome to stay, and at no additional charge. Also codified in High's new model is a clear conversion pitch, backed by church volunteers who are on hand and ready to support new converts with Christian reading material, counseling, and other resources.

Those leery of evangelicals and their forceful presence in the public square may find Brent High's campaign more threatening than ever under the new plan. Or, perhaps, they could find it motivating.

This much is clear: Don't count on team management putting the kibosh on faith days. Don't expect ticket-sellers to resist the lure of an extra 20,000 fans passing through the turnstiles on a given Sunday at the ballpark. And don't count on the Brent Highs of the sports world to go out of their way to work Jewish or agnostic speakers into the faith day lineup. Inserting themselves in the game, High points out, is a project those constituencies can undertake themselves.

As High seems to suggest, those outside of the evangelical universe need to assert themselves if they don't like being left on the sidelines. Let there be Free

24. http://www.njjewishnews.com/njjn.com/080907/sptMurrayChass.html

25. Fisher, "Unsavory Mix."

26. High, interview July–September 2008.

27. Telephone interview with a group sales manager for a Major League Baseball team, conducted August 6, 2008. The ticket official did not authorize the use of his or his team's name.

28. Telephone interview with a group sales manager for a Major League Baseball team, conducted August 6, 2008.

29. High, interview July–September 2008.

30. "Many Americans Uneasy with Mix of Religion and Politics," survey report published by the Pew Research Center for the People and the Press, August 24, 2006, http://people-press.org/report/287/.

31. "Many Americans Uneasy," Pew Research Center.

CHAPTER 7

~

For God, Country, and the Republican Party

The Conservative Politics of Jesus' Pro Sports Warriors

Draped in World Series glory, Curt Schilling was concluding his appearance on the popular network talk show *Good Morning America* and getting ready to make his final "pitch" of the 2004 season.

The previous day, Schilling and his Boston Red Sox had won the franchise's first World Series championship in eighty-six years, setting off delirious celebrations in a region that loved its baseball and knew disappointment like no other sports market in America. Schilling had pitched masterfully, besting the New York Yankees in a crucial game in the American League Championship Series and following it with another winning performance against the St. Louis Cardinals in Game Two of the World Series. He had also demonstrated remarkable grit, mental toughness, and pain tolerance to the many millions of Americans who were watching. He had pitched despite an ankle injury that would have kept many men watching from the dugout. As if to supply visual proof of Schilling's fortitude, a red badge of blood had appeared on his sock—leakage from an incision made for a stop-gap surgical procedure to fortify the ankle. "Thrilling Schilling," as some writers dubbed him, had also given one of the more impressive, high-moment religious testimonials that fans had ever witnessed. Twice, in the live, nationally televised post-game interviews following his heroic pitching performances, Schilling had earnestly professed his Christian faith and credited God with giving him the strength and courage to overcome the injury and take the mound.

Now, with the World Series championship still fresh and Schilling's star power at an unprecedented height—and a hotly contested presidential election just days away—the Christian superstar pitcher was ready to step up for another towering figure on the cultural landscape of 2004: George W. Bush.

"Make sure you tell everybody to vote," Schilling told program host Charles Gibson as he exited the *Good Morning America* set, "and vote Bush next week!"[1]

The moment furnished an unusually high-profile, big-stakes convergence of sports and Republican politics. But to those who followed baseball, Schilling's commitment to the re-election of the polarizing president—and, with it, the war in Iraq—came as anything but a surprise.

Three years before, in the immediate aftermath of the September 11 terrorist attacks, Schilling had branded himself a true-blue patriot, writing an open letter to baseball fans and the families of the victims, published on ESPN.com, that was drenched in national pride and a passion for payback. "To the victims and families of the tragedies inflicted on us this past week we send our hearts out to you, and our prayers that you will find some comfort, some solace in the coming weeks as this great country gets up on its feet and defends itself as the world's greatest nation, with the world's greatest people," Schilling had written. "We will proudly wear the great flag of this country on our uniforms, and it's something I hope baseball adopts forever." Schilling had added that he and other players would wear scrawled messages on their hats and uniforms to honor the victims and their loved ones.

"The flags in this country fly at half-staff to honor those that have fallen," Schilling had continued, "but the flags are the only thing going halfway in this country and it's my belief that that will not change. I believe our President when he says retribution will be swift and total; as an American it's all I can go on, but based on what I have seen done these past few days by other Americans it's more than enough."

To close, Schilling had offered a sentiment that would become ubiquitous at major league baseball games in the years that followed and, for that matter, at other sporting venues and across the broader popular culture. "God Bless America," Schilling had written, "and God Bless Americans everywhere."[2]

In that autumn of 2004 that would bring so much glory to Schilling and his Red Sox, the famed pitcher had already gone on the record as supporting the president's re-election despite the country's growing unease over the war and qualms about the president's performance. Weeks earlier, when Democratic nominee John Kerry had thrown out the first pitch before a Red Sox game at Fenway Park, Schilling had shouted "Go Bush!" to political reporters lingering in the Boston clubhouse after Kerry's departure. Schilling was also one of twenty-four current and ex-athletes who had signed and publicized an open letter endorsing the president's re-election. Joining Schilling as signatories were several pro-football Hall of Fame members known for their strong Christian belief: Roger Staubach, Anthony Muñoz, and Steve Largent, the latter a former Republican member of Congress. "The same qualities that make a great athlete," the athletes' statement said, "make a great President—the determination to do what is right, regardless of the latest polls, the personal strength to bear the weight of the nation on your shoulders, and the faith that a higher power will direct the actions of good people."[3]

Schilling and his wife, Shonda, had barely left the *Good Morning America* set before word of his Bush endorsement caught the attention of the president's people. Keen on dimming the Boston baseball-championship glow around the president's Massachusetts-based rival, the Bush campaign immediately posted Schilling's statement on its website and e-mailed word of it to reporters around the country. The campaign contacted Schilling and quickly scheduled him to make an appearance with the president in the battleground state of New Hampshire.

Schilling canceled that appearance, citing problems with his now-famous ankle injury, so he and the campaign had his always-ready mouth do the walking instead. Schilling recorded pro-Bush telephone messages for auto-dialing to voters in New Hampshire, Maine, and Pennsylvania. Said the message from the man nicknamed "Schill": "These past couple of weeks, Sox fans all throughout New England trusted me when it was my turn on the mound. Now you can trust me on this: President Bush is the right leader for our country."[4]

It was hardly shocking, of course, that Schilling, like so many of his fellow pro athletes, would align with George W. Bush. Here was a president who exhibited an affinity for pro sports, having begun his rise to prominence as the owner of a major league baseball team, the Texas Rangers, and who projected a vigorous athleticism with his well-publicized zest for running, mountain-biking, and chainsaw assaults on the underbrush at his ranch. Moreover, professional athletes, like sports culture more generally, trend conservative.[5] But for Schilling and the other Christian jocks endorsing the president, the allegiance with Bush had an even stronger force behind it: the president's own unabashed evangelicalism, which had done much to set the tone in American public life in the decade.

Much the same as George W. Bush, these athletic, Christian men united in support of the Bush re-election, and so many more like them in and around evangelical religion in sports, combine their theologically conservative faith with a set of political and cultural values celebrating rugged individualism, free enterprise, belief in America's virtue, and a tough foreign policy backed by a strong military. To separate the causes and effects—does faith fuel the political conservatism, or the other way around?—is a complicated undertaking. But one truth seems certain: For evangelicals in and around pro sports, their complex of religious and cultural values has invariably found its political expression in the Republican Party.

*

God, country, and the GOP: it is a seemingly inevitable trinity among evangelical Christians in professional sports. To shift metaphors, perhaps the three are natural peas in the American pod, as complementary and inexorable as baseball, hot dogs, and apple pie. To some, it might have a wholesome ring, a suggestion of things that are good, solid, and true in American life. But for the liberal- and progressive-leaning Americans who follow pro sports, the arm-in-arm march of sports world Christianity with conservative politics takes on an air of eye-roll-inducing cliché. As demonstrated by Schilling's pitch for Bush and innumerable other cases in point, Christian practice and ministry in pro sports often appear to be about something more than spreading the gospel of Jesus and providing religious and moral guidance to athletes. Often, too, evangelicals in sports move in ways political, and in doing so, they rarely if ever veer left.

"For the past generation, sports have been suffocated by corporate greed, commercialism, and military cheerleading," writes Dave Zirin, a progressive sports author and commentator known for his "Edge of Sports" sports-and-politics column and radio program.[6] Not that Democrats are pure on those scores—far from it—but to many observers of American culture and politics in the new century, nothing says "Republican" quite like corporate greed, commercialism, and military cheerleading. To that short list of GOP trademarks one might add religion—religion of the Christian Right, God-blesses-America variety.

In numerous instances this decade, those who stage major league baseball games, and other sports events, too, have marshaled a form of flag-draped religion to promote militaristic patriotism. Although the linking of sports, faith, and patriotism is hardly new, the ritual has been taken to lofty new heights—or depths, to cynics—since the terrorist attacks of September 11, 2001. By pushing into foul territory any expressions of dissent, this form of Christianity in baseball has contributed to "a disturbing suppression of democratic voice," writes Michael Butterworth, a communications professor at Bowling Green University who has studied the infusion of religion into major league baseball since 9/11 and subsequent American wars. "Through its many rituals of purification," Butterworth adds, "the nation is sanctified even as it marches toward war."[7]

Recall baseball's return to the diamonds, and limelight, following the tragic occurrences of September 11. The major leagues shut down for a week, and when the action resumed, it came drenched in fervent patriotism. The Stars and Stripes were everywhere—stitched onto the backs of players' uniform tops and the sides of their caps, unfurled on outfield fences, and handed out to fans in miniature version as they entered ballparks on flag-giveaway nights.

As a way to honor the thousands killed in the 9/11 attacks and heal the nation's psychic wounds, the ubiquitous flags served a noble and unifying purpose. There was something stirring about baseball's return, almost as an act of defiance. The surge of flag-waving patriotism was hardly confined to major league baseball; Walmart and other stores could scarcely keep up with Americans' demand for flags. But there was another dimension to baseball's literal and figurative flag-waving that, for many fans, laid it on a bit too thick.

The scene: A key playoff game at Yankee Stadium. The moment: The seventh-inning stretch. The Fox network stays live with its broadcast, delaying the customary commercial break, as Irish tenor Ronan Tynan strides to a microphone stand on the diamond to give yet another full-throated performance of "God Bless America"—the long version, that is, with the seldom-sung prelude. Once it is over, Fox play-by-play announcer Joe Buck enthuses about the beauty of the moment—"it resonates with you after you leave the ballpark," he glories on one such occasion—and finally the commercials roll.[8] Because of the intensity of the post-season, these Yankee Stadium moments stand out in the public memory, but recall that Commissioner Bud Selig had "God Bless America" sung at every major league game in 2002. Teams continue to have it sung today, although they usually reserve it for special occasions like Memorial Day and the Fourth of July.

Defenders of the practice will correctly note that the song is not explicitly Christian, that it is more an expression of "civil religion" and national pride than an overt act of promoting Christianity. But it is impossible to separate that staging of "God Bless America" from what was happening (and is continuing to happen) on the larger world stage: namely, a bitter Christianity-versus-Islam, good-versus-evil under-narrative in the ongoing struggle against terrorism, the wars in Iraq and Afghanistan, and the saber-rattling between the United States and Iran. Those "God Bless America" moments at Yankee Stadium, and many other sports moments like them, were nothing if not displays of religious nationalism, implicitly promoting a political argument in favor of the Bush administration's controversial policies, strategies, and actions. Adding another unsavory element to the decade's Yankee Stadium tableau was the apparently compulsory nature of fans' participation in the ritual—revealed when news broke of the ejection of a fan who had the temerity to attempt leaving the seating area to visit the bathroom during the "God Bless America" performance. (The New York police denied the charge, insisting that the man was booted out for drunk-and-disorderly behavior.)[9]

"Support the troops!" was the oft-heard rallying cry at major league parks during the Bush years, as in many other venues across American culture—code, often, for acceptance of the administration's pursuit of its controversial Iraq war. The Minnesota Twins, for example, have staged an annual "Armed Forces Appreciation Day" in recent years. Active members of the military receive free tickets to the game and see their service honored in numerous ways before and during the action: special hats worn by the Twins players and coaches, a musical performance by the 34th Infantry Division Red Bull Band, an infantry rappelling demonstration, a "multi-generational ceremonial first pitch featuring veterans of World War II, the Korean War, Vietnam War, Gulf War, and 'Operation Iraqi Freedom'" (as the team's press release phrases it), the public introduction of a "military starting lineup" featuring the children of soldiers deployed overseas, and a hot-air-balloons performance called "Freedom Flight."[10] Supporting the troops is well and good, but as critics might rightly ask, is it necessary to adopt the tropes of the Bush administration and plaster the word "freedom" all over the proceedings? One of the problems with the Iraq war, in the view of many Americans, is that it has *not* been crucial to the protection of American freedom and security, and perhaps even detrimental to those worthy objectives.

"Far from being the pastoral sanctuary it is so often purported to be," the scholar Michael Butterworth observes, "baseball has been implicated in the 'war on terrorism' from the moment major league games resumed on September 17, 2001. . . . Baseball's mythological investment in the tropes of innocence and purity has operated in conjuncture with the rhetoric of evil that motivates the 'war on terrorism.'" Baseball's use as a means of stifling dissent, Butterworth adds, dishonors a more democratic tradition running through the game's history, one that made baseball a democratizing pioneer in the inclusion of minorities and economic lower classes in the mainstream of national life.[11]

Butterworth's observations about faith and militaristic nationalism are specific to baseball, but much the same point could be applied to our other major league sports as well. In professional football, martial displays are commonplace at big games, especially the Super Bowl, and the players can usually be counted on to furnish the religion tie-in with their media comments and on-field displays. Basketball? The NBA's reputation is more hip-hop than lockstep, but Jerry Colangelo, a longtime major league sports executive and a leader in sports ministry and Republican politics, found a way to fuse war and basketball in illuminating ways in his capacity as the managing director of the U.S. men's basketball team in the 2006 world championships.

Colangelo, who was an executive with the Arizona Diamondbacks and Phoenix Suns before taking over the Phoenix entry in the Women's National

Basketball Association, brought to his U.S. basketball leadership a long list of accomplishments on behalf of evangelical sports ministry and conservative politics.

The onetime University of Illinois basketball player has been a reliable friend of the leading Christian ministries in pro sports, frequently speaking at events organized by Athletes in Action and the Fellowship of Christian Athletes. AIA has named an award for him, one that it gives out each year to the "NBA executive whose life and lifestyle impact and benefit the community both on and off the court." As Colangelo told the Christian magazine *Sports Spectrum*, "I learned a long time ago that there are priorities in life. A personal relationship with Jesus Christ has to be No. 1. . . . You have to stay in the Word."[12] Colangelo has emphasized one of the most scalding hot-button issues of our time in his forays to the intersection of his faith and his politics: abortion. Besides organizing a Suns' "Right-to-Life Day" in 2003, Colangelo and a cadre of fellow baseball executives and retired players launched "Battin' 1,000," a group that describes itself as seeking "to promote a culture of life through the endorsements and engagement of major league personalities."[13] The group also works to raise funds for the American Life League, which could never be accused of a wishy-washy stance on abortion; the organization opposes all abortion, even in cases where the pregnancy was caused by rape or incest or threatens the mother's life.

In the summer of 2004, when Colangelo was serving as deputy chair of the Bush-Cheney campaign in Arizona, he helped establish a national prayer campaign emblematic of the Bush years, when conservative politics and partisan-flavored religion merged to the point where they became nearly indistinguishable. The Presidential Prayer Team, created by Colangelo and allies in the aftermath of 9/11, has pursued a mission of "mobilizing millions of Americans to pray daily for our president, our nation, and our armed forces."[14] Colangelo did more than participate and lend his well-known name to the cause. As the journalist Max Blumenthal reported, the then-Diamondbacks executive helped bankroll a campaign to air radio advertisements on some 1,200 stations urging listeners to pray for President Bush in the summer before the 2004 election.[15]

So perhaps it was no surprise when Colangelo took action with USA Basketball that critics felt was one more step toward the complete politicizing of sports for conservative purposes. In the hope of inspiring his hoop troops—a constellation of young superstars like Dwight Howard, LeBron James, and Dwyane Wade, all in their early twenties—Colangelo and coach Mike Krzyzewski arranged for the squad to meet with some *real* troops. These were not wide-eyed newbies shipped in from the nearest training base for the meeting (a meeting televised on the NBA's cable network), but veterans wounded in hard action in Iraq. One solider had been blinded by a piece of shrapnel in his brain; another had lost part of his hand to an explosion.[16] As Colangelo had earlier explained to one sports columnist, he and "Coach K" (coach of the famed Duke University squad and the onetime coach at West Point) saw the Armed Forces as a natural connection. "Coach K and I were having dinner last summer and talking about ways to connect this team with America," Colangelo said. "We talked about engaging ourselves [with the military]: 'Can this become their team? America's team?' It seemed like a natural."[17]

Natural, given Colangelo's political profile and history—and disturbing, in the view of progressives like Edge of Sports pundit Dave Zirin. As Zirin opined in a column in the liberal journal The Nation, "To use a deeply unpopular war from which, according to a recent Zogby poll, 72 percent of troops want to escape, and using the injured for public relations purposes, feels more like exploitation than motivation, especially when spearheaded by Jerry Colangelo."[18]

If progressive-leaning fans can get past their understandable cynicism about Colangelo, this meeting of wounded veterans and the USA Basketball team makes sense on one level. Several of the players were reportedly moved to tears, and in view of young athletes' need for a more mature perspective, who could doubt the value of these pampered, super-rich NBA stars meeting face-to-face with people who truly knew about sacrifice and adversity? And if it could help the team's disparate parts set aside personal agendas and unite as a cohesive unit—always a challenge with all-star basketball ensembles—all the better.

Yet Zirin, and those whose resentments he articulated, are certainly justified in crying "foul" about the hoops-and-troops summit arranged by Christian Right warrior Jerry Colangelo. Given the larger context, what progressive would not see the event as an exploitive public relations stunt? This is especially so in view of the larger patterns into which the ballers-and-soldiers get-together fit: its creation by a right-wing Christian friend of the then-president, and by the almost-complete absence of counterexamples over time in which sports and its power structure have supported progressive causes. How, we might ask, would conservatives have reacted if the U.S. team's management had invited anti-war veterans to meet with the players and discuss the war's injustices with them? Or if Colangelo had brought in civil rights activists to discuss racism and make that the team's rallying point—or representatives of the American Civil Liberties Union to galvanize and unite the players around that ultra-American value known as freedom of speech?

When the faith-and-sports force is not striking a martial-sounding chord, it can often be heard playing in the minor key of homophobia. Through recent decades, the Christian sports establishment has stood firm with the Christian Right in resisting gay rights. To tease out the role of faith from the tangled matter of sports and homosexuality is very difficult; as academics like Butterworth, Michael Messner, and many others have written, sports culture is shot through with homophobia, even where religious faith is not a big part of the equation. Men's major league sports are, after all, one of the few remaining high-profile sectors in the country yet to have a single "out" gay person (although the same cannot be said about the women's game since WNBA star Sheryl Swoopes emerged from the closet in 2004). As anyone who has been around locker rooms can attest, men's sports are a realm of super-macho behavior where derogatory slang terms for gays are as common as the stories about sexual conquests of the opposite sex variety.[19]

Whether Christian ministry is an important factor in this aspect of sports culture is a story for another day. But it seems beyond doubt that ministry's leading agents reflect and reinforce intolerance of sexual minorities. For a case in point, admittedly an extreme one, consider Ron Brown of the Fellowship of Christian Athletes.

Brown is an assistant football coach at the University of Nebraska and former director of FCA operations in the Cornhusker State. He continues to host an FCA radio program and is the author of several books on Christian character. Brown also writes "Finish Strong," a regular column for the FCA magazine.

Brown devoted his November 2007 column to an issue he called the "elephant in the house"—rampant homosexuality in women's sports. Taking issue with ESPN commentator Stephen A. Smith, who had commended Swoopes for coming out of the closet, Brown wrote, "There's nothing heroic about endorsing sin or simply watching it take root without action and exposing it so that there can be confession, repentance, and rebirth."

No one could accuse Brown of political correctness or a mealymouthed retreat to nuance. "Homosexuality," he continued, "is, in fact, a sin according to God's Word (see Romans 1:26-27). Homosexuality, like lying, stealing, lusting, cheating, being prideful, and having sex outside of marriage, is sinful. Those who do not come to the cross for the forgiveness of their sins through the death of Jesus Christ alone will endure the wrath of God in hell."

As he made clear elsewhere in the column, Brown is quite convinced that Swoopes will have plenty of company by the Lake of Fire. He cited intelligence from one Linda Roh, an FCA-sponsored chaplain working with a major college women's basketball team and a former collegiate player herself. When Roh played, a "high number" of her team's supporters "were living in homosexual sin," Brown said, and fully a third of team members were doing likewise. An isolated case? No. "Homosexuality in women's sports is prevalent," Brown warned. "It's real. It's the elephant in the room that needs to be addressed!"

At least Brown could be credited with providing a measure of context by acknowledging that the go-to biblical teaching by the apostle Paul has "unnatural relations" nestled in with a host of other common sins: greed, malice, envy, murder, slander, insolence, rebellion against parents, ruthlessness, deceit, and pride. What Brown failed to note, in a manner indicative of the larger pattern in sports world religion and Christian Right politics, is the line Paul delivered at the beginning of his very next chapter: "Therefore you have no excuse, whoever you are, when you judge others; for in passing judgment on another you condemn yourself, because you that judge are doing the very same sort of sinful things."

One wonders how Brown had managed to misplace Paul's crucial admonition when he went on to write, in that same FCA column, that Christians in sports had an obligation to go on the warpath against homosexuality, and that Roh was a true hero for testifying to the sinfulness of homosexuality. "Women like Linda who love and follow Jesus," Brown wrote, "not only have a right to declare that the act of homosexuality is a sin but the responsibility to declare it."[20]

Picture it: Finger-wagging Christian players, coaches, and chaplains getting on their locker room soap boxes and warning lesbian players about the wages of their homosexual sin. Is that how Brown wants Christianity to be seen and known in sports? Given the context of the biblical quote he marshals, this must be asked, too: Is he also counting on Jesus' followers in sports to unleash the same fire and brimstone on fans, teammates, coaches, and management officials who are guilty of greed, malice, envy, murder, slander, insolence, rebellion against parents, ruthlessness, deceit, and pride? If not, his fixation on this one issue of homosexuality begins to take on the appearance of bigotry, of his picking on a certain group of people.

If Brown has fallen prey to an utter lack of proportion, he cannot be solely blamed. For this kind of thinking about homosexuality has been advanced by leading promoters of sports world Christianity for decades.

Minister and former NFL linebacker Ken Hutcherson, for one, has used his Kirkland, Washington, pulpit to strenuously resist gay rights. An African American, Hutcherson has strongly objected to the framing of homosexual rights as parallel to the struggle for blacks' civil rights in the 1960s. Wielding threats of a boycott, he pressured Microsoft to withdraw its support for a bill in the Washington state legislature that would have made it illegal for employers to discriminate on the basis of sexual orientation.[21]

Christian pro athletes are sometimes given to saying outrageous things about gay people that could only be called bigotry, even if one respects their right to personally object to homosexuality on biblical grounds. Longtime major league baseball pitcher and evangelism star John Smoltz, for example, linked gay marriage to bestiality, asking the Associated Press in a 2004 interview: "What's next? Marrying an animal?"[22]

The late NFL giant Reggie White, a sports world evangelist par excellence, condemned homosexuals with the same ferocity that he brought to the playing field. When it came to gay rights, the "Minister of Defense" was the "Minister of Intolerance," as one pundit called him, consistently rejecting any suggestion that the struggle of homosexuals bore any resemblance whatsoever to the drive for blacks' civil rights. Typical of White's rhetoric on gay rights was this statement at a 1999 Iowa rally called to oppose the governor's executive order banning discrimination against gays in executive-branch state agencies. "Every black person in America should be offended," White declared, "that a group of people should want the same civil rights because of their sexual orientation."[23] Appearing with White and others in the speaker's lineup was Gary Bauer, then a candidate for the Republican presidential nomination, who still today appears in any who's-who of hard-right Christian conservative leaders.

When Christian sports figures such as Hutcherson and White take up the anti-gay cause, they are hardly leaving the faith-in-sports reservation. Rather, they represent what has long been the movement's position on the matter. Indicative of the prevailing attitude is language appearing on staff applications for Campus Crusade, the parent organization of Athletes in Action, which warns that "indulgence in any lifestyle or pastime that is illegal or scripturally questionable or forbidden (for example, living or sleeping with a member of the opposite sex out of wedlock, homosexual practice, drunkenness, or refusing to pay legitimate bills) may result in termination."[24]

And so it goes with evangelical sports figures and their forays into the political arena: Kurt Warner, the one-time Super Bowl champion quarterback and evangelizing superstar, with his starring role in political ads opposing stem cell research in Missouri (which aired, fittingly enough, during St. Louis Cardinals World Series games); NFL kicker and Christian Jason Elam with his "Monday Night Jihad" novel and its tale of a Christian special-operations hero who foils a Muslim terrorist attack on a fan-filled football stadium; longtime FCA president Dal Shealy with his membership on the board of the far-right Council for National Policy, and more.

Yet for all their staunch advocacy for the Christian Right's causes and candidates, the Christian sports figures discussed above—Curt Schilling, Ron Brown, Ken Hutcherson, and others—cannot match the sledgehammer outspokenness with which onetime AIA basketball team member Ralph Drollinger connects sports and evangelical religion to the political sphere.

So committed was Drollinger to Jesus and sports ministry following his UCLA basketball career that he forsook the NBA and spent four years preaching the gospel and playing ball around the globe with AIA. The seven-foot-two Drollinger finally gave pro basketball a shot. He joined the newly formed Dallas Mavericks for their inaugural NBA season in 1980 but played in only six games, logging a grand total of sixty-seven minutes on the court, before a bad knee sidelined him for good.

Drollinger returned to sports ministry, and there he continued his work for the better part of the next two decades. Then he identified a different group of people to target with his gospel message: politicians. Since 1997, Drollinger and his long, tall frame have been a conspicuous presence in the California capitol in Sacramento, where the ex-UCLA star goes about his work for an organization called Capitol Ministries. Its purpose, as it explains on its website, "is delivering the gospel to every state legislator, in every state capitol, every year. Reaching elected officials and leading them toward maturity in Christ are our primary focuses."[25]

Drollinger, unfortunately, has at times pursued that mission in ways more likely to repel people than attract them to Christianity. He generated headlines in 2004 with his statement that it was sinful for female legislators with young children to leave the brood at home and travel to work in Sacramento. Several of the accused responded not by immediately retreating to their nests but by showing up for work at the capital wearing aprons with a scarlet "M" emblazoned on them. Drollinger's intolerant statements about Catholicism—the world's "largest false religion," as he called it—got him in hot water with the wrong Catholics: Governor Arnold Schwarzenegger and his wife, Maria Shriver.[26]

In one newspaper interview around the time, Drollinger rationalized his intolerance with this simplistic "reasoning": "I'm just trying to be true to the scripture. It's really just a matter of courage. Do you want to be popular in the capitol or do you want to be true to the scripture?"[27]

Of course, trotting out a series of examples cannot alone make the case that Christian sports figures are co-opted by Republican politics. (It is also important to acknowledge that all of the figures discussed above are complex human beings whose personal and public lives have many more dimensions than their divisive political stands.) Yet the picture becomes clearer when one examines the sports-faith-politics landscape for counterexamples—for instances of Christian athletes taking liberal positions—and comes away virtually empty-handed. To cite one possible exception to the evident rule, NBA veteran Derek Fisher, a man well known for his character and Christian devotion, joined several Los Angeles Lakers teammates in 2008 in videotaping testimonials about the genocide in Darfur. Of course, one might correctly point out that the dynamics of that issue probably transcend the liberal-conservative divide, and given the sheer magnitude of the disaster and the hold we would expect it to exert on the religious conscience, one might also ask: Why aren't *more* Christians raising their voices on the matter?

On the relatively few occasions when pro athletes have publicly aired progressive views in recent times—NBA players Etan Thomas and Steve Nash, outspoken opponents of the Iraq war, come to mind, as does baseball's Carlos Delgado—they are rarely if ever evangelical Christians. This, despite the fact that progressive evangelicals have become some of the leading voices of conscience on matters of war, torture, and poverty in the country's fast-changing political culture, demonstrating that publicly applied faith cannot be confined to a narrow, far-right band of the political spectrum.

Numerous participants in, and observers of, the faith-in-sports movement who were interviewed for this book confirm what has long been obvious to those in and around evangelical Christian engagement with big-time sports: When it comes to politics, Christianity in sports is no equal-opportunity player. Nor does the form of faith advanced in sports appear to be a *complete* Christianity, one that applies the teachings of Jesus wherever they might lead on the political spectrum. Rather, like tough, savvy rebounders in a basketball game, the promoters, supporters, and practitioners of evangelicalism in pro sports have generally boxed out any political manifestations of faith that fail to conform to the big-business, pro-Republican ethos of the conservative powers that be.

*

Why does stepping up for Jesus in the world of pro sports so often mean taking a stand for the Republican party and/or conservative politics?

Ed Uszynski, director of resource development for Athletes in Action, believes critics read too much into things if they see an intentional, conspiratorial allegiance between promoters of Christianity in sports and conservative political interests. "I don't deny the 'right-wing' connections between evangelical ministry and politics," Uszynski said in an e-mail exchange on the issue. "I just don't think the average chaplain/minister is thinking about political leanings. Some of the heavy-hitter [religious right] organizations—Focus on the Family, Liberty University, for example—made a name for themselves because they've had strong leaders who have a political agenda attached to their religious convictions. I'm not going to say this is wrong, but . . . it is not representative of most ministers and ministries. Given the choice between aligning myself with Republicans who are supportive of faith-based programs and Democrats who support groups like the ACLU—which tries to ransack ministries like the one I work for—well, the choice isn't a difficult one."

Uszynski later clarified his point about the ACLU and indicated "ransack" might have been too strong a word. Nevertheless, he confirmed the general point: When AIA has met resistance on separation-of-church-and-state grounds, the ACLU and like-minded liberal groups have invariably been involved. And the organizations and individuals friendly to AIA are typically conservative in their politics. "Resistance to 'conservative' ministries like AIA comes from the left, not the right, and it's easy over time to find one siding with 'right' causes whether intentionally or unintentionally," Uszynski explained. "There is no conscious alignment with right-wing, conservative causes in AIA that I'm aware of, although, in fact, a ministry that tends to be made up of white conservative folks will probably also find itself aligning with white conservative politics, whether intentionally or not. I've never heard of purposeful strategizing in AIA circles [about politics], though if you polled the majority of folks who work with us, I'd guess they were Republican."[28]

The point was acknowledged by Uszynski's onetime colleague John White, a scholar who has done extensive research and thinking on Christian engagement with sports and who, until 2008, served as sports ethics director for AIA. In their day-to-day work and lives, ministry representatives and Christian athletes are not first and foremost political agents, and they are probably not conscious of the political meaning of much of what they do or say, White said. He believes their conservatism is so ingrained as to be almost unnoticeable and often not intentional—and yet highly and inherently political just the same.

"Ed is right that [Christian players and ministry representatives] do not think how their political persuasions theoretically relate to how they do sport ministry—but that does not mean that they do not *pragmatically* relate," White said in an interview conducted during his final year on the AIA staff. "This is the point of much of the push-back by intellectuals, both Christians and non-Christians, about what they see as a serious disconnect in the U.S. between Christians beliefs and Christian behavior."

In other words, as critics are pointing out with greater frequency, something is off, or at least missing, when the sports world purveyors of the Christian gospel of love and compassion so seldom have anything to say about social ills like racism, poverty, and poor public health that undoubtedly cause massive suffering in America and around the globe.

White also voiced deep concern about sports ministry's fixation on business-style metrics, or measurable results, and a "Constantinian" approach to faith that is on the wrong side of the ages-old struggle between the downtrodden and the holders of political and economic power (as in the Roman Emperor Constantine, who made Christianity the official religion of the empire).

"It seems to me," White added, "that we often listen more to the business-men who give to the ministry than to the radical, costly gospel call to serve as the hands and feet of the compassionate Christ. Our staff, myself included, have been given much by many faithful donors, but where it becomes an ethical issue is when the amount given is matched more with the outcomes that yield marketable and measurable results. This reflects more of a Wall Street approach, where ministry and, hence, people become commodified like any other product. I do not think Jesus had any of the patrons of Rome investing [in his work] and determining what he did or did not do. Jesus' care for the poor, beggars, drunks, harlots, and publicans resulted in more disdain and doubt than denarii."

Before joining the faculty of the evangelical Cedarville College in Ohio in the fall of 2008, White lived in Scotland for two years while completing his Ph.D. and doing ministry work in Europe as an AIA staffer. He has become an outspoken voice against the co-opting of Christian ministry by athletic values, especially a fixation on "extrinsic" results like winning and money that White sees as nothing short of idolatrous. White sees a similar co-opting by conservative politics that has made sports ministry complicit in the protection and promotion of a status quo that prevents progress on racism in American society—an issue White approaches with deep and urgent concern—and on other social justice fronts.

White estimates that some 90 percent of staff members working for AIA and FCA favor the GOP, reflecting the political proclivities of the individuals and organizations that provide the ministry's financial support. This, he worries, leads not only to a business-style fixation on measurable outcomes—events held, conversions achieved, and the like—but to a skewed form of Christianity overly concerned with temporal power. "While [the staffs] might not contemplate the faith-politics relationship, they consistently value and do things that are consistent with Republicans," White says. "If that relationship goes unexamined, it is akin to a Constantinian brand of Christianity, certainly not worthy of living or reproducing. For no Christian should ever equate the veracity of his faith with a particular political party or nation."

Republican values, White elaborated, contribute greatly to ministry's historic failure to address social issues in sports, such as racism and equity for women. "Part of it is the unbelievably strong alliance between capitalism and sport. Republicans would not question this at all, but I beg to differ. This is a relationship that Christians cannot leave unaddressed."[29]

Regardless of whether liberal groups like the ACLU drove the organization into the arms of conservative politics, or whether Athletes in Action went there and remained with enthusiastic willingness, there is no question whatsoever about the conservative politics infusing the ministry's founding stories and pantheon of leaders.

The late Bill Bright, the founder of AIA's parent ministry, Campus Crusade for Christ, was a giant in far-right politics before his death in 2003. This is not intended to demonize a man who, upon winning the Templeton Prize for Progress in Religion, donated the entire $1 million-plus to causes promoting fasting and prayer and who funneled to Campus Crusade all royalties from his more than sixty books.[30] Yet to many moderates and progressives, Bright's legacy as a religious leader is indelibly marked—indeed *marred*—by his far-right politics. Poke around the constellation of organizations that have advanced the cause of the Christian Right the past quarter-century, and you will frequently find Bright among their supporters and leaders. Among Bright's roles: board member, Council for National Policy; founder, Alliance Defense Fund, which provides legal support to people and organizations engaged in high-profile courtroom brawls over conservative Christian prerogatives in the public sphere, and which once stated in fund-raising literature that the "radical homosexual agenda" was the principal threat to America; and founder, Third Century Publishers, created to publish books and study guides fusing conservative politics and Christianity.

One might point out that the fierce conservatism of the deceased founder of AIA's parent organization hardly proves a right-wing political bias on the part of Athletes in Action. But a look at AIA's executive and board leadership, and at its key benefactors, reveals that Bright's conservatism lives on.

Earlier this decade, for example, AIA President William Pugh, along with then-FCA president Dal Shealy, joined a lineup of Christian Right leaders and conservative pastors in resisting a more gender-neutral version of the Bible known as Today's New International Version (TNIV). Hardly radical feminists, the creators of the new translation were striving for more inclusiveness by changing the word "man" to "people" when the word referred to humans in the plural form, for instance. That was going too far for Pugh and Shealy, who signed a "Statement of Concern" with some one hundred other Christian leaders including such high-profile conservative icons as Albert Mohler Jr. of the Southern Baptist Theological Seminary, Charles Colson of Watergate infamy and Prison Fellowship, Donald Wildmon of the American Family Association, Pat Robertson of the Christian Broadcasting Network, and James Dobson.[31]

Ex-NFL star Anthony Muñoz is a leading supporter and promoter of AIA, serving on the ministry's board, speaking at numerous AIA events, and hosting youth camps. Muñoz has also been active in Republican politics over the course of this decade, heading the Bush-Cheney campaign in eight southwest Ohio counties in the 2004 election.[32] One of Muñoz' AIA board colleagues—and the

man for whom AIA's retreat center is named—is David M. Browne, the CEO
and president of Family Christian Stores. Browne is listed in SourceWatch as
a member of the Honorary Committee of the Presidential Prayer Team.

Donors and grant-makers "vote" their principles and agendas through their
choices of causes and organizations to support and, in so doing, say much about
the organizations on the receiving end of their generosity. Judging from its hefty
grants to AIA's parent ministry, Campus Crusade, the arch-conservative Arthur
S. DeMoss Foundation finds much to like about the shape and direction of the
work of Crusade and its various ministries, including AIA. A major supplier
of funds to Christian Right and evangelical Christian causes, the Florida-based
DeMoss Foundation has poured millions of dollars into Campus Crusade. In
2006, for example, the foundation made grants totaling $970,000 to Campus
Crusade's work in the United States and around the world.[33] DeMoss in
recent years has also supported the Fellowship of Christian Athletes, various
anti-abortion causes, and the Plymouth Rock Foundation, a group that is part
of the ultra-right Christian Reconstructionist movement and its campaign to
install strict biblical law in the United States.[34]

A review of the board members and the senior leadership of Baseball Chapel and the Fellowship of Christian Athletes reveals a similar pattern: Those
active politically are, like AIA's Muñoz, invariably associated with conservative
causes. Cases in point: Baseball Chapel board member Dave Dravecky, a former major league baseball pitcher who was a member of the notorious John
Birch Society in the 1980s, and Tom Rogeberg, FCA senior vice president of
communications and marketing, who before joining FCA in Kansas City was a
top executive of Coral Ridge Ministries, led by the late Christian Right warrior
D. James Kennedy.

Admittedly, a liberal's lament about the politically conservative direction of
Christianity in pro sports might sound like mere whining from a sore loser.
Conservatives might point out that all is as it should be—that Christianity in
sports veers consistently right because that is the direction of truth and virtue,
the direction of America, the direction of Christ. But developments across
the wider political/cultural landscape in the latter half of the decade makes
the proposition extremely difficult to support. For evangelical Christianity increasingly manifests all across the political spectrum in the closing years of the
decade, breaking away from a once-predictable conservative playbook into cen-
trist and even "liberal" areas of focus like climate change, poverty, treatment
of immigrants, and unduly aggressive American foreign policy and interroga-
tion tactics. On abortion and homosexuals' rights—the standard wedge issues
of the Christian Right—more theological conservatives are maintaining their
positions but doing so with a softer tone and a new recognition of the issues'

nuances and context. As for voting, exit polls and other opinion sampling in the 2008 presidential contest found large numbers of evangelical Christians voting for Democrats, and why not? The Christian religiosity of the two leading Democratic candidates greatly exceeded that of GOP nominee John McCain, who exhibited considerable discomfort and awkwardness talking about his faith. Yet the GOP is "God's Own Party" and the political destination where Christianity in sports naturally leads?

An increasingly clear picture of *complete* Christianity in politics is emerging, a picture in which Jesus' teachings confound attempts to apply "conservative" and "liberal" labels, and in which Jesus' message and followers show their faces all across the political spectrum, in ways surprising, idealistic, defiant, and at times frustrating to the political powers that be. Sociological research finds that 70 percent of evangelical Christians in America do not identify with right-wing political Christianity.[35] As the columnist and author E. J. Dionne has declared, the era of the Christian Right's outsize influence on national electoral politics is over.

If the rapid change in these closing years of the decade is good news for the integrity and well-being of faith—which I believe it is—the trends should be disquieting to those who have promoted or gone along with the skewed form of Christianity operative in the faith-sports relationship. The emerging trend certainly calls into question what has gone unquestioned for too long— the proposition that the path of Jesus, as it winds through American sports, culture, and politics, inevitably bears to the right.

As Christianity itself is demonstrating, it seems ever clearer that the skeptics and critics have been right all along: It's not primarily because of Jesus that Christianity in pro sports has been a servant to far-right politics. This has not been "mere Christianity," to cite the title of the seminal book by C. S. Lewis, the author revered by so many in sports ministry. Rather, a clear-eyed examination of religion in pro sports reveals that something in addition to Jesus' teaching has been shaping the political views and actions at the intersection of pro sports, faith, and the public issues of the day. When you scrape away the surface piety, you find devotion not so much to the stories and wisdom of Jesus, but to a set of ideas and objectives including these longtime staples of conservative politics: Support for big business; preservation of the status quo for the benefit of those enjoying its privileges; the deification of capitalism; American might; and the age-old pursuit of power.

Perhaps a case can be made for the rightness, or at least the inevitability, of these less-than-holy lodestars. Just don't look for it in the Bible.

Notes

1. Brian C. Mooney, "Schilling Delivers for Bush on 'Good Morning America,'" *Boston Globe*, October 29, 2004.

2. Curt Schilling, "Curt Schilling's Letter to America," ESPN.com, September 15, 2001.

3. Tom Krattenmaker, "Going Long for Jesus," *Salon*, May 10, 2006, http://www.salon.com/news/feature/2006/05/10/ministries/index.html.

4. Rick Klein, "Schilling Goes to Bat for Bush in 3 States," *Boston.com*, October 31, 2004, http://www.boston.com/news/politics/president/articles/2004/10/31/schilling_goes_to_bat_for_bush_in_3_states.

5. The 2009 Super Bowl and surrounding hoopla furnished a high-profile exception, with both the coach and owner of the champion Pittsburgh Steelers publicly expressing their enthusiasm for Barack Obama.

6. Dave Zirin, *Welcome to the Terrordome: The Pain, Politics, and Promise of Sports* (Chicago: Haymarket Books, 2007), 93.

7. Michael L. Butterworth, "Saved at Home: Evangelical Christianity in the 'Church of Baseball,'" a paper delivered at the 2006 annual meeting of the National Communication Association meeting, San Antonio, Texas.

8. Butterworth, "Saved."

9. Sewell Chan, "Seventh-Inning Stretch Turns Into Suit Against Police," *New York Times*, April 15, 2009.

10. "Twins and Qwest to host fifth annual Armed Forces Appreciation Day," Minnesota Twins press release, May 22, 2007, http://minnesota.twins.mlb.com/news/press_releases/press_release.jsp-?ymd=20070522&content_id=1979406&vkey=pr_min&fext=.jsp&c_id=min; see also the team's press release from 2005 announcing that year's event, at http://minnesota.twins.mlb.com/news/press_releases/-press_release.jsp?ymd=20050621&content_id=1098451&vkey=pr_min&fext=.jsp&c_id=min.

11. Butterworth, "Saved."

12. "Hot Corner Archives," *Sports Spectrum*, April 28, 2005, http://www.sportsspectrum.com/daily/-archives/050428.html.

13. See Dave Zirin, "Troops and Hoops," *The Nation*, August 20, 2006, and "Battin 1,000" web page, published by the American Life League at http://www.all.org/battin1000.

14. To its credit, and probably to the surprise of many skeptical progressives and secularists, the Presidential Prayer Team continued to function and pray for the President after the arrival of the nonevangelical Barack Obama in the White House, albeit in a manner consistently reflective of conservative values.

15. Max Blumenthal, "The Christian Right's Humble Servant," AlterNet, November 15, 2004, http://www.alternet.org/election04/20499.

16. Zirin, "Troops and Hoops," *The Nation*.

17. Zirin, "Troops and Hoops," *The Nation*.

18. Zirin, "Troops and Hoops," *The Nation*.

19. For a useful review of homophobia, misogyny, and sexual aggression in male competitive sports, see Margaret Gatz, Michael A. Messner, and Sandra J. Ball-Rokeach, *Paradoxes of Youth and Sport* (Albany, New York: SUNY Press, 2002).

20. Ron Brown, "Then a Hero Comes Along," *Sharing the Victory*, November 2007.

21. Sarah Kershaw, "Microsoft Comes Under Fire for Reversal on Gay Rights Bill," *New York Times*, April 22, 2005.

22. Paul Newberry, "Mixed Signals as Gays Try to Find Their Place in the Sports World," Associated Press, sports wire, July 2, 2004.

23. Dave Zirin, "The Death of Reggie White: An Off the Field Obituary," Common Dreams.org, December 28, 2004, http://www.commondreams.org/views04/1228-34.htm.

24. Campus Crusade for Christ Application for Employment; copies can be downloaded from http://www.ccci.org/opportunities/careers/applications/campus-crusade -hourly-salaried-job-application.pdf.

25. Capitol Ministries, "About" page, http://www.capmin.org/About/Vision.aspx.

26. Keith Whitmire, "Ex-Mavs Center Ralph Drollinger is now Living by the Book," *Dallas Morning News*, August 8, 2005.

27. Whitmire, "Living by the Book," *Dallas Morning News*.

28. Ed Uszynski, Athletes in Action, extended interview conducted via telephone, e-mail, and face-to-face between the fall of 2007 and summer of 2008.

29. John White, then of Athletes in Action, extended interview conducted by phone and e-mail between October 2007 and June 2008.

30. See Bill Bright biography page at Campus Crusade for Christ International website, http://billbright.ccci.org/staff/presskit/overview.htm, and the ministry's Bill Bright obituary at http://billbright.ccci.org/public.

31. "Statement of Concern about the TNIV Bible," published on the Internet by Bible Research at http://www.bible-researcher.com/tniv2.html.

32. "Former Bengals Player to Replace Allen as Head of Local Bush-Cheney Campaign," WCPO.com, September 8, 2004, http://old.wcpo.com/news/2004/local/ 09/08/munoz.html.

33. Arthur S. DeMoss Foundation, Form 990-PF, 2006.

34. Sourcewatch, published by the Center for Media and Democracy at http://www .sourcewatch.org/-index.php?title=Arthur_S._DeMoss_Foundation.

35. Jeremy Adam Smith, "Living in the Gap: The Ideal and the Reality of the Christian Right Family," PublicEye.org, published by Political Research Associates at http:// www.publiceye.org/magazine/v22n4/christian_family.html.

CHAPTER 8

~

Domesticated Christianity
The Political Acquiescence of African American Christians in Sports

> White folks like for us to be religious, then they can do what they want to with us.
>
> —Bigger Thomas[1]

It was, in the words of the network television commentator, a Super Bowl freighted with "social significance."

Whichever team won Super Bowl XLI following the 2006 season, the Chicago Bears or the Indianapolis Colts, the National Football League champions, for the first time ever, would be coached by an African American. That was due to another first that defied the odds in a professional football world where black head coaches have been, and remain, relatively rare: African Americans were the coaches of *both* teams.

Tony Dungy's Colts defeated Lovey Smith's Bears 29-17 at rainy Dolphins Stadium that evening in early February 2007. As the television personalities and league brass launched into the well-choreographed post-game ceremony, still before the massive television audience, the moment seemed alive with possibility for many of those concerned about the state of racial progress in the United States. How would Dungy use the opportunity?

Following a stirring introduction by the public address announcer, a coach from the Super Bowl pantheon, Don Shula, began his journey to the podium, where he would present the Vince Lombardi championship trophy. The grinning ex-coach strode through a gauntlet of victorious Colts players. Mostly African American, the young men whooped and shouted—"yeah, baby!"—and touched or patted the Lombardi trophy as Shula sauntered past with the prize he had won twice in his coaching career.

The retired coach ascended a short staircase to the circular podium decked out in the orange and light blue with which the NFL had branded this edition of the Super Bowl. As he mounted the platform, Shula joined an assemblage that included Commissioner Roger Goodell, CBS announcer Jim Nance, and three representatives of the champion Colts: owner Jim Irsay, quarterback Peyton Manning, and Dungy—the African American coach who during his collegiate playing career had the temerity to play the ultimate white-man position, quarterback, and who now had advanced the cause of blacks in sports even deeper into the white, inner sanctum by serving as the coaching brains of the champions of the NFL.

"This trophy," Goodell declared, "represents the greatest achievement in team sports. We're proud to give this to you, Jim. Your organization deserves it. Congratulations to you, Tony, and the rest of your organization, and your great fans."[2]

Irsay, having viewed the game from a well-sheltered stadium suite, looked dry and crisp in his dark suit, red tie, and neat goatee as he accepted the prize from the commissioner and held it up to the rainy sky amid a wave of cheers. "Thank you, Roger!" he exulted.

The victorious owner began on a solemn note, awkwardly voicing his and his team's concern for victims of tornados that had blasted central Florida in the run-up to the big game and pledging the Colts' support for recovery efforts. "The Colts will participate in helping, in partnershiping (sic) with that tragedy down there, and our prayers are with them tonight—we don't want to forget that."

A smile came over his face then as he raised the trophy again. "Now we're world champions!" he proclaimed, setting off a cascade of applause. Irsay then reprised the religious statement he had made two weeks earlier, when he had given the glory to God while accepting the trophy for the American Football Conference championship.

"There's an awful lot of shine and glory, even more than last time up here," he said, "but we're giving it all to God again, because that's what got us here. Sticking together, and believing that we could. And I know God has looked after us in this journey, and bonded us to such a tight family. . . . Big congratulations to all of Indiana, the city of Indianapolis, coach Dungy, [team president] Bill Polian. I'm so proud of my men. I love you, guys!"[3]

Dungy, wearing one of the white Super Bowl champion t-shirts passed out to the Colts following the final gun, held the trophy in his right hand as Nance congratulated him and his team.

"I'm so proud of our guys," Dungy responded in the calm voice that had contributed much to his reputation for wisdom and decency. "We took the hit early with Devin Hester [a Chicago kick returner who had shocked the Colts with a spectacular touchdown to start the game]. But we talked about it. We said there's gonna be a storm. We said the Lord doesn't always bring you directly through. Sometimes you gotta work for it, and our guys just hung tough and played so hard. I just can't tell you how proud I am of our group, our organization, and our city right now."

Nance proceeded to the crux of the matter, the "social significance" of the moment. What did it mean, he asked, to become the first black coach to win the Super Bowl?

"I tell you what—I'm proud to be representing African American coaches," Dungy replied, "and to be the first African American coach to win this. It means an awful lot to our country. But, again, more than anything—I've said it before—Lovey Smith and I are not only the first two African Americans, but *Christian* coaches showing you can win doing it the Lord's way. We're more proud of that."[4]

Dungy looked away, a closed-mouth smile on his face, as more applause rained down. Nance turned his attention to quarterback Manning, and the moment of "social significance" was over. Whether Dungy had delivered "in the clutch," to use the sports cliché, or fumbled the ball a step short of the goal line depended entirely on the religious and political perspective of the person judging.

Praise was quick to follow from leaders of prominent evangelical figures. Among them was Richard Land, president of the Ethics & Religious Liberty Commission of the Southern Baptist Convention, one of *TIME* magazine's twenty-five most influential evangelicals, who hailed Dungy for placing his faith above his race. "While commentators noted the game's historical significance with two African American head coaches on the sidelines," Land wrote in a guest column for the *Christian Post*, "it might well have been the first Super Bowl where the two head coaches . . . openly shared their Christian faith."[5]

Typical of the other point of view was this expression of disappointment: "It's just a shame," commentator Sarah Braunstein wrote for the sports website *The Bleacher Report*, "that [Dungy] didn't seize the moment." Dungy, she continued, "should have said something about following in the footsteps of players like Kenny Washington, who effectively integrated football in 1946, and Paul 'Tank' Younger, the first athlete recruited by the NFL from a historically black college. And he definitely should have mentioned Art Shell, the first African American head coach in the NFL. Instead, Dungy tried to circumvent race and claim it was more important that he'd won the Super Bowl as a Christian, thus giving credit and power to a group that had no lack of it."[6]

The champion coach's true religious and social allegiances became clearer still when, within days of the Super Bowl, he accepted an invitation to be the honored guest of the Indiana Family Institute (IFI) at its fund-raising banquet, scheduled for the following month. The IFI, a state-level version of Focus on the Family, was leading a drive to change the state constitution to ban same-sex marriage and campaigning to bar gay couples from adopting children.

To the leaders and followers of the Christian Right, Dungy had seized the moment—had seized it in spectacular form.

*

There was a time when some of the country's leading African American athletic figures, religious or otherwise, spoke out for racial justice and addressed the pressing social justice issues of the day. One of the most enduring images of "the black athlete" remains the photograph from the climactic moment of the 1968 Summer Olympics in Mexico City in which African American track stars Tommie Smith and John Carlos stand on the victory dais in their USA uniforms, each raising one black-gloved hand with his fingers clenched in a fist—the symbol of black power. The gesture, as historian Amy Bass writes, was threatening and upsetting to much of America, and it earned Smith and Carlos the harsh criticism of U.S. Olympic officials and many members of the public.[7]

Smith and Carlos were not associated with religiosity. But a survey of the social and athletic landscape of that era does find high-profile Christian black athletic figures involved in progressive political causes, including two of the leading luminaries of that time—Gale Sayers, a record-shattering running back and kick returner for the Chicago Bears, and Jackie Robinson, the African American who broke the major league baseball color barrier.

Gale Sayers describes his faith, his social conscience, and his first forays into activism in his landmark autobiography *I Am Third*. (The book's title speaks to the important role of religion in Sayers' life. As he explained its meaning, God was first, his family second, and "I am third.") Sayers, who began attending an Episcopal church during his collegiate career in Lawrence, Kansas, formed a friendship with the young Jesse Jackson in the late 1960s and began paying closer attention to race issues. Prompting some in football to label him a troublemaker or "militant," Sayers lent his visibility and voice to some of Jackson's causes. He helped promote Jackson's Operation Breadbasket and picketed with Jackson and his group at a supermarket located in a black neighborhood, protesting its discriminatory hiring and pricing practices. Also, Sayers became cochair of the Sports Committee of a legal defense fund for the

NAACP and was appointed a Chicago parks commissioner, a position he used to advocate for equal contract-bidding opportunities for black contractors and construction workers.[8]

The story of Christian faith and political activism is even more dramatic with Jackie Robinson. From his upbringing by a fervently devout mother in California, to his pact with the thoroughly religious Brooklyn Dodgers general manager who signed him to play in the major leagues, to his post-baseball career in business and activism, faith played a central role in Jackie Robinson's life.

Robinson's Christianity was deep in his heart, if not always on his sleeve. Biographer Arnold Rampersad describes Robinson's religious turning not as a point-in-time conversion in mold of today's popular evangelicalism, but as a process that began in his youth and accelerated when Robinson as a young man developed a mentor-protégé relationship with a dynamic pastor as his church, Karl Downs. "Downs became a conduit," Rampersad writes, "through which [Robinson's mother's] message of religion and hope finally flowed into Jack's consciousness and was fully accepted there, if on revised terms, as he himself reached manhood. Faith in God then began to register in him as both a mysterious force, beyond his comprehension, and a pragmatic way to negotiate the world. A measure of emotion and spiritual poise such as he had never known at last entered his life."[9]

Robinson's Christian faith, in combination with his determination and political instincts, manifested in his turn-the-other-cheek method of dealing with the racial taunts heaped upon him by opposing players and fans when he began playing with the Dodgers in 1947. It is important to note that "turning the other cheek," when seen in the context of Jesus' time as well as the politics of the mid-twentieth century, is best understood not merely as an act of passivity but also as a form of defiant nonviolent resistance.[10] Accounts of the history-making, pact-sealing meeting between Robinson and Dodgers general manager Branch Rickey make clear that this crucial turn-the-other-cheek teaching from Jesus' Sermon on the Mount played a crucial role in the strategy devised by the two men for dealing with the insults and epithets Robinson would hear on major league diamonds.

After his playing career, Robinson became more directly involved in politics. His involvement with Richard Nixon and the Republican party could give the impression that Robinson was a conservative, but that would be a vast oversimplification of Robinson's politics as well as party dynamics of a half-century ago. Certainly, on the matter of racism, Robinson was anything but a denier and status quo defender. Among his many roles, he was a spokesman for the NAACP; a supporter of and speaker for the Southern Christian Leadership

Conference; the founder of the Church Fund, which raised money to rebuild black churches razed in retaliation for their roles as centers for civil rights organizing and agitating; and, like Sayers, a board member of Jesse Jackson's Operation Breadbasket.[11]

Today, by contrast with Sayers and Robinson, African American Christian athletes overwhelmingly tend to remain mute on matters political, and on the rare occasions they do reveal themselves, the stripes they bear are usually conservative. Although many express a form of social commitment by working with youths, starting charitable foundations, and pursuing other forms of community service, today there are few instances of black Christian sports stars speaking out on race or other social justice issues, or publicly questioning a sports-industrial complex in which very few blacks secure employment in executive suites and owners' boxes despite performing the preponderance of the "labor" in football and basketball.

The social/political stance of black Christian athletes is typified by football running back Shaun Alexander, who during the height of his stardom earlier this decade modeled an approach to faith and sports dramatically different from that of Sayers and Robinson. For the hugely successful Seattle Seahawks running back, Christian commitment translated into a smiling, clean-living image, copious rushing yards and touchdowns, and an enthusiasm for talking about God at every opportunity.

Alexander's religious stance—and the way in which sports world promoters of evangelical Christianity seized it, packaged it, and used it to encourage others—was showcased in the December 2002 edition of the magazine *Sharing the Victory*, published by the Fellowship of Christian Athletes. The magazine's cover featured a large photo of Alexander in action and hailed him as an "ambassador to the kingdom" of God. Inside the magazine ran a photo of Alexander pointing triumphantly skyward in tribute to God as he raced into the end zone for a touchdown and, next to that, a shot of him standing alongside an ESPN interviewer. As the article text noted, Alexander was using the live, televised exchange captured in the photo to praise Jesus and glorify God.

Lauding Alexander's habit of memorizing Bible passages during his record-setting collegiate career at the University of Alabama, article writer John Dodderidge quoted his subject's thoughts on one of his favorite verses. "I went through the Bible looking for something with 37 because that was my football number," Alexander recalled. "I found Psalm 37 and picked out the fourth verse—*Delight yourself in the Lord and He will give you the desires of your heart.*" Related to that was Alexander's perception of being "chosen" by God for athletic success and fulfillment, a privilege that he accepted with a mixture of gratitude and pride. As he told *Sharing the Victory*, "[God] said, 'I'm going to take you and make you special, and you are going to give me all the glory for it.' I'm glad he chose me to do that because I really do love playing football. It's a lot of fun. I really love scoring touchdowns."[12]

The pages of *Sharing the Victory* and a similar Christian sports magazine, *Sports Spectrum*, are filled with numerous other examples of black athletes using their sports star status to proclaim their Christian faith. Fans see the same philosophy acted out each time these men turn television, radio, and print-media interviews into opportunities for faith testimonials—especially in live interviews, when journalists have less control over what makes it on the air and what ends up on the figurative cutting room floor. Generally absent from the public profile of Shaun Alexander and his fellow black Christian athletes, however, is anything resembling righteous resistance to the state of racial affairs in the United States and the conditions afflicting much of America's black community. Racism in America? To judge from the smiling countenance of Shaun Alexander and his fellows, all is well.

To be sure, scattered exceptions can be found. Foremost among them is Etan Thomas of the NBA's Washington Wizards, a religious man and passionate progressive activist. Another is Donovan McNabb of football's Philadelphia Eagles, who has identified himself as Christian (albeit in ways atypical among religious athletes, with McNabb once stating that God has no interest in the outcome of a football game). McNabb on several occasions has called attention to the different treatment accorded black athletes, particularly those playing his high-profile position of quarterback. Baseball home run king Barry Bonds made his Christian beliefs well known before his unceremonious and unwilling retirement, punctuating home runs with a gesture to the heavens, taking the field with a gaudy cross earring for a time, and invoking God in interviews. Bonds also spoke his mind in the media about racism in baseball and society, and his often-snarling public persona bore no resemblance whatsoever to the smiling demeanor of his football counterpart Alexander. The deeply Christian ex-footballer Troy Vincent, a star defensive back for the Dolphins, Eagles, and Bills before he became president of the NFL players union, was a signer of a Jocks 4 Justice declaration of solidarity with the "Jena Six," the black high school students from Louisiana charged with attempted murder in 2007 for beating up a white student following a series of racist taunts. The emergence of Barack Obama as a candidate and, eventually, as the nation's first African American president, brought forth more instances of black athletes, Christian and otherwise, voicing political sensibilities outside of the conservative norm (but without necessarily endorsing Obama's more progressive positions).

Yet these are exceptions that prove the rule. Far more common among the hundreds of African American Christians making their livings in pro sports in this generation is a political silence interrupted by occasional expressions of conservatism, and an all-is-well gratitude for the opportunity to earn millions playing a game and witnessing for God. As the FCA magazine enthuses, "Alexander cherishes the opportunity to share his faith in Christ, especially in front of a large television audience." And, in the words of Alexander, who named one of his children "Heaven," "it's awesome being an ambassador to the Kingdom."[13]

Why has the social consciousness of a Gale Sayers or Jackie Robinson generally been absent from the public stance of today's black Christian athletes? The reasons are myriad and complex, but they can be boiled down to the reality that the Christianity espoused by today's black Christian athletes differs in significant ways from the Christianity of Martin Luther King Jr. and similarly minded black Christian leaders from earlier generations—that it differs dramatically from the Christianity that has compelled many black Americans to act politically for racial and social justice. Rather, it has been a Christianity accepting of the political and social status quo, Christianity dedicated to self-improvement, evangelizing, and politically neutral service to the community. Indeed, the form of belief embraced by most black professional athletes today is a domesticated Christianity—a religion shorn of the prophetic and subversive force that helped propel the civil rights movement and that continues to galvanize many African Americans to act socially and politically.

One needs to be careful about oversimplifying. Strong though it is, the social justice tradition in black churches has always competed with quietist, otherworldly, and materialistic traditions. And the social conservatism represented by Dungy's endorsement of the Indiana Family Institute and its anti-gay rights campaign is consistent with a current of social conservatism that has run through black churches for decades.

Nevertheless, scholars universally agree that there has been a strong link, particularly over the latter half of the twentieth century, between black churches and the political fight for the uplift of oppressed African Americans, which to many black believers was clearly ordained by God. And the overwhelming majority of black Americans today, Christian or otherwise, side with the Democratic party.

"Black Christianity in the United States is self-consciously political and more and more comfortable with the fact," write religion scholars Robert Booth Fowler and Allen D. Hertzke. The primary focus of black politics, they add, is "improving the economic condition and opportunities for blacks. . . . The struggle of the 1960s put the black churches . . . on the liberal side of American politics."[14]

For their part, white evangelicals have tended at times to eschew politics altogether, and during recurrent periods of political engagement, such as that underway since the 1980s, they have tended to pursue a politically conservative agenda that has exhibited little if any concern for structural race issues.

By contrast, a prophetic stand against racial oppression has been a biblical imperative among African American Christians since slavery. "Historically," political scientist Jacqueline S. Mattis writes, "African American Christian theologians have used biblical exegesis to challenge and subvert American racial orthodoxy." This use of the Bible is hardly confined to theologians. African American slaves, Mattis says, drew from the Old Testament the conviction that they were "soldiers engaged in a war against outrageous injustice." She notes that this image remains popular among contemporary blacks, who see the struggle for racial justice as a war in which "God is construed as the ultimate ally who, in time, will assure victory for the righteous and the oppressed." On a practical level, she finds, black Christian churches are "political and politicized" institutions that not only motivate members to strive for justice, but that facilitate political involvement by serving as centers for political organizing, information-sharing, and networking.[15]

Why are these characteristics of the black religious experience so rarely evident in the behavior of today's African American athletes? One of the leading black commentators on issues of race and religion today is Michael Eric Dyson, an ordained minister and Georgetown University professor who has repeatedly voiced his frustration with leading black sports figures and entertainers for not devoting themselves more seriously to improving the conditions experienced by the broad sweep of American blacks. In his book *Open Mike: Reflections on Philosophy, Race, Sex, Culture and Religion*, Dyson points to a competing current in black churches today that has partially supplanted social justice concerns. Dyson cites a prosperity gospel that has been on the ascendancy, a materialistic form of Christianity that sees God rewarding true believers with health and wealth. It is a form of Christianity that appeals to many blacks, but it requires a steep "price of admission," Dyson says—they must leave their ethnic identity at the door. With reference to the black minister Fred Price, a proponent of this prosperity gospel, Dyson writes:

> The price of admission to the gospel of health and wealth, in this case, is the erasure of the racial marks and the ethnic identities that have nurtured and sustained black people for a long time. As I've said, roots are for nurturing, not for strangling. Still, we must feed from them in healthy ways, in ways that respect the integrity of the people produced by them. And I think one of the great disservices of the Word churches is that they for the most part destroy those racial

roots and then extricate those black traditional meanings from their original contexts. The racial rhetoric is neutered, so to speak. . . . The manner in which such Word church ministers recode black religious forms is deeply problematic because it obscures any continuity between ancient biblical worldviews and black traditions of struggle and faith.[16]

Dyson voices a similar lament about white evangelists Kenneth Hagin and Kenneth Copeland and, again, the "word churches," so named for their acceptance of the Bible as the literal and final word of God. Preachers like Hagin and Copeland "remove attribution," Dyson argues, "for the black religious sensibilities that hug their Pentecostal roots, only to feed them back to black people through the ideological apparatuses of evangelical conservatism, whose political effects are often disastrous for black communities." Among those political effects, Dyson goes on to explain, is the "pathologizing" of poverty and other urban problems—problems that obviously affect blacks disproportionately. Underlying that political stance is a conservative theology that frames such problems in terms of individual morality without paying attention to the "structural features" that affect blacks. That theology, Dyson notes, "has little to say about political practices, public policies, and social mechanisms that harm black life."[17]

Although he is not writing about black Christian athletes specifically, Dyson's observations apply very well to the words and deeds of today's African American sports stars. Black Christian athletes work and live in a religious environment dominated by the evangelical conservatism of which Dyson speaks, and they tend to exhibit the political sensibilities such a theology would predict. Like the health-and-wealth preachers criticized by Dyson, black Christian athletes tend to have "little to say" about the political forces that plague black life in America.

The potential for black sports stars, religious or otherwise, to exert leadership on race and other issues has been cited by Dyson and other prominent African American figures, including Jesse Jackson and football star-turned-activist Jim Brown. As these men note, there is little question that such leadership is dearly needed; progress on race issues has largely stalled since the civil rights movement of the 1960s. Although larger numbers of African Americans have achieved middle-class comfort and respectability since the civil rights movement, and a black man has won election to the White House, conditions remain nothing short of miserable for those left behind. By measures ranging from economic status to incarceration rates to educational achievement, African Americans face conditions far more grim than white America.

In the important area of education, for example, black children have far higher dropout rates than white children and take fewer advanced mathematics and science courses than whites, with obvious implications for careers.[18] Racial disparities are perhaps most glaring with respect to incarceration. Given current trends, a black male has an estimated one-in-three chance of going to prison in his lifetime, in contrast with a white male's one-in-seventeen chance.[19]

Given their faith and race, which in combination and in history might predict liberal-leaning political involvement, why do black Christian sports stars have so little to say about the sad state of much of the African American community and the forces causing it?

Black sportswriter William Rhoden identifies a likely factor: the phenomenon he calls the "conveyor belt." In his book $40 Million Slaves, the New York Times writer and onetime college athlete Rhoden describes a process by which promising young black athletes are groomed for big-time college and professional sports. This machinery, effective though it is at funneling athletic talent from poor black communities to college campuses and pro locker rooms, has two significant flaws: It is designed and operated primarily by whites, Rhoden observes, and as might be predicted by that fact, it is engineered "to dull any racial consciousness and eliminate communal instincts."

Rhoden continues:

> Instead, the Belt cultivates a culture of racial know-nothingness. Indeed, the act of "processing" athletes along the Conveyor Belt involves a significant and often subtle element of "deprogramming" potential troublemakers—black athletes who might be tempted to think of themselves, or their situations, in racial terms and who might want to use their prominence in the service of something other than enriching the institution. . . . On the Conveyor Belt, young athletes quickly learn that easy passage through a white-controlled system is contingent upon not "rocking the boat," not being a "troublemaker," and making those in positions of power feel comfortable with the athletes' blackness.[20]

Rhoden doesn't address religion in his perceptive analysis—perhaps an oversight given the large percentage of black sports stars who have embraced Christianity and typically express it in ways that often seem more consistent with white evangelicalism than the African American tradition. Whether religion is the destination or the means of propulsion (some of both, probably) the domesticated faith of so many leading black athletes is surely an important part of the dynamic.

Former NFL player Anthony Prior is one of the most outspoken critics of Christian practice in pro football. Prior, a defensive back for the Jets, Vikings, and Raiders from 1995 to 2000, cites a deep racism in a system in which whites hold most of the administrative positions of power, and in which young black men burn out their bodies in short, physically brutal careers like so many plantation fieldworkers. Religion, Prior says, is one means by which players are inured to injustices and encouraged to swallow the status quo. "It's mind-boggling the way they push Christianity on players," Prior, an African American, said in an interview. "It's packaged in a way to basically make players submissive."[21]

Dave Zirin, a progressive sports writer and author and the founder of Jocks 4 Justice, observes, "Athletes have a voice, but it's almost as if they've been conditioned not to use it."[22] Religion, he added in an interview, is one means by which this silence is achieved.

The smiling persona of Shaun Alexander, his speaking of the "amazing things" God is doing in his life, calls to mind another of Dyson's barbed observations about a tendency among black Christians: "There is today a kind of narcissistic preoccupation with the elevation of the individual black church member and not the amelioration of the collective black fate."[23]

Dyson's observations were borne out vividly in the early weeks of the 2007 NFL season in an episode that began with comments by Donovan McNabb about race and black quarterbacks. McNabb told the media he believed the relative scarcity of blacks in his position—only six of the thirty NFL teams had black starting quarterbacks at the start of the 2007 season, despite African Americans occupying two-thirds of the league's roster spots—saddled them with a heavy burden. "Because the percentage of us playing this position—which people didn't want us to play—is low . . . we do a little extra," McNabb said. White quarterbacks, he added, "don't get criticized as much as we do."[24]

Vince Young, the black, and Christian, quarterback of the Tennessee Titans, distanced himself from McNabb's comments, as did another young African American and Christian quarterback, Jason Campbell of the Redskins. "That is something I can't get caught up in," Campbell said. "[Quarterback] is a tough position to play. I don't look at it as a color issue; I look at it as all of us in a brotherhood together."[25]

Echoes of Dyson's critique could be heard in Young's flat refusal to follow McNabb's cue and discuss the race dynamics of playing quarterback in the NFL: "That," Young said, "is not my fight to fight."[26]

*

Tony Dungy's arrival at his moment of championship glory, and his stepping forward for God and a conservative political cause, culminated a five-decades-long journey through the complicated waterways of athletic, social, and religious history in America.

In one sense, the story begins in 1959 when a major football-playing university in the progressive state of Minnesota turned racial stereotypes on their head and recruited a black quarterback. According to conventional thinking at the time, any role for blacks in football should be confined to positions that emphasized speed and strength—never intelligence and leadership ability. And no position emphasized those more cerebral and "character" qualities like quarterback. Defying the stereotypes and prejudices, that barrier-breaking black quarterback, Sandy Stephens, led the University of Minnesota all the way to the national championship. Thus began a heyday for black athletes from the South who came to Minnesota to play football and basketball during the 1960s, when universities closer to home wanted no part of them. Carl Eller, Bobby Bell, and Charlie Sanders were among the African American young men who left the South for football opportunity in frozen Minnesota and, eventually, stardom in the NFL. Eventual pro basketball stars Lou Hudson and Archie Clark beat a similar path to Minnesota in the same decade.

Dungy was not from the South—he grew up in Jackson, Michigan, the son of two teachers—but it was Sandy Stephens' path that he followed to the playing field of Minnesota's Memorial Stadium. An option quarterback known for his heady playing style and dedication to film-study of opponents before games, Dungy passed and ran his way to record-breaking yardage totals while leading a Gophers football resurgence. When he ended his collegiate playing career in 1976, Dungy was fourth in total offense in Big Ten Conference history.

Pro football was next for Dungy. Like Warren Moon, a black quarterback from the University of Washington entering pro football around the same time, Dungy was asked to give up quarterbacking and devote his talent to defense. Unlike Moon, who chose instead to play quarterback in the Canadian Football League, Dungy accepted his reassignment to the lower-profile position of defensive back, and he went on to have a brief three-year career, primarily with the Pittsburgh Steelers. Cut by the New York Giants prior to the 1980 season, realizing that no amount of intelligence and preparation could make up for his lack of NFL-caliber speed, Dungy retired as a player. Coaching, he decided, was his true calling.

From his starting point as an assistant coach at his alma mater, and then as an assistant to Steelers head coach Chuck Noll, Dungy began his ascent through the pro football coaching ranks. Through the mid-1980s, Dungy served as defensive coordinator of the Steelers, the first black man to hold the defensive coordinator title in the NFL. Dungy's reputation grew with the achievement of his defensive unit, known for savvy play, over-achieving, and penchant for creating turnovers. It appeared far from certain, however, that Dungy's rise in the profession would lead to a coveted head coach position. In fact, at that time, the league had no black coaches, had indeed never had a black coach.

Was it his quiet demeanor, which some executives thought unbecoming a head coach in the NFL? His relative youth? His race? Whatever the reason, Dungy met with disappointment when he attempted to parlay his success as the Steelers's defensive coordinator into a head coaching job. In fact, his career took a downward turn just around the time pro football got its first African American coach. Following the 1988 season, Dungy accepted a demotion of sorts, leaving Pittsburgh for Kansas City and a job as the Chiefs' defensive backs coach. The league did achieve a race milestone when the Oakland Raiders hired a retired black player as its head coach. The honor went not to Dungy, but to Art Shell.

But Dungy was far from finished. After three years in Kansas City, he became a defensive coordinator again, this time with the Minnesota Vikings. The unit excelled as his Steelers unit had, ranking No. 1 in the league one season under his direction, and Dungy's name begin surfacing as a head coaching candidate. His opportunity finally arrived when the Tampa Bay Buccaneers—the laughing stock of the NFL through most of their history—named Dungy their head coach in 1996.

From his first season as a head coach in 1997, through to his ascension to the Super Bowl throne ten years later, Dungy stood apart from other coaches for his demeanor. Not a "screamer" like many of his fellows in the head coach ranks, Dungy earned a reputation for carrying himself and treating his players with a quiet dignity. Coaching "the Lord's way," as he would describe it, meant eschewing the shouting and challenging of players' manhood that characterizes the approach of many NFL head coaches. Dungy told one journalist that his Christian faith helped him maintain his unusually serene demeanor in the storm of emotion, drama, and testosterone that characterizes life in professional football. Part of it, he explained, was "realizing that there are things you might not ever understand and a lot of things you won't be able to control, so worrying about those things and getting frustrated is not fruitful."[27]

Dungy got instant results. His Buccaneers, already on the way up before his arrival, won their first five games in 1997. They not only made the post-season but won their opening-round playoff game before being eliminated by Green Bay in the conference semifinals.

More playoff appearances would follow. In his six years in Tampa Bay, Dungy took the team to the post-season four times and won a division title. Yet the Bucs' failure to reach the Super Bowl started to rankle Buccaneers fans and management, as did a conservative, defensive-oriented team personality that, to critics, lacked imagination. Were the Dungy-era Buccaneers *too much* a reflection of a coach who cut his coaching teeth on the defensive side and who, for all the virtues of decency and levelheadedness, possessed little in the way of flair or dynamism?

Tampa Bay ownership fired Dungy after the Buccaneers absorbed a playoff drubbing by Philadelphia to bring his sixth season to a close. Dungy told journalists that he questioned whether he wanted to remain a pro coach. He considered other career paths, including prison ministry. But when Indianapolis president Bill Polian gave him the chance to become head coach of the Colts, Dungy seized it. His taking the coaching reins in Indianapolis set up an intriguing scenario: How would the conservative defensive mastermind Dungy fare as the coach of the offensive-minded Colts and their superstar quarterback, Peyton Manning?

Very successfully, actually, the results suggesting that the moribund offense of the Dungy-era Buccaneers probably owed more to a lack of talent on that side of the ball than any coaching deficiencies. Indianapolis went 10-6 and reached the playoffs in Dungy's first season and took off from there, winning division titles the next four seasons with at least twelve regular season wins each year. By the time Dungy completed his Super Bowl season, he possessed an overall coaching record of 123-70 (114-62 in regular-season games), his .648 regular season winning percentage the best among active NFL coaches with at least fifty regular season victories.

The accolades about Dungy's character piled up like his victories, often with a religious flavor. As Colts punter, and devout Christian, Hunter Smith put it, "This is the way a Christian man should coach a team. I believe it's the way Jesus would coach a team."[28]

"The Lord's way." That's how Dungy described his coaching and his team's path to success, and he would soon use the term to justify his divisive entry into a political squabble in Indiana over gay rights.

A month after the Super Bowl triumph, Dungy and his wife, Lauren, strode to the podium in an Indiana ballroom to accept an award from the Indiana Family Institute. At the time of the event, the IFI was entrenched in a political battle to amend the state constitution to ban same-sex marriage. Dungy's very presence at the banquet was tacit approval of the organization and its political agenda. Would Dungy *explicitly* endorse the IFI's battle against gay rights?

Introducing the coach and his wife, Jim Freeman, vice president of the OneAmerica corporation (an IFI sponsor), hailed the Dungys for their Christian commitment and community service. Freeman cited Dungy's founding of the good-parenting group All Pro Dads and his support for numerous organizations including Mentors for Life, Big Brothers and Sisters, the Fellowship of Christian Athletes, and Athletes in Action. IFI President Curt Smith greeted the Dungys at the podium and presented them a framed page from an original King James Bible. The page was from John 9, which tells the story of Jesus restoring sight to a blind man.

With his wife looking on, Dungy warmed up the crowd with tales from the locker room and bits of self-deprecating humor. After arriving as the new coach of the Colts, he explained, he made it his first priority to establish a "family atmosphere" at team headquarters. "The first thing I did," he said, "is talk with the chaplain of the team. I said, 'I want you to come in and visit with me. I want us to see how we're going to map out this discipleship program.' We talked about how we're going to get Bible studies set up, how we'd run our chapel program, how I wanted him to minister to our team."

The coach then reflected on his own childhood in Jackson, Michigan, and his relationship with his now-deceased parents. By virtue of having summers off, his schoolteaching father had plenty of time to spend with his son, Dungy said—time for fishing, playing catch, shooting baskets. He acknowledged one of his own regrets as a parent. "I haven't got to spend as much time with my kids as my dad spent with me." There was an unspoken poignancy about the comment. As was known by most of the crowd, one of Dungy's children had committed suicide the year before at the age of eighteen.

"I want to finish by saying one thing," Dungy continued, working up to the pay-off moment. "There's been a little publicity about my coming here. There are some people who would really like me to say, 'Thank you . . . but the views of the IFI don't necessarily reflect my personal views.' A lot of people would love to hear me say that. They don't know me very well." Applause broke out.

"And they don't know that that's not the way I operate," Dungy said. "But there are some people who try to take one issue, of all the great things IFI is doing. They try to take one issue and spotlight that and say, 'Which side are you on?'"

By way of answering that question—and answering it emphatically—Dungy summoned a story from the Old Testament, a passage in which Joshua beholds a figure standing over him with a drawn sword. Joshua asks, in the King James translation: "Art thou for us, or for our adversaries?" Neither, replies the angel. Or, in Dungy's telling, "'I'm on the Lord's side.'"

"That," Dungy concluded, "is what I feel like telling people when they look at this issue of same-sex marriage. I'm not on anybody's side. I'm on the *Lord's* side." More applause erupted in the banquet room. "Because IFI is saying what the Lord says, you can take that and make your decision which way you want to be. I'm on the Lord's side. And I appreciate IFI for the stance they're taking, and I embrace that stance.

"Family is important, and that's what we're trying to support. We're not anti-anything else and not trying to hate anyone else. We're trying to promote the family, family values, the Lord's way. Just like I'm trying to win on the football field the Lord's way. I'm on the Lord's side when I'm on the field, and on the Lord's side when I'm off the field."[29]

Later, Ryan McCann, IFI's director of operations and public policy, said the group had not expected Dungy to endorse its political campaign against gay marriage and was quite pleased just to have him speak. His endorsement of IFI's campaign, McCann said in an interview, "was a surprise to us. We were ecstatic."[30]

Thus did Dungy complete his journey to the confluence of two powerful currents in American culture: pro sports and the politics of the Christian Right. Drenched in football championship glory, he had become a champion of the Christian social-conservative agenda and had stood up decisively for one of its pet causes, the fight against homosexual rights.

The rights and wrongs of it were a complex affair, and anyone's opinion of Dungy's decisions had everything to do with the political and cultural proclivities of the beholder.

On one hand, here was a decent and dignified man, by all accounts morally upstanding, an African American who had individually overcome race barriers for three decades by playing the white man's position of quarterback in college and, later, by making an even deeper foray into the inner white house of power by becoming one of the first black head coaches in the NFL. More stirring still, Dungy had not only become an NFL head coach, but had won the Super Bowl. As Dungy put it on the victory dais in Miami, it meant "an awful lot" to our country.

On the other hand, Dungy was also this: A wealthy man draped in evangelical Christianity who, in the eyes of many concerned about race, had forsaken his racial consciousness and squandered a tremendous opportunity to call public attention to the systemic racism plaguing millions of black people in America. To those supportive of gay rights, Dungy had done something worse than blowing an opportunity: He had deliberately taken action to *oppose* the expansion of equality.

As stated, these matters are never simple, never black and white. To Dungy's credit, his volunteer work in such areas as responsible fatherhood and prison ministry—which he has taken to even higher levels of commitment and distinction since his retirement as a coach in 2009—surely contribute to improving the lives and circumstances of many Americans, whatever their race. And his opposition to same-sex marriage is hardly a radical departure from the mainstream

of African American churches, which have a tradition of conservatism on social issues running alongside their more liberal stances on economic affairs.

Yet unlike many prominent African American Christians of a previous
generation, Dungy has had little to say about racial oppression and the politics behind it. By remaining mute, he has made it easier for the largely white
power structures of the sports world, and of the country at large, to convince
themselves that race in America is a solved problem. In so doing, he has helped
empower a status quo that blocks deeper progress toward equity.

Tony Dungy, like so many other Christian sports figures from the African
American community, has made important choices during his gradual passage to massive white approval. He has foregone anything that might raise a
prophetic challenge to the conservative powers that be. He has cloaked himself
in a politically domesticated evangelical Christianity that finds favor with the
mostly white men who run professional sports and society.

And what of the characteristics and commitments that Michael Eric Dyson
calls "the racial marks and the ethnic identities that have nurtured and sustained black people for a long time"?

In choosing what he calls "the Lord's side," Tony Dungy, and most of the
other black Christians who have made it in professional sports this generation,
have checked them at the door.

Notes

1. Bigger Thomas is the protagonist in Richard Wright's seminal novel *Native Son*
(New York: Harper, 1940).

2. Roger Goodell, remarks following Super Bowl XLI, February 4, 2007, as seen on
CBS television.

3. Jim Irsay, remarks following Super Bowl XLI, February 4, 2007, as seen on CBS
television.

4. Irsay, remarks, February 4, 2007.

5. Richard Land, "Faith by Example—Dungy, Smith," *Christian Post* (Nashville edition),
February 10, 2007, http://nashville.christianpost.com/article/editorial/128/section/
faith.by.example.%96.-dungy.smith/1.htm.

6. Sarah Braunstein, "Discriminating Choice: Tony Dungy's Missed Opportunity,"
Bleacher Report, February 7, 2007, http://bleacherreport.com/articles/707-Discriminating
-Choice-Tony-Dungy-s-Missed-Opportunity-070207.

7. Amy Bass, *Not the Triumph but the Struggle: The 1968 Olympics and the Making of the
Black Athlete* (Minneapolis: University of Minnesota, 2002), 240-247.

8. Gale Sayers with Al Silverman, *I Am Third* (New York: Bantam, 1970), 225.

9. Arnold Rampersad, *Jackie Robinson: A Biography* (New York: Ballantine, 1997),
52-54.

10. For an illuminating interpretation of Jesus' turn-the-other-cheek message as an act of nonviolent resistance, see Marcus Borg, *Jesus: Uncovering the Life, Teaching, and Relevance of a Religious Revolutionary* (New York: Harper Collins, 2006), 248-49.

11. Rampersad, *Jackie Robinson*, 445.

12. John Dodderidge, "An Ambassador to (sic) the Kingdom," *Sharing the Victory*, December 2002, 6-9.

13. John Dodderidge, "An Ambassador to (sic) the Kingdom," Sharing the Victory, December 2002, 6-9.

14. Robert Booth Fowler and Allen D. Hertzke, *Religion and Politics in America: Faith, Culture, and Strategic Choices* (Boulder, Co: Westview Press, [1995], 2004), 157, 160.

15. Jacqueline S. Mattis, "Religion and African American Political Life," *Political Psychology* 22, issue 2 (2001): 267-71.

16. Michael Eric Dyson, *Open Mike: Reflections on Philosophy, Race, Sex, Culture and Religion* (New York: Basic Civitas Books, 2003), 317.

17. Dyson, *Open Mike*, 316-18.

18. "Status and Trends in the Education of Blacks," a report by the National Center for Education Statistics, September 2003, available online at http://nces.ed.gov/pubsearch/pubsinfo.asp?pubid=2003034.

19. Gail Russell Chaddock, "U.S. Notches World's Highest Incarceration Rate," *Christian Science Monitor*, August 18, 2003.

20. William Rhoden, *Forty Million Dollar Slaves: The Rise, Fall, and Redemption of the Black Athlete* (New York: Random House, 2007), 177-78.

21. Tom Krattenmaker, "Going Long for Jesus," *Salon*, May 10, 2006, http://www.salon.com/news/feature/2006/05/10/ministries/index.html.

22. Scoop Jackson, "Yes, There Are Heroes in Sports," ESPN.com, August 20, 2007, http://sports.espn.go.com/espn/page2/story?page=jackson/070816.

23. Dyson, *Open Mike*, 291.

24. Mike Freeman, "McNabb on the Money: Black QBs Have to be Twice as Good," CBSSports.com, September 18, 2007, http://www.cbssports.com/print/columns/story/10359541/2.

25. Dan Steinberg, "Jason Campbell on McNabb's Comments," D.C. Sports Blog, published at Washington Post website, September 19, 2007, http://voices.washingtonpost.com/dcsportsbog/2007/09/jason_campbell_on_mcnabbs_comm.html.

26. "McNabb Sticks to His Guns about Race Remarks," Associated Press, September 19, 2007, http://nbcsports.msnbc.com/id/20835710/.

27. Tony Dungy biography, published by Gale e-research and publishing, at http://www.gale.cengage.com/-free_resources/bhm/bio/dungy_t.htm.

28. Art Stricklin, "Tony Dungy Voices the Pain and Lessons from His Son's Suicide," *Baptist Press*, February 3, 2006.

29. Tony Dungy, remarks at the "Friend of the Family" banquet of the Indiana Family Institute (IFI), March 20, 2007, Indianapolis, Indiana. The author based the material on a video recording of the event provided by IFI.

30. Ryan McCann, e-mail exchange March 2007.

CHAPTER 9

~

A Match Made in Heaven–or Hell

The Dissonance between the Values of Jesus and the
Values of Big-Time Sports

If you ain't cheatin', you ain't tryin'.

—an old saying in sports

At the apex of his college football coaching career, Bill McCartney led the University of Colorado Buffaloes to a share of the national championship. But college football was not the only venue in which "Coach Mac" led men as mentor, commander, and inspirational force. In 1990, the same year Colorado reached the pinnacle of sports success, McCartney launched an organization that would make him "coach" to a massive swath of the American male population.

As founder and leader of Promise Keepers, a Christian men's organization that attracted hundreds of thousands of participants and followers, McCartney became a pre-eminent–and polarizing–religious and moral leader. His call to men to live up to their responsibilities as fathers and husbands, to live by their word and reconcile with one another across racial barriers, had a unifying, uplifting appeal, and helped transform numerous lives for the better. McCartney's conservative stances on social issues also made him highly suspect in the eyes of progressives and secularists. Feminists vigorously objected to his teachings about gender roles, which deemed males the masters of their households. His outspoken opposition to abortion and homosexuality rankled, as did his requirement that all his players join in pre-game prayers, which was successfully challenged by the American Civil Liberties Union.[1]

According to the founding philosophy of Promise Keepers, men of God had seven promises to keep: honoring Christ through obedience to God's word; forming vital relationships with other men; maintaining spiritual, moral, ethical, and sexual purity; building strong marriages through biblical values; supporting the mission of one's church; overcoming "racial or denominational barriers" to achieve biblical unity; and obeying the New Testament's Great Commission; that is, "make disciples of all nations." In founding the organization, McCartney "was imagining a revival among Christian men who were willing to take a stand for God in their marriages, families, churches, and communities," according to the organization's literature.[2] A revival there was, with annual Promise Keepers rallies filling football stadiums, and with its "Stand in the Gap" rally on the National Mall in Washington, D.C., attracting one of the largest crowds ever assembled in that space.[3]

The dictionary definition of "integrity," McCartney once explained, was the origin of his movement's memorable name. "Way back before Promise Keepers had a name, we looked up the word 'integrity' in Webster's Dictionary," McCartney recalled. "[It] gave six definitions: 'utter sincerity, honesty, candor, not artificial, not shallow, no empty promises.'"[4]

Highly successful as a college football coach and as an ambassador for a masculine brand of evangelical faith, McCartney stood precisely at the confluence of high-profile spectator sports and popular evangelical Christianity. Even those who might argue with his theology and political conservatism had to concede his constructive influence, his calling innumerable men back to their commitments to their wives, families, and communities, and his rare ability to appeal across racial divides. If his persona suggested rigidity, he showed heart and compassion, too, eventually accepting into his graces and affections the dying young man who had earlier impregnated McCartney's daughter.[5] In many ways, Bill McCartney seemed the very model of how faith and sports harmonized with one another. Unfortunately for his legacy, he has also come to represent the unmistakable disharmony that also exists between Christianity and sports, and the price that pursuit of victory can often exact from the possession that McCartney and his Promise Keepers valued most: their integrity.

Colorado was in the running for the national championship in the fall of 1990, its title hopes in the balance with the clock draining and the Buffaloes locked in a tight game with Missouri. Trailing 31-27 with less than a minute to play, Colorado found itself inside the Tigers' 10-yard line, in position of the ball and in prime position for the winning touchdown. That's when the confusion began. The officials failed to flip the down marker after Colorado's Eric Bieniemy was stopped short of the goal line on second down, which made all the difference two plays later after the Buffaloes' quarterback spiked the ball to stop the clock on what *should* have been the fourth and final down. Instead of losing possession and their fondest championship aspirations, McCartney's

Buffaloes received the strangest of football blessings: a fifth down. Colorado seized the opportunity, scoring the touchdown and winning the game.

As the game and conference officials sorted out the mess in the hours and days after the final gun, an eerie coincidence hung over the proceedings and the quickly ensuing ethics debate. As the religion scholars Tony Ladd and James Mathisen astutely note in their book *Muscular Christianity*, it was the fiftieth anniversary year of a similar fifth-down episode involving a national power from the Ivy League; officials' inadvertent gift of a fifth down had helped Cornell defeat Dartmouth 7-3 and continue its impressive 18-game undefeated streak—until, that is, Cornell's coach and president followed their consciences and, three days later, forfeited the victory.[6] Would McCartney do the same as the pressure bore down in the aftermath of the Buffaloes' fifth-down triumph?

The Colorado coach, joined by university president William Baughn, stood firm, refusing to forfeit the game. Initially, the coach rationalized the acceptance of that crucial fifth down by citing the slippery conditions of Missouri's field. "We slipped and slid all day," he said, "or we would have put more points on the board." Later, in a television interview, McCartney invoked the Bible in justifying the win. "I have to answer to my team. I can't answer to everybody out there. And there is a verse in Scripture—it's 1 Corinthians 4:4—and it says, 'My conscience is clear, but that does not make me innocent. It is the Lord who judges me.' And, you see, only the Lord can judge a man's innermost thoughts."[7] Colorado went on to win its remaining games and the Associated Press poll for the national title. (The rival Coaches Poll declared Georgia Tech the winner, taking some of the shine off the Buffaloes' championship.)

McCartney's suggestion that he had to "answer to my team" reveals much about the sports world values that drove his decision. The coach had a point: Imagine the heartbreak, anger, and frustration his players and the fans would have felt had he given back the victory and, with it, any hope of the holy grail of the national championship. After all, victory is the overarching objective in major collegiate and professional sports, the organizing principle, the imperative that supersedes fair play, fidelity to the rules, the aesthetic quality of the performance, and, most poignant for McCartney, the maintenance of one's integrity. Unfair fifth down or not, Colorado had won within the framework of the game as administered by the officials. Clearly, it was not McCartney's or his players' fault that the officials committed a colossal blunder. From the perspective of sports values, McCartney had done what anyone would do.

As suggested by McCartney's biblical verse, observers cannot know what is inside a man's heart. Judging from McCartney's later action, however, one can make the educated guess that his heart became the site of considerable conflict and turmoil following the infamous game. In 1998, more than three years after his retirement as the Buffaloes' coach, at a Promise Keepers event in the same Missouri city where the Buffaloes had received the ethically challenged fifth down, the ex-coach admitted he was "truly remorseful" about the episode.[8]

Perhaps it was fitting that this champion of integrity needed three years' separation from the coaching profession before he could clear his conscience and acknowledge the lack of integrity he had displayed in that championship run in 1990. Resisting the call of sports world values is no easy thing, even for the most religiously and ethically rigorous among us. And even for deeply Christian leaders who stake their claim with character and integrity.

*

Listening to evangelical ministries and athletes can easily leave one with the impression that, together, Christianity and big-time sports create a sweet harmony. As onetime NFL superstar (and Christian) Deion Sanders philosophized, faith and sports go together like peanut butter and jelly.[9] The eagerness with which evangelicalism has embraced the world of big-money baseball, football, and basketball suggests that Christianity finds its natural expression on the professional diamond, gridiron, and court—and that the better one performs at sports, the better qualified one is to represent Christianity. Thus, the notion so frequently articulated by pious players that God elevated them to athletic stardom so that they might proclaim the Lord's truth from the sports mountaintop. That they play so they might pray—for the cameras.

"The language of victory in sports is identical to the Christian faith," says Pat Williams, the Orlando Magic executive and longtime leader of the Christianity campaign in pro sports. "Think about what it takes to be a great athlete: discipline, hard work, sacrifice, selflessness, teamwork, respect, trust, loyalty, humility, influence. All those words cross right over. The athlete understands that language. The two worlds fit together."[10]

Certainly, religion and professional sports demonstrate some degree of surface convergence. The character traits traditionally emphasized by the church, as Williams observes, are often the same as those drilled into players by the coach: hard work, selflessness, teamwork, and perseverance, not to mention obedience to a higher authority, whether that is God or team management. Calvinism, the school of Christian thought that casts its large shadow over popular theology in America, holds that one's material success is indicative of good Christian living and God's favor, with obvious implications for society's "losers." In accommodating the capitalist, get-ahead ethic, this popular theology creates a large swath of common territory for religion and the philosophy of today's religious athletes, who often imply—and even outright declare—that God himself willed their success and the copious material benefits accruing thereto.

If God loves sports, it is probably only natural that churches do, too. A far cry from the day when preachers frequently objected to sports on Sunday and, before that, when they viewed sports as something of a devil's workshop, churches today generally accommodate sports, even bless them. They move service times to accommodate football-viewing; some even host Super Bowl parties, seeming to elevate pro football to a level of cosmic significance a 1950s fan could scarcely have imagined. Some ministries go a step beyond merely accommodating Sunday sports. They encourage members to host evangelistic Super Bowl home viewing parties, where they can gather their unconverted or wavering friends and use the break between halves to show a special ministry-supplied video and share their faith in Jesus.

Perhaps what all of this suggests is that evangelical Christianity and sports share one trait above all others: They both are big in American culture and ever intent on getting bigger.

Those of Pat Williams' viewpoint can accurately cite a list of traits shared by sports and Christianity. But to describe the two as thoroughly compatible amounts to spin or, worse yet, astonishing blindness to fundamental characteristics of pro sports and Christianity that are seldom acknowledged by those bringing faith to our stadiums and arenas. Do Christianity and pro sports go together like peanut butter and jelly? Or are they more like oil and water?

Consider some of the ways in which values of faith and values of sports create not a sweet harmony, but a grating dissonance.

*

Christianity projects an ethic of sharing, of compassion for the least powerful; sports, one of ruthless defeat of the opponent and glory to the victor.

One of the best-loved, most-told stories in the New Testament is the parable of the loaves and fishes, from John, chapter 6. Christians know the story well: Jesus finds himself with a large and hungry crowd of followers, numbering some five thousand, and no food to share with the multitude save for the five little barley loaves and two small fish possessed by a boy who has just been spotted by the disciple Andrew. How to resolve the issue of who gets lunch and who does not?

Consider how the enterprise of sports might resolve the matter. The sports world ethic is one of competition in which the strongest, or wiliest, competes for and wins the spoils. Think of how pro sports leagues are organized. Thirty teams vie for one prize, the championship—and there can be no sharing. One team experiences ultimate success; the others go home with varying degrees of disappointment and failure. Every game in sports has underneath it the same ethic of competing for a scarce resource: Two teams take the field; just one can win. In sports, we want our team to possess a "killer instinct" and dispatch the opponent without regard for the negative consequences it will suffer. As fans, we would be appalled if our team enjoyed a big lead in the game or the standings and then fell prey to compassion and let the opponent catch up. Or if the World Series champions, in the champagne-drenched locker room following the final out, decided they felt badly for the losers and forfeited the title. That is not how sports work, not how they *should* work.

Imagine the scene if Jesus were to have applied a sports model to his problem with the hungry multitude—if the meager supply of bread and fish had been doled out through some means of competition. Perhaps the wealthiest would simply have paid the most money, outbid the rest of the assembled throng, and taken possession of the food. Maybe the issue would have been resolved through physical strength; the toughest men there, perhaps the best-armed, would have used force or the threat of it to seize the barley loaves and fish. Popular jock theology often imagines Jesus as something of a sports lover. So perhaps God's son would have organized an athletic competition—a race, maybe, or discus-tossing— with the food conferred to the winner. Whatever the case, a sports model would require competition, a zero-sum battle for a scarce resource.

The Bible's resolution of the issue could not be more profoundly different. In the parable of the loaves and fishes there is no competition for the paltry supply of food. There is only sharing—sharing so profound that what appeared to be a pathetic shortage miraculously becomes an abundance, with enough bread and fish for all and much left over besides. Leave it to the enterprise of theology to explore the many nuances of the parable and its deeper meaning for living a Christian life. What seems beyond doubt, however, is that the loaves-and-fishes story teaches believers that God's salvation is universal, a "championship" granted to all who believe, not just those strong enough or powerful enough to out-do a rival for the eternal prize. Also irrefutably clear is that the Christian ethic, as expressed in the loaves-and-fishes parable, is one of compassion; it rejects competition for a finite prize and, through generosity, finds that somehow there is enough for all.

This is not to say sports are bad, but to demonstrate that, at their core, they operate according to rules and values radically different from central themes of the religion of Jesus.

*

Religion teaches morality; in sports, the message says: Cheat if you must, so long as you get away with it, and so long as you win.

Steve Courson was an offensive lineman for the Pittsburgh Steelers and Tampa Bay Buccaneers from 1978 to 1985. In his first two seasons with the mighty Steelers, Courson experienced the best the football life can give: the Super Bowl championship. But as Courson would later claim in the title of his book, it was all *False Glory*. He and many of his teammates were juiced on steroids, he revealed—a practice he said was known and tolerated by team management.[11] Ashamed of his involvement with steroids cheating, Courson dedicated himself after his playing career to pulling back the curtain, revealing the unethical practice inside NFL locker rooms, and persuading young athletes to resist the powerful temptation to get bigger, stronger, and faster through the wonders of chemistry.

But what made Courson especially unpopular in the pro football world (which essentially blackballed him) was his having the audacity to question what has long been held up as a sacrosanct truism: that big-time sports somehow inculcate character among the young men who play them. The *New York Times'* Jere Longman reflected on the since-deceased Courson and his message in a July 2007 article exploring the triple-threat scandals that had rocked the sports world that summer: The Michael Vick dog-fighting case; the assault on Henry Aaron's career home runs record by Barry Bonds, a God-saluting slugger widely perceived to be a steroids cheater; and an NBA referee's game-manipulation scandal.

Courson, Longman wrote, "said it was time to acknowledge that the values taught in youth sport bore no resemblance to the values of elite sport. He suggested that childhood values were ethical fungo drills, for practice only, not applicable between the lines of big-time sport, where athletes seek any edge they can get—from doping to stealing a catcher's signs—and it isn't considered cheating if you don't get caught."[12]

It wasn't long after the triple-crown scandals of the summer of 2007 that another massively publicized cheating incident afflicted the professional sports world. Bill Belichick, the brilliant, obsessive coach of the league's highest-achieving franchise, the New England Patriots, was outed for having his staff videotape the opponents' sidelines during games for the purpose of deciphering and stealing their play-calling signals. Let it not be said that Belichick (nicknamed the "Mad Monk" by some for his dour persona and habit of wearing a hooded sweatshirt during games) got off Scot-free. The NFL fined him $500,000 and nicked the team for an additional $250,000 and a pick in the next year's draft.[13]

Belichick's transgression was puzzling in a Nixon-Watergate way. Given his Patriots' superiority over the New York Jets team it was crushing that day, why would he go to the trouble, and incur the risk, of cheating? But what truly stood out in the endless debriefing by the columnists, TV analysts, sports-talk radio pontificators, and blogosphere sages was this truth about big-time spectator sports in our age. As the old saying goes: "If you ain't cheatin', you ain't tryin'." Perhaps fans share much of the blame because of our insistence that our teams give their ultrabest effort—more than 100 percent if possible—to thrill us with a victory. If it requires a little cheating, so be it. Sports world values, in other words, tolerate, even expect, a certain degree of cheating. Just don't get caught.

Religion? One need go no farther than the Ten Commandments—the foundational teachings of Christianity and Judaism—to learn what the Bible teaches about cheating, which is nothing if not a form of dishonesty: To quote the Ninth Commandment: "Thou shalt not bear false witness."

Of course, the Christian argument against cheating goes farther and deeper than the Decalogue. John White, a Christian scholar and the former sports ethics director for Athletes in Action, cites a long list of other Christian teachings and ideals that forbid cheating in sports and other walks of life: Jesus, whose model believers strive to follow, never cheated or lied in the Bible; in his Sermon on the Mount he stressed the imperative to "hunger and thirst for what is right" in relationships with other people, which would certainly include, White notes, one's athletic opponents; the call of the prophets to strive always for fairness and justice; and, finally, the deeper theological/philosophical imperative that calls on people to abide by the rules they believe are justified, and that they expect others to follow.[14]

One could go on. Suffice it to say that Christianity does not tolerate cheating. Even *if* it's the big game.

*

Sports, especially football, involve considerable violence; Jesus taught love and modeled nonviolence.

Love is hard to find in the following tale: Andre Waters was a 44-year-old man, the father of three children, who shot and killed himself in 2006, just three days before Thanksgiving. Waters had been one of the "lucky" ones. Against the long odds that face every American youth with his eye on the prize of a pro sports career, and the difficult hurdles that await an undrafted free agent trying to catch on with a team, Waters had made it in the NFL, playing a dozen seasons as a defensive back for the Eagles and Cardinals.

But in the end, it became clear that Waters had not been so thoroughly lucky. As a forensic pathologist discovered after Waters' suicide death, the retired footballer had brain damage so serious that his test results were similar to those of an Alzheimer's patient on the north side of eighty years old.[15] Waters' brain had been scrambled by repeated concussions, all the result of the blows to the head that are commonplace in the physical warfare that takes place on the fields of the NFL on any given Sunday.

What made the Waters revelations tough to shrug off were the larger, league-wide pattern to which they pointed. As the media reported as part of the

Waters coverage, a University of North Carolina study of former NFL players had discovered a direct link between the number of concussions sustained by a player and the incidence of diagnosed, clinical depression.[16]

Other stories similar to Waters' were surfacing, too. Freshly retired Patriots linebacker Patriot Ted Johnson went public with his post-retirement struggle, which found the onetime model citizen and player reduced to racking depression and erratic behavior—all the result, Johnson told the *Boston Globe*, of football concussions. "I've been dinged so many times," he said, "I've lost count." He accused team management of making his situation worse by rushing him back to the field after documented concussions.[17]

And there was the pathetic tale of Hall of Fame center Mike Webster. He played in the 1970s and 1980s, primarily for the Steelers, before the league limited the "head-slapping" that defensive linemen typically employed against centers (who were particularly vulnerable because the process of snapping the ball to the quarterback occupied their hands and thus limited their ability to ward off blows to their helmets). Before his death in 2002, Webster's life took a bad turn. Disabled by amnesia, depression, dementia, and acute bone and muscle pain, he could not keep a job or his wife, and he slept in his car and train stations despite offers by friends and former teammates to find housing for him.[18]

Leading Christian figures in sports rarely if ever publicly acknowledge the tension between their religious teachings and the often-brutal play that characterizes pro sports. But on this score, are the two spheres as compatible as the rhetoric might suggest? The folly of insisting "yes" is especially clear when attention turns to a pair of Christian football safeties, Donovin Darius and Rodney Harrison, who are well known for both their piety and their reputation for dangerous and/or dirty play.

Darius, then with the Jaguars, was fined $75,000 by the league in 2004 for administering a patently dangerous clothesline hit that temporarily paralyzed its recipient, Green Bay's Robert Ferguson.[19] This, from the same Donovin Darius who proudly told NFL Films not long before the incident, "This game provides a great platform—the greatest show on Earth! Anytime you can give God the glory . . . it's important. And if by celebrating [with religious gestures on the field]—something I've done—if that's a way to be a witness for God, that's what I'll do."[20] As skeptical observers must ask, was Darius' illegal and injurious hit on Ferguson part of his "witness for God?"

Those keen on leveraging Jesus-professing players for the advancement of the evangelical faith have to cringe when one of their vanguard is named the league's dirtiest player. That unflattering laurel has been bestowed upon Harrison via polls of both coaches and players in the league[21]—on the same Harrison who has spoken publicly and enthusiastically about his Christian faith. "Without my faith in the Lord, there is no way I would be here," Harrison told the press at the pre-Super Bowl media day in 2005. "I have to start my morning out right with devotion, prayer, and reading God's Word. I can't start my day without it. I pray about becoming a better dad, a better husband, a better person in Christ."[22]

Football is our most physically brutal sport, but basketball occasionally reveals a brutal side, too. No NBA incident was uglier than the sprawling melee that broke out at a Piston-Pacers game in 2004, with multiple players squaring off before Indiana's Ron Artest and Stephen Jackson went into the seats and began throwing roundhouse punches at Pistons fans. After the game was called with forty-six seconds left on the clock, the Detroit faithful drenched the Indiana contingent with drinks, ice, popcorn, and other debris as the Pacers scrambled off the court. An advertisement for religious virtue this was not.

Baseball has its share of fights, too. To be sure, they often amount to little more than dugout-emptying spectacles consisting of opposing players shoving and cursing. But those showy "brawls" are often an extension of more serious rough stuff that happens during the action: pitchers drilling batters with pitches, sometimes intentionally, and occasionally with devastating consequences if the head happens to be the part of the body absorbing the blow; and base runners barreling into the catcher at home plate or the fielder at second base to break up would-be double plays. It was in the context of the commonplace collision at second base that a Christian ballplayer once made an infamous remark about what Jesus would be like if he lived in our time. Fritz Peterson, a pitcher for the Yankees and two other clubs in the 1960s and 1970s, offered: "I firmly believe if Jesus Christ were sliding into second base, he would knock the second baseman into left-field to break up the double play."[23]

It might be difficult to find a serious theologian to vouch for Peterson's claim. The New Testament is full of instances in which Jesus chose the route not of physical confrontation, but of nonviolence. To cite just a few, Jesus instructed his followers to throw out conventional wisdom about "an eye for an eye, a tooth for a tooth." If slapped on the right cheek, he taught, one should not slap back—but should offer his left cheek as well. When Jesus was apprehended in the garden of Gethsemane, and a disciple attempted to resist by use of the sword, Jesus criticized him for resorting to violence—"All who live by the sword," he famously said, "shall die by the sword." Finally, in perhaps the greatest display of nonviolence imaginable, Jesus voluntarily submitted to his own execution.

None of this is to suggest that pro athletes should cease from going hard into second base or shy way from bone-crunching tackles on the football field, but only to remind us that professional sports are not—and shouldn't be—the purely Christ-like enterprise conjured by those who evangelize to and through sports. In significant ways, the deeds of our athletic warriors on and off the field are just the opposite.

*

Christianity teaches sexual and moral purity; the spectacle of pro sports is awash in beer and babes and, for the television-viewing throng, spiced with commercials for erection-inducing pharmaceuticals and numerous other less-than-virtuous products.

The hosts of those aforementioned come-to-Jesus Super Bowl parties had better be employing their TiVO or DVRs and viewing the game on a delayed basis so that they can fast-forward through the commercials. Otherwise, the would-be Christian converts attending these parties are being exposed not just to Jesus, but to an almost nonstop series of profane messages that clash with the message about faith and morality. Among the less-than-holy pitches: Succumb to materialism and buy this car or that TV. Have lots of sex—even if you're a bit older and need a pharmaceutical boost to rise to the occasion. Drive a bigger, more masculine (and more gas-guzzling) vehicle. Drink beer! Be selfish and stupid and place the refrigeration and consumption of said beer above petty concerns like the result of your wife's pregnancy test. (Yes, a Coors commercial was promoting precisely that for a time in an attempt at humor, prompting one to wonder about the brewing giant's commitment to the "family values" so often proclaimed by the conservative political movement to which the iconic Coors name is attached.)

The marriage between sports and crass sex-selling was consummated at the 2004 Super Bowl, the site of the infamous "wardrobe malfunction" that caused the baring of Janet Jackson's breast for the massive live television audience. Pious politicians and much of the public reeled in exaggerated horror, as though a woman's breast were a weapon of mass destruction, and NFL officials vowed to clean up their act. But sports can't seem to help themselves: It was just a year later that the web-hosting company GoDaddy.com riffed on the incident with a Super Bowl TV commercial featuring a well-endowed young woman in tight jeans and a skimpy tank top wiggling for a lineup of suit-wearing old men at a faux Senate indecency hearing.[24] Her top falls off, naturally, for the titillation of the harrumphing senators—and those of us in the viewing audience (who, alas, see only an indirect reference to the exposed body part).

The NFL voiced concerns about the migration of erectile dysfunction-remedy ads from a medically oriented sales pitch to a lifestyle message—from health to fun, in other words—and announced in 2006 it was distancing itself from such sales pitches.[25] But the fun-loving "E.D." commercials continued to run nearly nonstop on sports telecasts, none more blatant than the "Viva

Viagra" spots that prompted the AIDS Healthcare Foundation to allege that E.D. marketers were encouraging use of Viagra as a party drug.[26]

In view of the way pro football and basketball are staged, the heavy promotion of erection aids makes sense. After all, the older, largely affluent male fans who can afford NFL and NBA tickets might well need some assistance if they are to act on the stimulation provided by the cheerleaders and dance teams during breaks in the action. Be clear: These are not spirit-raising displays by the wholesome, sweater-clad cheerleaders of a more innocent age in sports, but highly sexualized performances by attractive young women whose outfits are as tight as they are skimpy.

The pro football spectacle is "sending a message all the time," says Irving Fryar, a longtime pro football receiver who became pastor of a Pentecostal church in New Jersey after his player career. "It's boobs and beer. It's the 'sex sells' message."[27]

Christian sports ministries certainly do not endorse the sex- and alcohol-peddling that are such a part of the pro sports spectacle, and in their work with individual players, and in their literature and teachings, they encourage morally pure living. Yet nowhere in the work and rhetoric of Christianity in sports can one find any sustained prophetic and public voice against these blatantly profane aspects of sports, or the profit orientation that is the underlying force behind each beer pitch, E.D. commercial, and titillating dance-team move. The ministries' public silence on the sports industry's promotion of skin and beer—and on the moneymaking motive behind it—does seem to signal their acceptance of the reality of the party-time and big-business aspects of professional sports, as well as a perception that sports ministry is neither obligated nor able to do anything about the situation.

Those in ministry have still more reason to remain quiet about the pro sports industry's inherent character flaws. For one, it stands to reason that ministries' privileged access to major league locker rooms and their inhabitants depends in part on their acquiescence to the basic premises of professional sports; ministry agents might justifiably fear the consequences of their mounting a serious critique of pro sports—consequences that could well include the loss of access they prize so highly. Also, the promoters of faith in sports depend on the games remaining basically what they are—including profane and morally tainted—lest they lose their ability to command the massive audiences the ministries want to reach.

Kevin Harvey, the Fellowship of Christian Athletes staff member and Philadelphia 76ers chaplain profiled earlier, seems to recognize the futility of doing more than working around the margins of the pro sports industry. "We talk at chapel," he said in an interview, "about how it is to be a follower of Christ in an environment that is anti-God in a lot of ways. We'll talk about how we have to be a part of the culture but can't allow culture to suck us in.

"It's not that we have to remain quiet [about irreligious aspects of the sports industry]," Harvey added. "There are just so many things in our culture these days that are not consistent with any faith. I always tell the guys they're not there to point out sin but to uplift Christ . . . expressing that there's a better way to live."

Harvey was asked about the likely consequences were he to approach Sixers' management with concerns about the deeply irreligious qualities of the staged spectacle of an NBA game. "I would be busy every day if I were pointing out all the injustices of society," he said. "That's not what we're called to do. The gospel teaches us that God's word is alive, that *God* changes hearts. It's our job to be faithful."[28]

Shirl Hoffman, an emeritus faculty member at the University of North Carolina–Greensboro and a leading scholar of the religion-sports relationship, likens the sports chaplains' approach to the traditional role of military chaplains. "Their role is not to question the war but to help the soldiers adapt to the war that they inevitably must fight," Hoffman says. "That's what you find with chaplains in sports. From the organization's standpoint the chaplains' job is to help athletes adapt to the pressures, ethos, and values that are presented to them on a daily basis—not to challenge them. You can't have soldiers question the value of the war. And you can't have an athlete, with the help of his team chaplain, challenge values of athletics.

"The value of sports for evangelizing," Hoffman adds, "hinges on them staying pretty much as they are." Don't expect the ministries to suggest any fundamental changes in big-time sports, Hoffman adds, like "reinventing them in form of the Sermon on the Mount. That would change sport in such a way that it would not be a commodity anymore. If it doesn't sell, you don't have the hook for your evangelization. There's a real conflict of interest. So the ministries have accepted that sports aren't going to change, and they're going to do what they can to work around the edges."[29]

The foregoing has touched upon some of the most conspicuously impure personality traits of professional sports. To the cheating, violence, materialism, hedonism, and the promoting of sex we could add gambling, which flourishes in and around professional sports, often in illegal form, at the same time that socially conservative Christians are frequently mounting political opposition to pro-gambling legislation. To this list of transgressions we could add pro sports' systemic "sins" of exploitation, such as wealthy owners virtually blackmailing communities to construct new stadiums on the taxpayers' dime, their devaluing of young men's educations and conventional (i.e., nonathletic) career preparation, and many more. But perhaps the most glaring of all these irreligious characteristics, and the one least frequently mentioned, is the mammoth *distraction* provided by pro sports—their availability as a means of diverting too much of our attention away from caring for our families, neighbors, churches, communities, nation, and world.

In their conceptions of God and games, the promoters of faith in pro sports generally take it for granted that Jesus would accept the basic premises of the athletic mega-industry, maybe even join in as another rugged competitor on the diamond, gridiron, or court. But is it not more likely that Jesus would challenge our obsession with our games? Perhaps he would call on the legions of fans to restore a proper perspective on pro sports, to reduce them to something other than the focal point of our spare time and the part of life where we look for our biggest thrills and deepest meaning. Perhaps he would fault us for pouring our time, energy, and resources into sporting spectacle, like so many Romans in our coliseums with our empire crumbling around us. Perhaps—just perhaps—he would do something even more radical and occasionally empty the stadium and arena and send the multitudes out to serve humanity.

As religion-in-sports scholar and critic Robert Higgs sees it, "You can't imagine Jesus up in a box seat. You can't do it."[30] You'd more likely find Jesus outside the stadium, says Higgins, coauthor of a book called *Unholy Alliance* that critiques the faith-sports relationship. You'd find Jesus not in the sky box or the suite with the well-stocked bar and wealthy wheeler-dealers, Higgs believes, but in the bad part of town, mingling with the outcasts, passing out food to the poor.

*

Sports, at their best, unite people—the players on a team and the members of the communities that host and support franchises. Evangelical Christianity, to degrees varying with the style of evangelizing, can be highly divisive.

When the management of baseball's Colorado Rockies went public in 2006 with their philosophy about building a faith-based major league baseball team, general manager Dan O'Dowd admitted some nervousness. "It's the first time we ever talked about these issues publicly," O'Dowd told *USA Today* while going on the record about the team's strategy of building the franchise on what it perceived to be foundational Christian principles. "The last thing we want to do is offend anyone because of our beliefs."[31]

Judging from their reticence on the subject following the appearance of the *USA Today* article and their later attempts to backpedal from a story they called overblown, O'Dowd and the rest of the Rockies organization regretted being so candid with the newspaper. The Rockies' nervousness about religion in the organization and the relative silence about it following the *USA Today* revelation are instructive. In truth, league and team managements in baseball, football, and basketball are generally loath to discuss the subject of religion in the game beyond a few platitudes about players' right to practice their religion. In the experience of this writer, executives and public relations officials from the franchises and league offices would prefer that the subject simply not come up, and their response to pointed questions and concerns is frequently to ignore them.

One case in point: Following the public flap over the Washington Nationals' chaplain and his apparent teaching that Jews go to hell, Bud Selig publicly expressed his dismay and promised a review of the matter—and then proceeded to pretend as though none of it ever happened, issuing not a single follow-up statement in the several seasons that followed, despite being repeatedly pressed for the outcome of his promised review.

Two years later, Selig's league raised eyebrows with its apparent editing of God-talk from the Rockies' Matt Holliday in a delicate context. The now-you-see-it, now-you-don't episode stemmed from the delirious, champagne-soaked clubhouse celebration of Colorado's extra-inning victory over San Diego in a one-game playoff for the right to advance to the post-season. The live edition of the Holliday interview, seen by the national television audience, included his thanking God for the victory and the season's many blessings. That Holliday would voice this religious gratitude was understandable given his Christian faith and the storybook quality of his team's rise from obscurity to stunning success. But there was something troubling about the story, too. Controversy clouded Holliday's game-winning run in the bottom of the thirteenth inning. Television replays made it appear that the young star had never touched home plate in his effort to elude the catcher's tag, prompting the *Los Angeles Times* to ask in the headline of a subsequent op-ed: "Bad call, or God's will?" As noticed by several sharp-eyed newspaper reporters, Holliday's religious comments were nowhere to be found on the version of the interview mounted on MLB.com—an editing decision that a league spokesman attributed to the need to provide information on the web in the "clearest and most concise way possible."[32]

Another example of management's wariness about religion involves the NBA's Milwaukee Bucks and their sharpshooter guard Michael Redd. Redd is a minister's son who talks about God as frequently and easily as breathing, working his faith into interviews without prompting. After watching Redd glorify God with particular zeal in one live post-game interview, I asked the team's media relations office for an opportunity to interview Redd about his faith and its application to his career. After several days came the obviously untrue reply that Redd considers his religious beliefs a private matter and would prefer not to discuss them with media members. But credit is owed to the Bucks' public relations people for at least having the courtesy to say "no." In almost every other instance, this writer's requests for comment from team and league officials have been ignored.

Why are those running pro sports so reluctant to talk about faith in the game? The reason, apparently, is their perception—a correct one—that evangelical Christianity is a touchy subject, one with the potential to stoke controversy and possibly repel a significant portion of the fan base. And that, of course, is because evangelical Christianity, at least in the form popularly practiced and promoted in American society in this era, can divide people as well as attract them. As the scholar Hoffman notes, people generally do not appreciate being informed, by declaration or implication, that their religious beliefs are deficient and likely to consign them to hell.

At the core of the conundrum is the reality that American society, despite survey data showing religion holding some sway over the vast majority of the population, is quite diverse on matters of faith. One-truth evangelical Christianity, despite the higher profile it has assumed in American culture and politics in recent decades, still claims only a sizeable minority of the population. Many among the nonevangelical majority—whose ranks include liberal and moderate Christians, followers of Judaism, Islam, and other faiths, and significant numbers of atheists and agnostics—resent to varying degrees the experience of watching sports only to be subjected to a form of Christianity that denies the validity of their own beliefs.

Just as evangelical Christianity can drive a wedge between teams and fans, so can it sometimes cause dissension on teams—an unfortunate situation for coaches intent on creating clubhouse unity. To be sure, dynamics around religion vary significantly from team to team and season to season, with many clubhouse cultures maintaining a religiously tolerant and inclusive atmosphere. Yet stories frequently circulate about Christianity becoming an issue that divides the men in a locker room.

John Feinstein's *Next Man Up* provides an inside look at the Baltimore Ravens' frustrating 2004 season, in which Baltimore began with Super Bowl aspirations and finished out of the playoffs at a disappointing 9-7. The Ravens dealt with numerous setbacks and bad breaks during season—injuries to key players, friction between coaches, subpar performances by players who management thought were ready to shine—and all of it under the keen eye of the veteran reporter/writer Feinstein, who was granted rare access to the inner workings of an NFL franchise.

One source of disagreement was religion; specifically, the direction it would take and under whose leadership. Two seasons earlier, one faction of Christian team members grew dissatisfied with team chaplain Rod Hairston, who was affiliated with Athletes in Action, and pushed to start a ministry under the leadership of a preacher from Champions for Christ. In the world of muscular Christianity, Champions for Christ is the steroids version of Christian minis-try, known for its aggressiveness and its fundamentalist theology. Hairston and the players supporting him—not exactly religious liberals—objected to Champi-ons for Christ being granted a piece of the action.[33]

The dispute eventually escalated to the office of coach Brian Billick, who sided with Hairston while expressing his annoyance at having to deal with the matter. As described by Feinstein, Billick is quietly religious himself and frequently collaborated with Hairston on subjects to address in the customary Saturday night fellowships, receiving an outline of Hairston's planned message each week and making his own suggestions. Billick told Feinstein, "Rod is the team chaplain. He works with me during the season, and I'm comfortable with the messages he's trying to send to the players. I certainly can't control what players do away from the facility. . . . But anything that was happening in our locker room . . . was going to go through Rod. But I told them if they couldn't all work together, I'd just abandon the whole thing completely. Religion should unite people, not divide them."[34]

A similar episode unfolded during the 2004 season when Deion Sanders, a superstar who had lived a glitzy, hedonistic life before finding Jesus, attempted to bring in a different speaker—the aforementioned Irving Fryar—for the Ra-vens' Saturday night fellowship. Again, friction with Hairston and, again, Bil-lick stepping in to back his team's official chaplain.[35]

Billick's comments reflect the headaches that religion can sometimes cause for team management despite the good it does in promoting individual moral-ity. That episode involved a disagreement between theologically conservative Christians and even *more* conservative Christians. There was also the friction between the believers and secular-leaning members of the team, a problem ex-acerbated by the ultrareligious personality of team leader Ray Lewis in his role as both a hard-hitting linebacker and no-holds-barred prayer leader.

Lewis' pray-as-you-play style has been captured several times by television crews that received his permission to "mic him up"—attach a small microphone to his uniform—and play back snippets of his banter. Via one such clip, the public is treated to a scene in which Lewis, while seated on the bench, exults after a fortunate turn of events for his team and gazes upward, exclaiming, "Thank you, Father, Jesus, another opportunity to show your *glory!*" Lewis appeared on the cover of *Sports Illustrated* in a prayerful, folded-hands pose next to the cover-story headline: "The Gospel According to Ray Lewis: God's linebacker."[36] Inside the magazine, Lewis is shown preaching at a church, and the accompanying article describes his practice of anointing some of his fellow defensive players before kickoff by tracing a cross on their foreheads with consecrated oil.

In *Next Man Up*, Feinstein recounts several scenes in which Lewis laces his pep talks to his teammates with religion. The problem was that not all team members were comfortable with Lewis' religiosity, which left them with a difficult decision: Go along with the fervent Christianity of the leader, or remain outside the team's inner circle? Star cornerback Chris McAlister chose the latter, and by season's end he was chirping with annoyance to the media about cliquishness on the team.[37]

To be fair, religion does not always or necessarily become an issue in locker rooms, even those with a critical mass of outspoken believers. For example, Robert Smith, an atheist and former Minnesota Vikings running back, said in an interview that team religious practices were never offensive to him during his time with Minnesota, from 1993 to 2000. Vikings leader Cris Carter, a devout Christian, voiced his religious exhortations in a friendly way that did not alienate his teammates, according to Smith. Then-coach Dennis Green brought in religious leaders whose messages and prayers were not explicitly or exclusively Christian. "Some players would make [religious] comments," recalls Smith, who retired at the relatively young age of twenty-eight and expressed deep skepticism about pro sports culture in a subsequent book, *The Rest of the Iceberg*. "With Cris Carter, it was more in a joking sense than overbearing. You know, 'You need to stay out of the nightclub and come to Bible study.' We had a diverse, interesting locker room, a lot of different philosophies and different types of characters. That's the way Denny designed it."[38]

But so, too, can religious practice cause friction and dissent, sometimes in even more dramatic fashion than that chronicled by Feinstein in his season with the Ravens.

For a time in major league baseball, outfielder Chad Curtis became notorious for his heavy-handed proselytizing. "If I have something that I believe is the truth and it's necessary for other people to come to some type of a recognition . . . of that truth, then I want to share it," Curtis once explained.[39] Curtis complained to ESPN that his preaching-the-one-truth style contributed to the Yankees' trading him to Texas following the 1999 season (which then-Yankees general manager Brian Cashman denied).[40]

Curtis took his sledgehammer evangelizing with him to Texas, where it caused trouble with some of his new teammates. When he confronted shortstop Royce Clayton about the music he was playing in the clubhouse, a heated argument ensued. Both players spoke about it with ESPN. Said Curtis: "There was a lot of foul language, and I'm a guy that just, you know, I don't really care to hear that and I know there's other guys that are the same way and we have

Notes

1. Michael Romano, "Conservatism is McCartney's Game," *Seattle Times*, February 16, 1992.

2. "History of Promise Keepers," published by Promise Keepers on the Internet at http://www.promisekeepers.org/about/pkhistory.

3. Linda Wheeler, "Unofficial Estimates Point to Crowded Day on the Mall," *Washington Post*, October 5, 1997.

4. "History of Promise Keepers," at PromiseKeepers.org.

5. For McCartney's own telling of the story of his and his daughter's relationship with Sal Aunese, see his autobiography, *From Ashes to Glory* (Nashville: Thomas Nelson, 1990), with Dave Diles.

6. Tony Ladd and James A. Mathisen, *Muscular Christianity: Evangelical Protestants and the Development of American Sport* (Grand Rapids, MI: Baker Books, 1999), 201.

7. Ladd and Mathisen, *Muscular Christianity*, 200–1.

8. Associated Press, "McCartney 'Remorseful' about Fifth-Down Play," Sports Illustrated/CNN Internet site, http://sportsillustrated.cnn.com/football/college/news/1998/06/20/mccartney_fifthdown.

9. Richard C. Crepeau, "Holy Touchdown!" PopPolitics.com, July 2001, http://www.poppolitics.com/-archives/2001/07/Holy-Touchdown.

10. Pat Williams, telephone interview conducted July 23, 2004.

11. Jon Saraceno, "Ex-Steeler Courson's Resolve against Steroids Still Echoes," *USA Today*, March 31, 2005.

12. Jere Longman, "The Deafening Roar of the Shrug," *New York Times*, July 29, 2007.

13. Judy Battista, "Sideline Spying: NFL Punishes Patriots' Taping," *New York Times*, September 14, 2007.

14. John White, then of Athletes in Action, extended interview conducted by phone and e-mail between October 2007 and June 2008.

15. "Pathologist Says Waters' Brain Tissue Had Deteriorated," ESPN.com, January 19, 2007, http://sports.espn.go.com/nfl/news/story?id=2734941.

16. Alan Schwartz, "Study of Ex-NFL Players Ties Concussion to Depression Risk," *New York Times*, May 31, 2007.

17. Jackie MacMullan, "Plagued by Post-Concussion Syndrome and Battling an Amphetamine Addiction, Former Patriots Linebacker Ted Johnson is a Shell of His Former Self," *Boston Globe*, February 2, 2007.

18. Greg Garber, "Wandering through the Fog," fourth installment of a five-part series on Mike Webster published at ESPN.com, January 27, 2005, http://sports.espn.go.com/nfl/news/story?id=1972288. See also Part One, Garber, "A Tormented Soul," at http://sports.espn.go.com/nfl/news/story?id=1972285.

19. United Press International, "Jaguars' Darius fined $75,000 for hit," December 21, 2004.

20. "Football & Religion," NFL Films, 2004.

21. See *Sports Illustrated* players poll, published October 12, 2004, at http://sports illustrated.cnn.com/-2004/players/10/12/poll.dirtiest/index.html and "Coaches Validate Harrison's Rep as NFL's Dirtiest Player," EPSN.com, July 1, 2008, http://sports.espn .go.com/nfl/columns/-story?columnist=sando_mike&id=3439800.

22. Joni B. Hannigan, "Football Provides a Platform for Patriots' Players," *Florida Baptist Witness*, February 10, 2005, http://www.floridabaptistwitness.com/3840.article.

23. Philip Yancey, *The Jesus I Never Knew*, (Grand Rapids, Michigan: Zondervan, 1995), 19.

24. The ad may be viewed at the GoDaddy web site at: http://www.godaddy.tv/ gdshop/media/-play.asp?isc=bpshdr001&mediaID=sb05&ci=11204&tab=sb.

25. Theresa Agovino, "NFL, Marketers of Erectile Dysfunction Drug Part Ways," *USA Today*, January 1, 2006.

26. Allison Linn, "Viva Viagra?" MSNBC.com, July 31, 2007, http://adblog.msnbc.msn .com/archive/-2007/07/31/298668.aspx.

27. Mark Moring, "Fumbling Religion? When it Comes to Christians and Churches, the NFL Doesn't Always Have a Good Game Plan," *Christianity Today*, September 11, 2007.

28. Kevin Harvey, series of interviews between from 2004 and 2006, initially begun May 11, 2004, Marlton, New Jersey.

29. Shirl Hoffman interview, telephone.

30. Andrea Adelson, "Debate Continues: What Place Does Religion Have in Sports?" *Orlando Sentinel*, February 24, 2008.

31. Bob Nightengale, "Baseball's Rockies Seek Revival on Two Levels," *USA Today*, June 1, 2006.

32. Vince Bzdek, "You've Gotta Have Faith? Colorado Rockies at Play in the Fields of the Lord," *Washington Post*, October 24, 2007.

33. John Feinstein, *Next Man Up: A Year Behind the Lines in Today's NFL* (New York, Boston: Little, Brown, and Company, 2005), 268–69.

34. Feinstein, *Next Man Up*, 269.

35. Feinstein, *Next Man Up*, 270.

36. *Sports Illustrated*, November 6, 2006.

37. Feinstein, *Next Man Up*, 468.

38. Tom Krattenmaker, "Going Long for Jesus," *Salon*, May 10, 2006, http://www .salon.com/news/feature/2006/05/10/ministries/index.html.

39. ESPN, "Outside the Lines," April 23, 2000, transcript available online at http:// sports.espn.go.com/-page2/tvlistings/show4transcript.html.

40. "Outside the Lines," April 23, 2000.

41. "Outside the Lines," April 23, 2000.

42. Shmuel Herzfeld, from a series of interviews held from 2005 to 2007, the first of which took place face-to-face at Ohev Shalom synagogue, Washington, D.C., November 2005.

43. Andrea Adelson, "Debate Continues: What Place Does Religion Have in Sports?" *Orlando Sentinel*, February 24, 2008.

CHAPTER 10

~

The Salvation of Sports

"Getting it Right" in an Emerging New Era of Faith in Sports

Objections to the shape of Christianity in professional sports might seem easy to dismiss when they are voiced by the usual (read: secular and liberal) critics. The concerns and the criticisms—the "Jon Kitna was sacked for your sins!" catcalls—might seem like fodder for the trash heap when they come, as they most often do, from the usual rogue's gallery of snarky comics, Internet loudmouths, and more-secular-than-thou sophisticates. But what if the "foul" were called by the man who probably did more than anyone to usher in this era of conspicuous Christian religiosity in pro sports? What if the questions were raised by the man lionized like none other for his Christian love toward his fellow football men, a man with an unparalleled talent for bringing down ball-carriers and quarterbacks, the man with a heart so big for his Christian faith, and a voice so ready to preach it, that he earned the moniker the "Minister of Defense"? Would the issues be worth considering then?

I could scarcely believe my ears when I first heard Reggie White disavowing most of what he stood for as the poster man for preaching from the sport star soapbox. Reggie White saying he had been "prostituted" by religious leaders looking to leverage his fame? Reggie White admitting it was just Reggie, not God, who decided he should leave Philadelphia and sign with Green Bay, contrary to what he'd said when he made the move back in 1993? Did Reggie White, the quarterback-sacking, thirteen-time Pro Bowler, the massive defensive lineman who seemingly saw every post-game interview as an opportunity to proclaim the get-Jesus message, really say that God didn't need football to make his presence known to the world? And that the spoon-fed faith that nourished him as an evangelizing player no longer satisfied—that following God wasn't about saying the right things, but *living* them?

He did.

Yet since White's "confession," Jesus' most visible representatives in pro sports have seemingly gone on as though it never happened. And White, sadly, has not been among us to raise his uniquely credible voice against those aspects of sports world Christianity in need of change. For as fate or God or his cardiac arrhythmia would have it, White died mere days after his change of heart became widely known to the sports-consuming world.

The revelation of White's new turn reached the airwaves in late 2004. The 43-year-old White, who had retired in 2000, appeared as an interview subject on an NFL Films program about religion in pro football. Among the remarkable revelations made by the contemplative, chastened Reggie White: "Sometimes when I look back on my life, there are a lot of things I said God said. I realize he didn't say nothing. It was what Reggie wanted to do. I do feel the Father . . . gave me some signals . . . but you won't hear me anymore saying God spoke to me about something—unless I read something in scripture and I know."

White also questioned a practice at the very heart of the Christianity in sports, one he did much to popularize: the perceived imperative for the star athlete to use his stature to spread the evangelical message. It was one of the foundational concepts motivating the formation of the Fellowship of Christian Athletes more than a half-century ago, and it remains a major thrust of athletic Christianity today, acted out every time a player points to the heavens after a touchdown or home run, credits God in an interview, or puts his fame to work in front of a church congregation or youth gathering. This star endorsement form of preaching, White suggested, was really more about celebrity worship than Jesus-following. "I was an entertainer," White said. "People seemed to want to be entertained rather than taught."

About the ministers and ministries keen on leveraging his fame, White made this incredibly blunt comment: "Really, in many respects I've been prostituted. Most people who wanted me to speak at their churches only asked me to speak because I played football, not because I was this great religious guy or this theologian. . . . I got caught up in some of that until I got older and I got sick of it.

"I've been a preacher for twenty-one years, preaching what somebody wrote or what I heard somebody else say. I was not a student of scripture. I came to the realization I'd become more of a motivational speaker than a teacher of the word.

"Maybe I was wrong," White continued. "I used to have people tell me, 'God has given you the ability to play football so you could tell the world about him.' Well, he doesn't need football to let the world know about him. When you look at the scriptures, you'll see that most of the prophets weren't popular guys. I came to the realization that what God needed from me more than anything is a way of living instead of the things I was saying. Now I know I've got to sit down and get it right."

In the final chapter of his life, White was doing something astonishing for a man who professed a deep dislike of reading: He was learning Hebrew from a Jewish scholar he had met on a trip to Israel. His aim: to study the Old Testament/ Hebrew Scripture in its original language. "I came to the realization," White said, "that if I'm going to find God, I'd better find him for myself."[1]

White's new direction was apparently not well received by all in the Christian community who had known and loved—and exploited?—the old Reggie. He told NFL Films that some Christians found his study of Hebrew objectionable and his searching attitude heretical. Some ministers, he said, warned other Christians to stay away from him. There was considerable confusion: Was he converting to Judaism and turning away from Christianity? In truth, White was not jettisoning Christianity—just, apparently, the simplistic practice and preaching of it that has become all too common in professional sports.

Those who disapproved of the new Reggie might have done well not to dismiss his new stance and message, but to listen and consider his point. They, and all of us with a stake in pro sports (and religion), would be well advised to take his cue and strive to "get it right"—to return to original sources, so to speak, and rescue a deeper understanding and application of faith from a culture of jock religion that has too often trivialized Christianity in its zeal to promote it, and that has too often narrowed it in ways harmful to the broader public interest. As White apparently came to realize, little justice is done to the Christian religion by victorious players chattering on camera about God-given football victories or by sports heroes who hit the church-world speaking circuit with little more than their celebrity and a pocketful of evangelism bromides, sports world metaphors, and ill-considered right-wing political ideas.

Days before White's posthumous induction into the Pro Football Hall of Fame in the summer of 2006, I opined in one of my *USA Today* columns that the football- and Jesus-loving public ought to remember all of Reggie's story, including his remarkable, albeit challenging, change of heart—which, as far as I could see, few had been doing since his untimely death. From the appearance of things, those in and around ministry were still invested in holding onto the Reggie White of his playing days and keen on acting as though his jarring disavowals and new way forward had never happened. It appeared that White's study of Hebrew, his observation that "God doesn't need football to let the world know about him," and his claim of being prostituted were the rhetorical equivalent of the crazy aunt or uncle who gets locked in a room upstairs when the family's company comes calling.

In that newspaper column, I noted that the occasion of White's Hall of Fame induction would be used to extol—appropriately so—Reggie's quarterback-sacking prowess, service to the community, love for his fellow players, and commitment to his family and Christian faith. "Amid the deserved praise that will pour forth in the speeches and media coverage," I wrote, "there probably won't be much, if anything, said about another important but less easily swallowed chapter of White's story—namely, his post-retirement disavowal of much of what he stood for as the Jesus-praising champion of jock evangelism."[2] The prediction proved correct. Perhaps understandably, those fondly remembering the fallen giant on the television and radio, and from the microphone at the induction ceremony in Canton, Ohio, skipped mentioning the final move of White's public career.

But that final move deserves attention. Reggie's parting shots may have been surprising, perhaps hard to process, but they were not shameful, and they hardly represented his going to the theological dark side. White had something important to say, and a unique vantage point from which to say it, on an issue that is far from settled—the appropriate role of religion in pro sports.

If anything, evangelical Christianity in our major professional leagues has become even more forceful and conspicuous, and the attendant issues more urgent, since White retired from the National Football League for good after the 2000 season. Baseball faith nights and faith days have arrived on the scene, first across the minor leagues, and now in the majors, raising a host of questions about the rights of nonevangelicals in the communities that support franchises. New stadiums—new venues for Christian evangelism in the minds of sports world faith promoters—have continued to rise on the taxpayers' dime while other public resources have too frequently gone neglected, and while America's religious diversity has continued to grow. Exercising a right born of sports' crucial antitrust exemptions, Congress has become more deeply involved in investigating pro sports' sins, as if to demonstrate that, yes, in a very real sense, the industry is responsible to the public.

Naturally, one needs to be careful not to superimpose his own politics and theology over Reggie White's disillusionment and change of heart; in truth, we don't know exactly where his journey would have taken him had premature death not cut him short. But his story does, at the very least, challenge us to rethink sports world Christianity. What if we were to take Reggie's cue and reimagine religion in pro sports? How, to use Reggie's term, might we "get it right"?

With those questions in mind, I traveled to the heart of evangelical sports ministry. And there, in Xenia, Ohio, at the headquarters of Athletes in Action (AIA), I was surprised to find a lot of people thinking in a not-so-dissimilar way.

*

My encounter with Athletes in Action began with a friendly e-mail from a man then serving as the ministry's director of sports ethics, John White. He had seen a newspaper column I'd cowritten about the tension between the values of Christianity and the values of big-time sports. He contacted me with an invitation to exchange views. I told myself that it was probably significant that White e-mailed not from AIA headquarters in Ohio, but from across the Atlantic Ocean in Scotland, where he was working on his Ph.D. at the University of Edinburgh. Maybe that time away from America had changed his perspective, I told myself, and led to his wanting to engage me, the nonevangelical writer and sometime critic of religion in sports, in an open-minded dialogue about greater possibilities for Christian sports ministry. In any event, I was surprised by White. I had harbored some unflattering stereotypes about evangelicals in and around sports: their (supposed) intolerance of those not subscribing to their religious and political beliefs, their (supposedly) closed minds, their (supposedly) unquestioning acquiescence to big business and Republican values and complete lack of interest in conversation with someone from outside their camp. John White seemed to defy those stereotypes with everything he said.

As I came to learn more about White's background—his career as a highly scrupulous drug-free competitor in the doping-plagued sport of cycling, his perception-altering ministry experiences on the campus of a historically black college and in Europe, and his academic writings on sport culture's "idolatrous" fixation on winning—I realized I had to set aside my preconception that all Athletes in Action missionaries were close-minded apologists for the conservative status quo in sports and society. Here was a deep-thinking man who was interested in reform and open to new ways of conceiving of faith in sports.

White put me in touch with his colleague Ed Uszynski, who had been serving as director of AIA's ministry training center and was in the midst of fashioning a new position at the ministry that would allow him to publicly address ethical and moral issues in the game. It turned out White was not alone; Uszynski, too, expressed to me dissatisfaction with aspects of Christianity in sports and with his own ministry's impact on sports' character flaws.

Through a series of telephone and e-mail exchanges, Uszynski and I developed a measure of mutual understanding and trust. Out of that was hatched an idea that I would have dismissed as impossible a few weeks before. This progressive-leaning religion columnist from the People's Republic of Portland, the nonevangelical who was on the record with various critiques of evangelical engagement with sports, would make a pilgrimage of sorts. I would travel to Xenia, Ohio, and spend two days with Ed Uszynski and company on the campus of Athletes in Action.

*

Norman Rockwell. The late artist's wholesome Americana seemed alive and right in front of me as I drove down Xenia's main strip and found my way, just blocks from downtown, to Home Avenue and the rolling campus of the Legacy Center, a complex of Christian organizations occupying the large site of what used to be a state-run orphanage and, later, a juvenile detention center. Families were sledding on the remnants of a recent blizzard on a steep grade near the center entrance. Driving in, I passed a series of large banners bearing biblical verses, then a small Christian school, and, off in the distance, a complex of snow-covered athletic fields, before pulling into a parking spot alongside the AIA headquarters building—named, fittingly, for the famed Campus Crusade founder and leader, the late Bill Bright.

A town of forlorn stone and brick buildings, Xenia sits east of Dayton in southern Ohio. It has a middle-of-nowhere feel, but looks can be deceiving. Xenia is barely an hour's drive from Columbus, the site of a college football juggernaut known as *the* Ohio State University, and a mere sixty miles from Paul Brown Stadium in downtown Cincinnati, the home of the NFL's Cincinnati Bengals.

Xenia, by virtue of its location in Ohio, has been very much at the center of things politically as well. A key state in the 2000 and 2004 presidential elections, Ohio, like the nation itself, was very closely and contentiously divided between the red and the blue, Republican and Democratic, conservative and liberal, and a state with a muscular Christian Right presence. Ken Blackwell, a conservative Christian who had since moved on and joined the staff of Tony Perkins' Family Research Council, had served as Ohio secretary of state from 1998 to 2006 before an unsuccessful run for governor as the first African American ever to receive a major party nomination for that high Ohio office. To many progressive Americans caught up in the political and cultural warfare of the decade, Blackwell was emblematic of much of what ailed Bush-era Republican politics. Blackwell was infamous for alleged conflicts of interest owing to his status as both the chief elections official and the honorary cochair of the Bush re-election campaign in Ohio. The dual roles, combined with a flap over his refusal to count provisional ballots cast in the wrong polling locations, spawned an onslaught of voter disenfranchisement charges and lawsuits in the aftermath of an election that swung to Bush on the strength of the Ohio vote.[3]

Blackwell, in his labors against abortion, gun-ownership restrictions, and same-sex marriage recognition in Ohio, and in his bid for the governorship in 2006, had a staunch ally in one Russell Johnson. The head of a group called the Ohio Restoration Project and the assembler of a band of "Patriot Pastors" from across the Buckeye State, Johnson was a rising star in the Christian Right and, to progressives, the very personification of the excesses and abuses of hard-edged Christian conservatism. It was this pastor, Johnson, who had been railing from Ohio pulpits that true believers must oppose America's "secular jihadists" and consign them to the "dustbin," and it was Johnson who had been linking evolution to Hitler and abortion to the practice of children murdering their parents.[4] It was Johnson who declared that the Iraq war was not a "geopolitical skirmish" so much as a labor to establish "a foothold for Christ in a country whose people have been enslaved."[5]

I was now in Russell Johnson and Ken Blackwell territory. I was on the turf of the sports branch of the Campus Crusade organization that made progressives shudder for its reputation as an anti-gay, anti-abortion, anti-liberal, anti-separation-of-church-and-state, and anti-pretty-much-everything-progressives-cherish bulwark. Would I be treated as a "secular jihadist"? Was I the enemy? Were my hosts going to question the validity of my beliefs and give me the hard sell for theirs?

No, actually.

My welcome was warm. As I went through a day of interviews with a half-dozen AIA staff members, Ed Uszynski and his colleagues patiently explained their operations and objectives, told their coming-to-faith stories, and asked with genuine curiosity about my writing and beliefs—not to start an argument or mount their defenses, but to learn another perspective.

I had an eye- and mind-opening conversation with Mark Householder, coordinator of AIA's international ministry operations and the former director of its pro sports outreach (and a man who in 2009 would be named AIA president). Householder had recently returned from the Africa Cup soccer competition in Ghana; it was one of many Africa trips taken by Householder, who exuded deep concern for the African continent and racial reconciliation in his own country. Householder spoke earnestly about his personal journey in the area of race, his dawning realization that AIA was distressingly unsuccessful at attracting ethnic minorities to the organization's staff. His concern for Africa, and his desire to connect successful African American pros to the continent of their ancestors, had inspired him to take a contingent of black NFL players to Zimbabwe and South Africa; he was proud that one of those men had taken up Africa as his own cause, following up with donations and trips of his own. Householder was eager to show me a photo he had taken on one of a dozen-odd trips to Africa. It captured something that truly galled him, that mocked his ideals about Christian justice: a Christian chapel at a castle that used to be a way station for captured Africans bound for slavery in the Americas.

Householder noted the great progress AIA had made in attracting African Americans to serve as chaplains with NFL clubs. In the mid-1990s, just one of the approximately sixteen AIA staffers serving NFL clubs was black, despite African Americans' making up the majority of the teams' rosters. "We decided enough was enough," recalled Householder, director of AIA's pro sports ministry from 1989 to 2001, "and started an aggressive change process to identify and place qualified African American chaplains." The ministry recruited, trained, and helped place seven black chaplains over the next ten years. Householder spoke hopefully about reigniting diversity efforts in the ministry now. He said it had become increasingly clear that the ministry's "normal ways of operating" were not sufficient to attract significant numbers of nonwhites to the AIA staff. So, among other changes, AIA was in the process of modifying its requirement that all staff members fund-raise for their own salaries, in the hope of attracting more minorities to the organization.

Like most of the other ministry staffers I met, Householder was keenly aware of the larger religious/political/cultural milieu in which his ministry operates. He was familiar with a new book that was prompting considerable self-reflection in Christian circles that fall and winter: *UnChristian: What a New Generation Really Thinks about Christianity . . . and Why It Matters*, by Gabe Lyons and David Kinnaman. (Based on a massive public opinion survey by the Barna Group, the book explores the image problems of the conservative church—a group increasingly seen as "unChristian" by young believers.)

"The methods that were effective over the past twenty years now are not working," Householder told me. "The culture has shifted. People are getting their information in different ways. People have different values. The church isn't doing a great job of representing the gospel when we're too tied up with criticizing lifestyle choices."

With that statement, Householder could have been alluding to, among other things, conservative Christians' seeming fixation on homosexuality, and the public's—especially the young public's—disdain for the Christian Right's out-of-proportion fixation on gay people.

Householder moved on to something else that worried him: the way Christian pro athletes represent the faith. It was hardly the case that Householder and his colleagues wanted players to be quiet about Jesus. Anything but. But he *was* questioning the when and the how of evangelizing. "We live in a culture that requires greater discernment," Householder explained. "I would question the [practice] of athletes' witnessing in post-game interviews. How effective is that in today's culture? I'm not saying athletes [should refrain from talking about their faith]. But there is definitely a shift in organizations like ours in thinking through what is the most effective way of reaching people with the Gospel."[6]

Uszynski, the man ending his stint as the ministry's training director, was undergoing a shift in his thinking, too, one he explored with me at his comfortable old house on Xenia's main street. The very fact I was welcomed into his home for dinner with his wife, three children, and him—for the pre-meal prayer, the family chatter over the young girl's dentist visit, the lasagna and the salad—was significant to me. Was this any way to treat a "secular jihadist"? After dinner, Uszynski and I made a conversational foray into a matter that has dogged sports ministry for decades. Why was a pro sports industry teeming with Christians seemingly so bereft of Christian morality in certain crucial ways? Why had ministries like AIA not stood more firmly as a prophetic force against the abuses of sports, against sports' propensity to exploit and discriminate, against the sports world's out-of-proportion obsession with winning and the fuel this provided to so much that ails pro sports?

Uszynski had been thinking along similar lines—not necessarily in all the same ways as his progressive journalist guest, but in a manner that was probing how his ministry and he might become more of a public voice for decency in a sports culture seemingly gone too far. He announced himself ready to take up the challenge. And in the months that followed, he took the first step as he began developing his new public affairs position at AIA and writing a blog for the organization's website dedicated to restoring perspective, good sense, and morality to the crazed, winning-is-everything sports sector. (The explicit evangelism pitch, such a stock in trade in sports ministry publications, have been conspicuously absent from Usynski's pieces—evidence of the new direction of which he and several colleagues have been speaking.)

At the next day's all-staff meeting—just before the diversity workshop, not insignificantly—I witnessed a vivid reminder of a powerful and absolutely central focus of Athletes in Action, of something that was not up for renegotiation. "Evangelism, evangelism, evangelism," William Pugh avowed as he held forth in front of a banquet hall full of AIA staffers assembled from across the country. Pugh, AIA's president since 2001, was at the microphone giving his troops a refresher course and pep talk against a backdrop of large screens bearing the ubiquitous AIA motto: "One language, one victory."

"It's evangelism to the *core*," Pugh declared, proceeding to remind the assembled of how their founder, Bill Bright, professed to waking up every morning thinking about how he would fulfill the Great Commission, on that day and every day.[7]

Evangelism, evangelism, evangelism. Doug Pollock was thinking that way, too, as might be expected of the man serving as AIA's evangelism director. But when Uszynski introduced me to Pollock during a short break, I learned within seconds that Pollock was in the midst of reinventing how to go about fulfilling the Great Commission. Pollock gave me a business card that announced his "God's GPS" website, and he used that concept of a GPS—a Global Positioning System navigational device—to explain his conviction that the old evangelism, particular to a different place and time, was becoming obsolete. Pollock likened the situation to a GPS that received data from only two of the twenty-four satellites employed by GPS systems, receiving only a limited—a *very* limited— revelation of truth.

In a subsequent conversation, Pollock elaborated:

"Many evangelicals operate from an us-versus-them mindset. If you don't have the right language, vote Republican, see the world the way we do, then you're one of *them*. Maybe Christians need to realize that we're all just fellow sojourners in this thing called life. Maybe we've had some special experiences with God that we like to share with others, but an us-versus-them mentality prohibits that from happening. When we withdraw from culture and lob our truth grenades over the wall of the morally superior fortresses we've created, we tend to alienate rather than attract people to the good news that we say we have in the Gospel."

Pollock, the author of a book on effective evangelism called *God Space*, due out in the summer of 2009, also said something impressive for its lack of defensiveness and, more important, for its clear truth. "We have not," he said, "brought salvation to the sports world."

Christian ministry failing to bring salvation to the sports world? It was a startling admission from a representative of Athletes in Action, which has been hard at work for more than forty years to bring Jesus to athletes and the multitudes who watch them. Pollock went on to explain that the agents of Christianity in sports would champion the faith more fully if they went farther and deeper than just saving individual souls and dedicating themselves to saving the soul of the sports colossus itself. "Sports ministries like ours," he concluded, "must bring the *whole* gospel to the world of sport if we are going to save it from what it has become."[8]

The possibility of this saving, and recognition of the failure of sports ministry to pursue it, are anything but new ideas, of course. It has been more than thirty years since the famed sportswriter Frank Deford published one of the seminal critiques of Christianity in sports—"Sportianity," as Deford called it—in a three-part *Sports Illustrated* series. As Deford observed in the closing passage of the series' first installment, sports were an enterprise rife with exploitation. Yet Christian ministry, fixated on using sports as an evangelism vehicle and scarcely concerned about the morality of the industry itself, amounted to little more than an exploitation of the exploiters. As Deford wrote:

> Sportianity casts stones at players like Joe Namath for their personal behavior. . . . But no one in the movement—much less any organization—speaks out against the cheating in sport, against dirty play; no one attacks the evils of recruiting, racism, or any other abuses. Sport owns Sunday now, and religion is content to lease a few minutes before the big games. Religion seems to have become a support force for athletics, like broadcasters, trainers, cheerleaders, and ticket-sellers . . . John Morley, a British statesman, wrote, "Where it is a duty to worship the sun, it is pretty sure to be a crime to examine the laws of heat." As long as it can work the territory, Sportianity seems prepared to accept athletics as it is, more devoted to exploiting sport than to serving it.[9]

Is the time finally coming when Christian sports ministry devotes itself to something deeper than "working the territory," as Deford put it? Is the time coming when religion in pro sports more fully addresses the large-scale ills that concerned Deford in the late 1970s and that continue to vex the sports-industrial complex today?

Getting there will not be easy. The truth of Deford's observation, and the dedication of the ministry old guard to resisting social justice–oriented change, are illuminated by an encounter John White recalls from the time when he and his wife, Cindy, were launching AIA's sports ethics department. Questioning the need for such a department, a Campus Crusade leader looked at White with a blank stare and said: "What do ethics in sports have to do with the *Gospel?*"

Yet White thinks a spirit of change is beginning to rise. "There's a fresh wind, a new day," White said by telephone from Scotland, the site of his Ph.D. studies at Edinburgh University's School of Divinity. White acknowledged that critical self-reflection was not a hallmark of parachurch ministries like AIA. But that did not mean that they could not take the occasional hard look in the mirror. Such a re-evaluation, he assured, was under way. "Right now, this is where God has us," White said, "and we're trying to bring change from within."

Steeped in academia and the vastly different European environment, White was on the sports-ministry frontier both geographically and philosophically. For his dissertation, he was immersing himself in the writings of Augustine and Pope John Paul II. Working across the Atlantic Ocean had left him no choice but to reconceive the evangelism model, a la Doug Pollock and his GPS analogy. Because of the different culture in Europe, the common American practice of "exploiting the platform" for evangelism was a nonstarter, White explained. European-style ministry was focused more on tending to the well-being of athletes and building relationships with them, he said, with the Jesus message shared subtly, and later in the process.[10]

It is illuminating—and entirely logical, it turns out—that an evangelical Protestant like John White would draw from the thinking of a Catholic pope in developing a more meaningful Christian engagement with sports. For in articulating the problems and promise of sports, in addressing what one Catholic organization calls the "moral crisis" in the game, the Catholics have made serious advances.

"Mega-million-dollar salaries for players, illegal drug use, and unsportsmanlike behavior on and off the field have helped tarnish the golden image of the ideal athlete: healthy of body, mind and spirit." So read an article by the Catholic News Service announcing the formation of the new church-and-sport unit of the Pontifical Council for the Laity in 2004.[11] A statement by the Pontifical Council explained that the new church-sport office would strive to promote "a culture of sport" in which athletics serve "as a means for bringing about well-rounded growth of the person and as an instrument of peace and brotherhood among peoples."[12]

Also, from Pope Benedict XVI came this articulation of what sports, at their best, might accomplish for humanity. In an address to the Vatican general audience in 2005, Benedict declared that sport, "if practiced with respect for the rules, becomes an educational instrument and a vehicle for important human and spiritual values." The pope called on the assembled pilgrims, including on that day representatives from two European soccer federations, to work to "ensure that sport contributes to building a society characterized by mutual respect, loyalty of behavior, and solidarity between peoples and cultures."[13]

It is not that America's sport-fan nation never gets a glimpse of the virtuous fruits of sports. But who would contest the proposition that pro sports regularly bring out not the best in us, but the gloating, win-at-all-cost, break-the-rules-if-necessary, demonize-the-opponent *worst* sides of us? And who with a straight face would argue that the pro sports industrial complex, intent as it is on entertaining the masses and making money, is sincerely devoting itself to the project articulated by the pope—serving to advance important human and spiritual values, and contributing to society's capacity for respect, loyalty, and solidarity?

That such an unedifying state of affairs should prevail in a sector with so much religion, one teeming with so many good men acting in the name of a Christian religion of love and compassion, ought to stir considerable distress—

and motivation—on the part of the people and organizations dedicated to promoting Jesus to and through the sports world.

In truth, sports ministry has tremendous potential and a unique opportunity to inject more heart and decency into a pro sports world in dire need, and into the communities "served" by pro sports. Those on the forward edge of the evolution—people like AIA's Ed Uszynski and John White and the increasingly active Catholics—are already sketching what a faith-based reform agenda might look like. Taking some of their cues, and applying the insights earned from countless hours researching and thinking about Christian engagement with sports, I am convinced that a more thoughtful, more constructive engagement between faith and pro sports must take on some of the following challenges.

*

Christian ministry in pro sports must address sports' pressing race issues.

This is not to dismiss the very real gains that are realized when a black evangelical football coach like Tony Dungy rises to the top of his profession—a coaching profession in which black ex-players have enjoyed precious few opportunities—and does so in a manner that models intelligence, class, and human decency. But in addition to celebrating and promoting Dungy's feats as they have done, the agents of Christianity in sports could serve as a prophetic force for wider, deeper progress on redressing the racial injustices that plague the industry, and the nation. A look at the church's powerful role in the civil rights movement might convince even skeptics of the ability of prophetic Christianity to tweak our consciences and galvanize our collective insistence on equal opportunity for African Americans (and Latin Americans, for that matter—no small concern when baseball's demographics are considered). Also encouraging is the evident truth that Christians in America today embrace the anti-racism legacy of the church with near unanimity, from progressive Jesus followers like Jim Wallis of left-learning Sojourners all the way through to Christian Right activists of the Tony Perkins and Family Research Council ilk. If there is anything that seems beyond argument and controversy, it is the righteousness of the cause of equal opportunity for racial minorities.

May Jesus' representatives in sports become known for their passionate stand for fair treatment of aspiring black coaches in football—in big-time college football as well as the professional game. Unless we are ready to pronounce African Americans inherently lacking in the skills and attributes needed for coaching success, it is difficult to explain why the National Football League—in which some two-thirds of the players are black and whose retired-player ranks are loaded with African Americans with "combat experience"—has only a handful of black coaches. It is probably even harder to justify the situation in Division I college football, where, as of 2007, just 6 of the 119 teams had black coaches.[14] Hand in hand with that, may those in and around ministry work against the fans' and media's tendency to deal in racial stereotypes and apply double standards in their evaluations, and too-quick condemnations, of black players.

May Christians in sports likewise address aspects of the pro sports machinery that contribute to the use, misuse, and abuse of human beings—often black and Latino—whose desperation for professional sports success, and perceived lack of more practical options, make them vulnerable. Writers such as William Rhoden and Dave Zirin have laid bare the most prominent exploitation "sins" that ought to gnaw at the Christian, and American, conscience—Rhoden, with his "conveyor belt" analogy to explain how young African Americas are lured into going all-in for sports as though they were the only route out of their often-rotten circumstances, groomed for college and pro sports stardom, separated from the concerns of the black community, trained for social/political apathy and silence, and left stranded, their educations and life skills atrophied, if they're not one of the lucky few to have a long and lucrative career; and Zirin, with his damning critique of major league baseball's "strip-mining" of Latin America, of baseball teams' now-standard practice of establishing development academies, particularly in the Dominican Republic,[15] where pre-teenagers, lured by the multimillion-dollar successes of fellow countrymen like David Ortiz, clamor for admission, forsake their educations, and stake everything on the ultrathin chance of making it big in the American major leagues—and usually end up discarded like an obsolete piece of equipment with nary a day in the big leagues, a life of menial labor and economic struggle ahead of them. As if to tie the whole tawdry mess in a big, nasty bow, there came the news in the 2008 baseball season that federal authorities (and baseball itself) were investigating the widespread skimming of Dominican prospects' signing money by MLB employees.[16]

As Zirin asks, doesn't the highly profitable enterprise of major league baseball bear a responsibility to cushion the fall for the vast majority of the academy prospects who never reach the American professional ranks, and some responsibility to the societies from which these aspiring players come? To give back to a region that has given so much to American pro baseball—to provide at least for the individual young men affected—seems a responsible, decent course of action. It could take the form of support for education and job training, for instance, or philanthropic work to improve social conditions in the aspiring players' countries. Sadly, major league baseball does little in this regard now.[17] More to the point, it seems fair to expect some accountability from the Christians who capitalize on baseball to market their cause to the vulnerable Latin American youth. To its credit, Baseball Chapel does mount a presence in the

Dominican Republic—including at the baseball youth academies—and in other Latin American countries. But promoting Christian faith in impoverished baseball-factory communities, whatever it might do for the development of character and self-esteem in teenage ballplayers, falls well short of dealing with the waste piles of injustice caused by the major leagues' mining of the "Republic of Baseball" in search of the next Pedro Martinez or Vladimir Guerrero.

The other forms of exploitation in major league sports are legion: the propensity of the sports machinery to use up men's bodies and force players, explicitly or implicitly, to rush back from injuries before they're ready—an issue especially poignant in light of new findings about rampant concussions in football and their profound long-term effects; the dynamics that allow wealthy owners, buoyed by a precious public good known as their antitrust exemption, to virtually blackmail communities into building taxpayer-financed stadiums while so many other public resources, from libraries to public hospitals to roads and bridges, fall into neglect; the use of colleges as pro leagues' free-of-charge training grounds and farm teams in ways that seriously detract from higher education's mission and the education of "student" athletes. The list goes on. . . .

Yet, as Deford noted decades ago, evangelicals in and around professional sports have offered little in the way of sustained public witness against sports' irreligious, unethical exploitation of human beings. Admittedly, change on this score will not come easy. Apart from sports ministry's dependence on the good favor of management to maintain access to athletes, and its understandable aversion to risking that access, there is always the doctrinal hurdle: the common belief among evangelicals that salvation comes through God's grace alone, that good works are of little avail in a hopelessly fallen world.

Yet one suspects their savior would consistently stand up for "the least of these" who suffer the bitter human consequences of a profit-hungry pro sports machine. Ministry should, too.

*

Christian ministry in sports must challenge the worship of winning and all that follows it.

The admonition against worshiping gods other than *God* is so foundational to monotheistic tradition that it is emblazoned in the Ten Commandments. Yet, as sports-ministry pioneers like John White point out, pro sports culture indeed has proclaimed a rival god: the god of victory. Once a person or industry bows before that false deity and gives full power to the lust for the Almighty Victory, unethical, unseemly behavior of almost every variety becomes more temping, harder to resist, and easier to rationalize.

Cheating has plagued the game since the dawning of the big-sports era in America. Yet, there is a growing recognition in this time of football spying, steroid scandals, and college-sports recruiting misdeeds that things have gone horribly awry—that lying and rule-breaking are not the exceptions that prove the rule, but the rule itself. And with that is coming a new awareness that a win-at-all-costs mentality reflects and reinforces similar forms of "cheating" that permeate so many other aspects of American life, from business and politics to literature and its new genre of made-up "memoirs." As the writer Robert Lipsyte has observed, "There's a connection between cutting corners to win a football game and to start a war. For many Americans, certainly for the majority of American boys, the most vivid and lasting lessons are learned in the sports they play and watch. Jock Culture is the incubator of most definitions of manly success."[18]

Wouldn't we expect that a sports world alive with conspicuous Christian piety—a sector with a decades-long relationship with society's most enthusiastic Christians—would be more consistently *moral* on these scores? Let Jesus' representatives in sports apply the teachings of their faith more fully to the out-of-bounds winning obsession of our sports culture. Not that sports ministry ignores these issues now; their literature and teachings frequently address these matters head-on. What they have failed to undertake, however, is a much-needed *public* witness against victory addiction and the many ills that ride its coattails.

Thinking beyond evangelism. Understanding athletes and those who follow them not principally as targets for conversion, but as complicated and often-hurting human beings. Standing up consistently for the well-being of a population—athletes—plagued by sky-high rates of doping, addiction, marital failure, and injuries with long-term consequences for mental and physical health. Engaging with pro sports in a manner aimed at transforming them into an entity that serves communities and, in the parlance of the pope, helps build a society characterized by respect, loyalty, and solidarity between peoples and cultures.

These are the principles of the new form of sports ministry now in the process of being invented by the movement's pioneers. Not that all aspects of this agenda have been neglected; many pro-team chaplains have been hard at work helping athletes manage the unique pressures and stresses of their lives and careers. May this compassionate agenda become not just the byproduct of evangelism to and through athletes, but the norm—indeed, the *point*—of Christianity in professional sports. And may it extend beyond the lives and souls of individual professional athletes to the industry, to the community, and to the country.

*

Christian ministry must share the territory with those who believe differently.

In the run-up to the 2008 National Day of Prayer, controversy broke out in a way that is most instructive for those concerned with creating a fair and level religious playing field in the world of pro sports.

As the May 1 prayer day approached, a group called Jews on First cried foul over the prayer day being "hijacked" by evangelical Christians. The Jewish group pointed out that the official organizing committee—led by none other than the wife of Christian Right warrior James Dobson and housed at Dobson's Focus on the Family headquarters—had brought exclusiveness and divisiveness to the once-ecumenical event by insisting that volunteer coordinators around the country signal their acceptance of evangelical doctrine (i.e., Jesus is the son of God and the only means by which people can gain salvation). As the Jewish group indignantly pointed out, organizers were forcing applicants for volunteer coordinator positions to pledge that the Day of Prayer activities in their cities would be conducted by Christians. What of non-Christians? "Those with differing beliefs," the application form said, "are welcome to attend."[19]

How kind of the Christians to allow Jews and other nonevangelical Christians to attend! (And to hear their own beliefs marginalized in the process.) Such an approach, obviously, does not live up to the principles of fairness and inclusiveness that one might expect from a *national* prayer event endorsed by what is supposed to be a religiously neutral government. Yet a similar ethos prevails in pro sports, where theologically conservative Christians have cornered the market like the Dobson devotees who took over the national prayer day. Confronted with the charge that the evangelical Christianity they dispense is exclusive, promoters of the faith often reply with something to this effect: "Of course we're inclusive. Anyone can accept Jesus and join us."

That glib response simply will not do. Inclusiveness is not achieved by allowing others to join you by becoming *like* you. Inclusiveness is achieved only by welcoming others as they are and adjusting the environment such that their rights will be respected. If that means ecumenical prayers in chapel services conducted for the whole team—prayers that tone down the salvation-through-Christ-alone message—so be it. Surely, there will remain a time and a place for evangelicals to share their Jesus-only message. But exclusive doctrine should not be dispensed at religious functions designed to serve the collective, and not in the presence of Jews, Muslims, or other religious minorities who seek spiritual counsel without the get-Jesus pitch. Nor should the religious agenda be pursued in a manner that will marginalize nonbelievers on the roster, in the team administration, or in the community.

If Christianity in sports is to serve consistently as the "salt and light" of which evangelicals often speak, it must do so in a way that respects the reality that America is not only the most religious country in the western world, but also the most religiously diverse. "Getting it right" means sharing the territory. Those who run our pro sports leagues and teams must insist that the evangelicals working the locker rooms and clubhouses respect the rights of Catholics, moderate and liberal Protestants, Jews, Muslims, and followers of any number of other faiths, as well as people who are not religious.

A good start would be the adoption of a different model of religious chaplaincy, in which religious counselors meet individuals on their own spiritual turf, as has been traditionally practiced at hospital chapels and in the military. This would mean providing religious resources and support appropriate for nonevangelical players as well as their evangelical teammates, and eschewing the now-too-common practice of chaplains using exclusively Christian prayers. It would mean the provision of stadium chapel services that forego exclusive evangelical teachings. It would mean prohibitions against chaplains promoting teachings that consign nonevangelicals to hell, as well as strictures against proselytizing—against evangelism that crosses the line separating good-hearted invitation from aggressive, even coercive pressure to convert.

Admittedly, this proposition might sound like a case of swimming upstream given the changes in religious practice and chaplaincy in the armed forces (among other sectors) that have made them ever more a hotbed of evangelical Christianity and high-pressure proselytizing—and of much-publicized litigation against the same.[20] On the ground of religious freedom, defenders of evangelizing military chaplains proclaim the right of those chaplains to pray in Jesus' name. But such reasoning, whether applied to the military or pro sports, seemingly forgets the essentially selfless purpose of chaplaincy. Chaplains are deployed in a given setting not primarily to satisfy their own need for religious self-expression or to advance their particular faith, *but to serve the clients*, whether they happen to be grieving family members at a hospital, stressed and struggling soldiers, or professional athletes.

The responsibility to ensure this service-first form of chaplaincy falls on those who run our professional leagues and teams, who have every right, and every responsibility, to insist on a level religious playing field. The responsibility falls, too, on those in evangelical Christian ministry who enjoy the privilege of access—access they have no doubt earned with their energy and hard work, but access that brings with it an obligation to respect the religious diversity in the stadium and the community surrounding it.

Nonevangelicals committed to greater inclusiveness would do well to accept an important practical reality and a course of action suggested by it: Those left out now cannot merely depend on others to create the constructive change that will serve their interests; inclusion is a two-way street. As discussed in previous chapters, moderate Christians, religious minorities, and nonbelievers would do well to take a page from the evangelicals' book and insert *themselves* into the action.

Raising a prophetic religious voice against racism and exploitation, bringing decency and perspective to a sports culture in the thrall of victory and blind to the many misdeeds committed as a result, respecting our communities' religious diversity—these are the beginnings of an agenda for reformed Christian sports ministry. These are starting points for a new form of faith in sports that heeds the call of the late-great Reggie White "to get it right" by living faith, and not just preaching it. These are foundations being laid by new-century reformers like John White who are drawn not to the Christ of corporate and political power, but to the Jesus who served the outcasts and the poor. These are the new directions for a sports ministry that strives toward the vision articulated by the pope—a sports sphere characterized by its ability to bring us all together, not wedge us farther apart.

*

Some, in the final analysis, would prefer that religion be kept out of sports. After all, as some ask, what does religion have to do with sports, anyway? But a complete separation of church and sport is neither practical nor fair. Religion permeates nearly all aspects of public life in America and will continue to do so for the foreseeable future. The installation of complete secularity in and around pro sports hardly constitutes a fair and neutral playing field for diverse America. The challenge, rather, is to create a *pluralistic* environment in professional sports, where no one form of belief or nonbelief takes over, but where all are welcome, and all are free to act and speak in accordance with their creeds and beliefs, so long as they do not blatantly infringe on the rights of others.

As ought to be abundantly clear by this point, this book is not against religion in sports. If anything, it is a call for *more* religion in professional sports—if by "more" we mean religious practice that is more inclusive of Americans of faiths other than evangelical Christianity (or of none), more devoted to prophetic witness against the abuses and excesses of sports, and more committed to fulfilling the potential of sports to serve as a positive force for human beings and communities.

In the words of the ministry representative and former major leaguer cited in chapter 5 (a man who agreed to comment on the condition that his name not be used), the Christianity practiced and expressed in professional sports too often misrepresents the faith. Christian players do not serve their religion well, the ex-player says, with their chatter about God helping them win games, with their product-endorsement model of evangelism. "I think the problem with sports ministry is the problem with the American church in general," reflects the retired pro athlete, who completed advanced theological training after his playing days. "We look for celebrities to promote a brand name. In my understanding of the Gospels, this is the antithesis of the method Jesus used while on earth."[21]

Evangelicals in sports likewise perform a disservice to the faith, we might add, when they reduce Christianity to a simplistic and exclusive theological proposition—accept Jesus or else—and use sports, this entity that belongs to the whole lot of us, to hammer home the point. So, too, do they commit a foul when they bring their faith to the broader public sphere in a highly skewed manner that makes Christianity look like an apologetic for big business and the Republican Party.

Encouragingly, the evangelical church itself is changing as we near the end of this first decade of the new century. As Christians branch out with new perspectives and energy to serve the poor, stand for peace, protect the planet and vulnerable populations, and undertake countless other projects of compassion—not instead of but in addition to the narrower agenda of the Christian Right—they demonstrate what it looks like when Christianity shows up fully in the public sphere. They're showing that their religion doesn't wear just the conservative stripes that so many skeptics have come to resent, but stripes of every imaginable hue. If Christianity in sports is going to be a *complete* Christianity, let its representatives follow in these directions, too.

That the muscular Christians might attempt to harness the messy, profane, and (still often) wonderful colossus of professional sports to advance their cause is testament to the energy and ambition of evangelicalism in our time—impressive, but problematic, too. Pro sports don't belong to them to use in this fashion that is contrary to the interests of the nonevangelical majority of us.

The funny thing is, big-time sports, like society itself, could really use what the Christians have to offer, if only they would heed Reggie White's admonition and live it as much as they talk it. May Jesus' followers in sports bring the best of their religion to the pro sports sector, to communities and a country in need of moral force and compassionate acts. May the Christian missionaries who work the territory serve as the *conscience* of sports—not just another set of hangers-on looking to capitalize on sports to promote yet another product.

A word to Christians in sports: The vision sketched above is not intended to silence you. If anything, your message will come through louder, and resonate more clearly and with far more listeners, when it is expressed through your ethical witness in addition to your get-Jesus evangelism. The nonevangelical rest of us will be more likely to relax our defenses and engage with you in an open, hospitable manner if you consistently lead with your hearts rather than a rigid theological proposition about Jesus, heaven, and hell that will inevitably exclude and alienate large numbers of us. You have something broader and grander to offer: a great religion, rich with transformative teachings and stories, that can help heal that which is broken in pro sports, as in society. You don't need to start from behind; the pioneers and innovators on your leading edge already have you in the race.

Pro sports could really use more of your heart and your conscience. So could the community, the nation, and the world of people touched by sports.

Onward.

Notes

1. "Football & Religion," NFL Films, 2004.
2. Tom Krattenmaker, "Reggie's (Whole) Story," *USA Today*, August 3, 2006.
3. Frances Fitzgerald, "Holy Toledo: Ohio's Gubernatorial Race Tests the Power of the Christian Right," *New Yorker*, July 31, 2006.
4. Susan Page, "Shaping Politics from the Pulpit," *USA Today*, August 2, 2005.
5. Dan Gilgoff, *The Jesus Machine: How James Dobson, Focus on the Family, and Evangelical America are Winning the Culture War* (New York: St. Martin's, 2007), 202.
6. Mark Householder, Athletes in Action, interview conducted March 10, 2008, at Athletes in Action headquarters, Xenia, Ohio.
7. William Pugh, remarks at Athletes in Action staff event, March 11, 2008, Athletes in Action headquarters, Xenia, Ohio. William Pugh left the AIA presidency in 2009.
8. Doug Pollock, Athletes in Action, extended interview conducted by telephone March 25, 2008, and via subsequent e-mail exchanges.
9. Frank Deford, "Religion in Sport," *Sports Illustrated*, April 19, 1976.
10. John White, then of Athletes in Action, extended interview conducted by phone and e-mail between October 2007 and June 2008.
11. Carol Glatz, "Off and Running: New Vatican Office Aims to Promote Culture of Sport," *Catholic News Service*, August 6, 2004, http://www.catholicnews.com/data/stories/cns/0404317.htm.
12. Glatz, "Off and Running," Catholic News Service.
13. "Pope Suggests Sport Can Build Respectful Society," *Catholic News*, September 22, 2005, http://www.cathnews.com/news/509/126.php.
14. Elia Powers, "Mulling Ways to Add Minority Coaches," *Inside Higher Ed*, March 1, 2007, http://www.insidehighered.com/news/2007/03/01/coaches.
15. Dave Zirin, "Say it Ain't So, Big Leagues," *The Nation*, November 14, 2005.
16. Mark Fainaru-Wada and T.J. Quinn, "Sources: Bowden, Rijo Investigated in Pair of Probes of Dominican Signings," ESPN.com, July 12, 2008, http://sports.espn.go.com/mlb/news/story?id=3483972.
17. For an analysis and critique of Major League Baseball's practices in Latin America from a human rights perspective, see: Arturo J. Marcano and David P. Guevara, *Stealing Lives: The Globalization of Baseball and the Tragic Story of Alexis Quiroz*

(Bloomington: Indiana University Press, 2002). MLB's media relations office did not respond to a request for information on and examples of the league's efforts to assist Latin American communities.

18. Robert Lipsyte, "Jock Culture Permeates Life," *USA Today*, April 10, 2008.

19. "Explicit Religious Discrimination by Christian Right Group that Controls the National Day of Prayer," News release by Jews on First organization, March 27, 2008, http://www.jewsonfirst.org/08a/-national_prayer_day08.html.

20. For background on allegations of coercive evangelism in the military academies, see: Neela Banerjee, "Religion and its Role Are in Dispute at the Service Academies," *New York Times*, June 25, 2008.

21. Interview by e-mail, November 2005. Name withheld by request.

Index

~

About the Author

Tom Krattenmaker is a Portland, Oregon-based writer specializing in religion in public life. A member of the *USA Today*'s board of contributors, he contributes frequently to the newspaper's weekly On Religion series, and his work has also appeared in the *Philadelphia Inquirer*, *Los Angeles Times*, and *Salon*. Krattenmaker was a winner in the American Academy of Religion 2008 journalism awards.